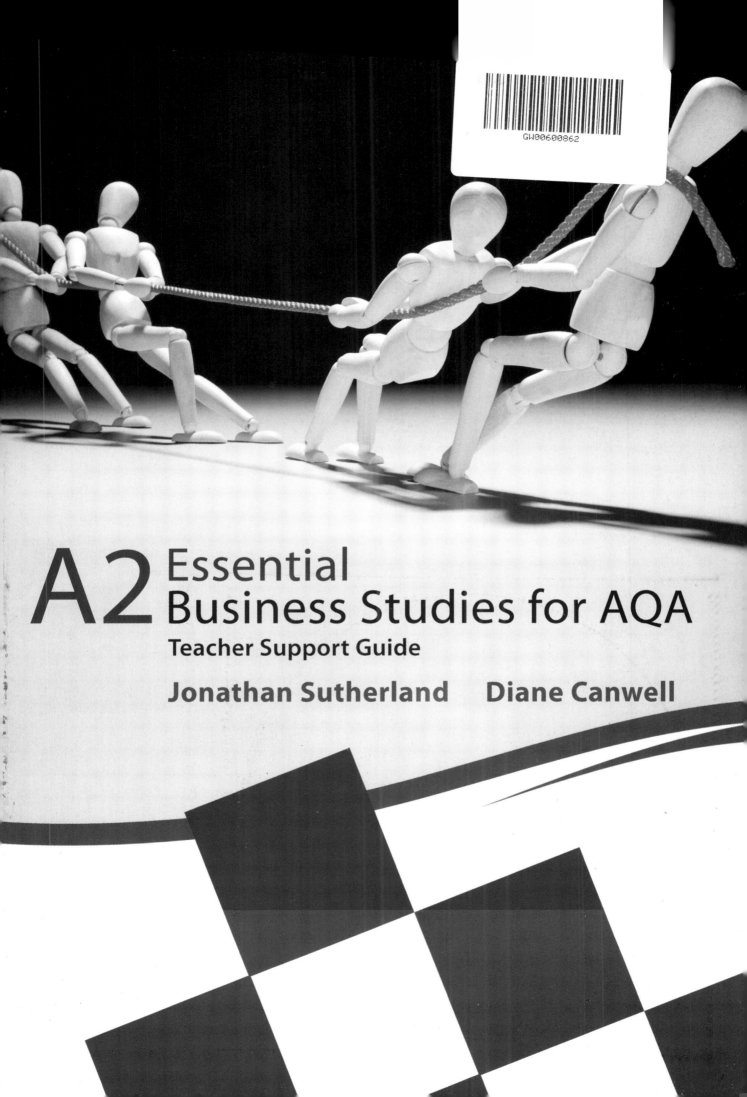

A2 Essential Business Studies for AQA

Teacher Support Guide

Jonathan Sutherland   **Diane Canwell**

United Kingdom: Folens Publishers,
Waterslade House,
Thame Road, Haddenham,
Buckinghamshire, HP17 8NT
Email: folens@folens.com

Ireland: Folens Publishers,
Greenhills Road, Tallaght, Dublin 24
Email: info@folens.ie

Editor: Louise Wilson
Project development: Rick Jackman, Jackman Publishing
    Solutions Ltd
Design and layout: Patricia Briggs
Cover design: Jump to! www.jumpto.co.uk

First published 2009 by Folens Limited

British Library Cataloguing in Publication Data.
A catalogue record for this publication is available from the British Library.

ISBN 978-1-85008-363-4
Folens code: FD3634

PICTURE CREDITS

The publishers would like to thank the following for permission to reproduce images in this publication.

p.1: Kingfisher plc; p.2: © Lai Leng Yiap–FOTOLIA; p.3: Kingfisher plc; p.12: © absolut–FOTOLIA; p.13: © endostock–FOTOLIA; p.15: © Leah-Anne Thompson–FOTOLIA; p.27: © Les Cunliffe–FOTOLIA; p.37: PA Photos; p.38: PA Photos; p.43: © senor nunez–FOTOLIA; p.50: courtesy of MCS; p.51: courtesy of FireAngel Ltd; p.64: PA Photos; p.76: © Anton Zhukov–FOTOLIA; p.85: © Dreef–FOTOLIA; p.89: © TebNad–FOTOLIA; p.90: © Mario Ragma Jr.–FOTOLIA; p.95: © kentoh–FOTOLIA; p.96: © David Humphrey–FOTOLIA; p.110: Nationwide Building Society; p.124: © Gudellaphoto–FOTOLIA; p.128: © Scott Maxwell–FOTOLIA; p.129: © c–FOTOLIA; p.131: © pmtavares–FOTOLIA; p.132: www.nikebiz.com; p.138: © sharply_done–FOTOLIA; p.143: © LVDESIGN–FOTOLIA; p.144: © Douglas Freer–FOTOLIA; p.153: © mr.REPORTER–FOTOLIA; p.158: © Sergey Galushko–FOTOLIA; p.159: (l) © Orlando Florin Rosu–FOTOLIA, (r) © The Third Man–FOTOLIA, (b) © Letty–FOTOLIA; p.168: © cornelius–FOTOLIA; p.169: Woolworths Group Plc; p.184: © petrol–FOTOLIA; p.186: © Csaba Peterdi–FOTOLIA; p.187: © Alan Heartfield–FOTOLIA; p.194: © CHEN–FOTOLIA; p.195: © Carl Durocher–FOTOLIA; p.201: © Srecko Djarmati–FOTOLIA.

Every effort has been made to contact copyright holders, but if any have been inadvertently overlooked, the publishers will be happy to make the necessary amendments at the first opportunity.

In the case studies in this teacher support guide, some businesses, people and products are given their real names and have genuine photographs as well, but in some cases the photographs are for illustrative or educational purposes only and are not intended to identify the business, individual or product. The publishers cannot accept any responsibility for any consequences resulting from this use of photographs and case studies, except as expressly provided by law.

CONTENTS

TOPIC 4 OPERATIONAL STRATEGIES

FOCUS ON UNDERSTANDING OPERATIONAL OBJECTIVES

FOCUS ON SCALE AND RESOURCE MIX

FOCUS ON INNOVATION

FOCUS ON LOCATION

FOCUS ON LEAN PRODUCTION

TOPIC 5 HUMAN RESOURCE STRATEGIES

FOCUS ON HR OBJECTIVES AND STRATEGIES

FOCUS ON DEVELOPING AND IMPLEMENTING WORKFORCE PLANS

FOCUS ON COMPETITIVE ORGANISATIONAL STRUCTURES

FOCUS ON EFFECTIVE EMPLOYER/EMPLOYEE RELATIONS

UNIT 4 THE BUSINESS ENVIRONMENT AND MANAGING CHANGE

TOPIC 1 CORPORATE AIMS AND OBJECTIVES

FOCUS ON UNDERSTANDING MISSION AIMS AND OBJECTIVES

A2 ESSENTIAL BUSINESS STUDIES FOR AQA

INTRODUCTION

Welcome to the support pack for *A2 Essential Business Studies*. This pack and the accompanying textbook have been designed to cover the demands of the AQA A2 Business Studies syllabus.

The textbook itself has been created to provide full coverage of the syllabus, using carefully designed double-page spreads with features, case studies, questions and activities that build together to deliver the two units.

The textbook assumes that students have already studied the AS Business Studies units. The features of this pack aim to deliver the content and knowledge required, as well as giving students the chance to experience the assessment procedures.

All the activities, case studies and questions in the A2 textbook have been designed to reflect the type of assessment questions that students are likely to encounter in the examination. This allows students not only to test their understanding of the content of the syllabus, but also, at the earliest possible stage, to appreciate how questions will be asked and how they are expected to answer them. Every question in the textbook has a set of answers or guidelines in this pack.

There are 53 worksheets, covering each of the focus areas of the textbook. Depending on the complexity of the focus area, there are between one and four worksheets. These are designed either to provide class-based, independent learning, revision or reinforcement, or to be photocopied and handed out as homework assignments. Answers are provided for all the worksheets at the end of the pack.

As an essential part of the revision aspect of this pack, there are also sets of mind maps, which can be used in conjunction with the revision checklists in the textbook. And, as a further revision aid, there is also a full set of answers at the end of the pack to the mock examination papers that can be found on the unit summary pages in the textbook.

Lastly, there are two new mock examination papers – one for each unit – which have been specifically written and designed to mimic a real examination paper. Full answers and guidelines are provided for these two mock papers.

FOCUS ON USING OBJECTIVES AND STRATEGIES

Functional and corporate objectives ▸ textbook pages 5–6

CASE STUDY – KINGFISHER'S B&Q STRATEGY

1 What do you think is meant by an operational driver? Explain what you think is meant by the four examples given by B&Q. (*12 marks*)

Considering the hierarchy of terms, this would be a specific divisional objective. Collectively, these are part of the overall objective of increasing sales. Price competitiveness refers to monitoring and evaluating the prices charged by key competitors and adjusting prices to match or beat competitors by either making price pledges or offering to match prices if necessary. Customer service refers not only to the availability of staff and their product knowledge, but also to generally assisting customers and encouraging additional sales and repeat visits to the store. Introducing new products and services in the store means that the product mix is constantly changing and providing an opportunity for new customers to be attracted and for existing customers to try out new product lines. All these are designed to increase sales and profitability. Changing the store environment to make it easier to find products, to move around the store, eliminate bottlenecks and generally make the shopping experience more enjoyable and problem-free is again a key component in encouraging increased sales.

2 If the four elements are operational drivers, the 25% improvement in sales can be considered as what type of objective and why? (*6 marks*)

This would be a divisional objective, which directly contributes to a major corporate objective of providing a good rate of return for investors in the Kingfisher group. It is not clear whether B&Q was given the target of achieving a 25% improvement in sales, but it does appear that the group expects at least this level of improvement given the investment in revamping all of B&Q's larger stores. It is part of a rolling programme to revitalise B&Q and to ensure that it remains competitive and makes as large a contribution as possible to the group's sales turnover and profits.

FOCUS ON USING OBJECTIVES AND STRATEGIES

Functional objectives and strategies ▶ textbook pages 7–8

CASE STUDY – KINGFISHER'S WAY OF MANAGING RISKS

Kingfisher has identified eight principal risks in managing the business and its development. In each case, suggest at least one functional strategy that could be used to minimise the likelihood or impact of each risk. (*24 marks*)

There is a wide variety of acceptable answers. Typically:

- Economic and market conditions – SWOT analysis, analysis of market trends and environmental scanning.

- Entering new markets – SWOT analysis, market research, joint ventures with businesses already in that market.

- Competitive product ranges, prices and customer service – market analysis, analysing and monitoring competitors' prices, looking for new trends, product innovations and initiatives to improve customer service, both in-store, online and over the telephone.

- Innovation in big, developed businesses – their initiative to revamp all of their larger stores can be seen as part of this process, specifically changes to the B&Q stores in order to make them a more pleasurable environment in which to shop, as well as providing a broader range of products and services and better customer service.

- Attracting and retaining the best people – largely through a coordinated human resource strategy, in order to attract the best possible candidates for job roles and then to provide them with an attractive overall package and support, in order to retain them. Training schedules and updating is an integral part of this process.

- Financial resources – this is a joint responsibility crossing over into many functional areas of the organisation. Initially the stores would provide the sales income, but this needs to be managed by the accounts department. Decisions need to be made about the appropriateness of investments, possibly using cost benefit analysis, budgets and targets. The business will need to have sufficient working capital and will need to set aside retained profits in order to fund future or ongoing projects.

- Crises affecting trading and Kingfisher's reputation - through contingency planning and by assessing possible future impacts of different trading conditions on the business, supporting and protecting Kingfisher's reputation through marketing and public relations initiatives, such as sponsorship and support for local community projects, etc.

- In-store safety – this can be seen as being part of the overall improvement in stores, but externally the business has to comply with relevant health and safety legislation in each of the countries in which it operates. It needs to be aware of future health and safety concerns and impending legislation, and be ahead of those requirements, to avoid disrupting trading.

FOCUS ON USING OBJECTIVES AND STRATEGIES

Case studies, questions and exam practice ▶ textbook pages 8–9

KINGFISHER'S INTERNATIONAL EXPANSION

1 Comment on the key principles behind Kingfisher's international expansion. How have these contributed to ensuring continued success? (*15 marks*)

Kingfisher always begins by identifying markets that offer the opportunity for growth and financial return. This means that the business analyses the current state of the market and tries to anticipate future growth trends. The research incorporates not only the trends but also the existing and potential future activities of the competitors. As part of this analysis the business would also consider other factors that could directly or indirectly impact on the market, such as legislation, the current economic climate, changes in government, etc. Kingfisher works very closely with specialists in the local market, particularly those that have an intimate knowledge of the potential customer base and ways in which business is conducted in that market. The company gives these local teams a degree of autonomy (freedom) in order to make their assessments and plans. However, on to this it superimposes group-wide key performance indicators (essential indicators that identify the progress and success of initiatives and plans underway). Having worked in a number of different markets for a period of time, Kingfisher has a wealth of ideas, resources and contacts with current suppliers. This allows its successful business model to be adapted to suit the local market. Kingfisher is pragmatic in the sense that having made an investment in developing a new market it will not be frightened to exit that market if the economic situation does not appear to be sustainable or the business model is not working.

2 B&Q is the market leader in Britain and is almost twice as large as its nearest rival. To what extent do you think this gives B&Q a competitive advantage and why might this be the case? (*12 marks*)

In Britain, B&Q has a 15% market share of a market worth £26bn. It is an established and respected business name that attracts the lion's share of Kingfisher's capital investment due to its continued success. In the last year it was given £182m to expand. It has a unique format that resembles a warehouse. Its staff-to-customer ratio is relatively low and it offers the broadest possible range of products and services in its store. In order to assist customers in making purchasing decisions there are room sets that display completed DIY projects. All products and services that would be required to carry out this work are available under the same roof. Broader and more specialised products can be ordered at the help desks. As B&Q has established itself as market leader and receives continued support from Kingfisher, it has a considerable advantage over the competition, as competitors would have to replicate the format and start at a far lower base, requiring an enormous investment to try to overhaul B&Q.

FOCUS ON USING OBJECTIVES AND STRATEGIES

MINDMAPS

CORPORATE AIMS AND OBJECTIVES

↓

CORPORATE MISSION
(MISSION STATEMENT

↓

DIVISIONAL OBJECTIVES

↓

DEPARTMENTAL OBJECTIVES

↓

SPECIFIC INDIVIDUAL TARGETS

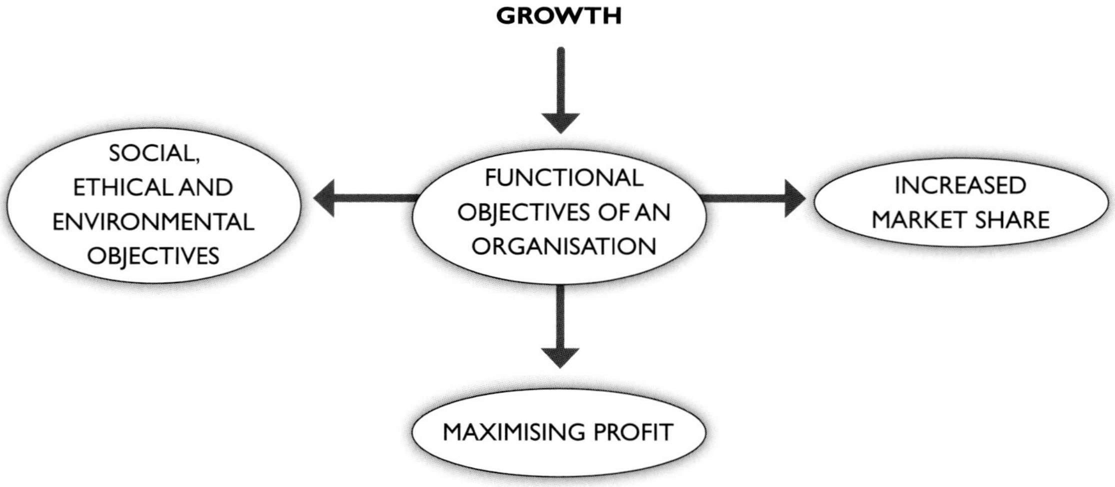

GROWTH

↓

SOCIAL,
ETHICAL AND
ENVIRONMENTAL
OBJECTIVES ← FUNCTIONAL
OBJECTIVES OF AN
ORGANISATION → INCREASED
MARKET SHARE

↓

MAXIMISING PROFIT

FOCUS ON USING OBJECTIVES AND STRATEGIES

MINDMAPS

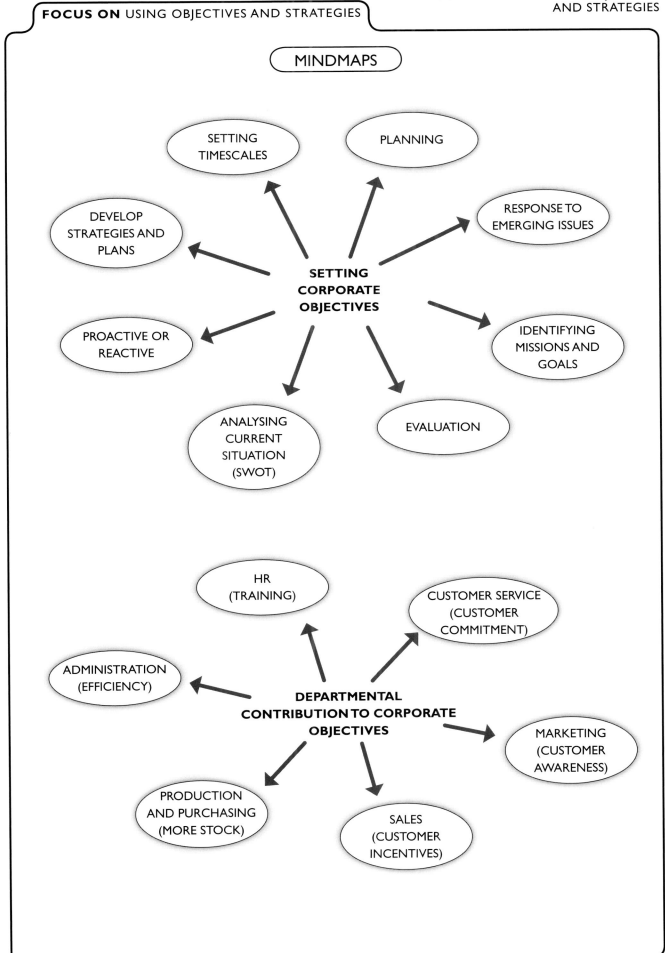

FOCUS ON USING OBJECTIVES AND STRATEGIES

(WORKSHEET)

1 What do you understand by the term 'corporate objectives'?

_____

_____

_____

_____

_____

_____

_____

_____

_____

2 Briefly explain what you understand to be key functional objectives of an organisation.

_____

_____

_____

_____

_____

_____

_____

_____

_____

3 How might a business transform its objectives into workable strategies?

_____

_____

_____

_____

_____

_____

_____

_____

_____

_____

Answers ▶ page 221

A2 ESSENTIAL BUSINESS STUDIES FOR AQA

FOCUS ON UNDERSTANDING FINANCIAL OBJECTIVES

Financial objectives ▶ textbook pages 12–13

CASE STUDY – PRELIMINARY RESULTS

1 Why might the profit have fallen even though sales were up? (*4 marks*)

The business might have to have discounted products in order to generate the additional sales, or they may have simply been responding to price changes by key competitors, or the cost of purchasing from suppliers may have increased.

2 Calculate the percentage change in both the pre-tax and after-tax profits. (*4 marks*)

These are fairly straightforward calculations. It is important for the student to appreciate that the figures should be displayed in brackets. The percentage changes for the pre-tax profit was (2.8%) and for the after tax profits (4.3%).

3 As an existing investor in the business, what would be your decision about retaining or selling the shares and why? (*8 marks*)

Sales are very buoyant and have increased by nearly 8%, which is very encouraging. The actual drop in profit of just (1.2%) is not that significant and is only actually a £6 million difference. What is perhaps slightly more concerning is the drop in the full year dividend by over 3p per share. The business would probably argue that the drop in profit has caused this, but there is an underlying difference, as the drop in dividend is actually 31.9%. This indicates that the business is making considerable investments by retaining profit for investment, rather than allocating it to shareholders. Therefore, it would probably be in the short-term interests of the shareholder to sell. But, in the longer-term, they can expect higher dividend payments as a result of these investments. The fact that the business has a property portfolio worth over £3.5bn is very encouraging, as these are tangible assets that could be realised if necessary.

Assessing internal and external influences on financial objectives

▶ textbook pages 14–15

CASE STUDY – THANET DISTRICT COUNCIL FINANCIAL SERVICES

1 What is meant by 'to maintain a balanced General Fund Budget'? Explain how the Council intends to achieve this. (*6 marks*)

A balanced budget means that expenditure matches income. The council would achieve this by calculating its total possible income and then allocating budgets to the different departments, so that total expenditure does not exceed income. They propose to chase any debts that are due to the council, minimise arrears and minimise the writing off of debts.

2 Why might the Council require a contingency reserve? (*4 marks*)

This is to cover any unexpected costs that could occur during the financial year, which have not been incorporated into the budget, such as a

major disaster, an expensive repair or some other crisis. The contingency fund is retained until needed and carried over if not used.

3 How does the Council intend to balance additional spending and why are the options uncertain? (*4 marks*)

The council suggests that it will try to increase income, or identify budget savings. Both of these are uncertain. Firstly there is no guarantee that it could increase income (although it proposes to increase council tax levels). Budget savings may not be possible either, as it is unknown whether the council has already made budget savings and the departments are running at a minimum budget at the moment.

FOCUS ON UNDERSTANDING FINANCIAL OBJECTIVES

Case studies, questions and exam practice ▶ textbook pages 16–17

CASE STUDY – CHELSEA'S FINANCIAL OBJECTIVES

1 Explain how Chelsea FC intends to break even and why this may not be as easy as the club suggests. (*12 marks*)

On the income side, match day revenues are up and overall revenues are up by 40%. They also intend to control costs by making their net spending on transfers far lower than it has been in previous years. They plan to reduce the percentage of turnover spent on wages. Achieving a high position in the Premiership each year guarantees prize money, as does involvement in competitions such as the Champions' League. However, Chelsea's ability to make money is limited by the size of its ground, Stamford Bridge, which in order to provide the club with a higher match-day revenue needs to have a greater capacity.

2 Explain what is meant by 'spread the cost of a player across the length of his contract'. Why might this not be appropriate for many other types of business? (*6 marks*)

The purchase of a player can be equated to the purchase of an asset. Most businesses would either buy the asset outright or spread its cost over a period of years in the form of installment payments. In most cases, purchasing a player requires almost immediate full payment. Yet the purchase cost of the player is spread out over the three, four or five year's contract period that has been signed by the player. This is in addition to their wages. This artificially spreads the cost over a period of years and also artificially reduces the costs on paper in the financial year in which the player was purchased. It is only because Chelsea is financially rich that it has sufficient funds to pay in one year, yet spread the cost over a number of years. This is not usually an option open to many businesses.

3 What are the internal and external influences on Chelsea's financial objectives? (*8 marks*)

In terms of the internal influences, the only major influence is that of the owner, who is a 100% shareholder. He has made enormous investment, approaching £600m. However he has put in place several key personnel whose responsibility it is to move the club into a break-even position. A key external influence on the club is the price charged for replacement players and the expectations of players in terms of their weekly wages. The club has also increased its global prominence, which is increasingly giving additional revenue from abroad. Ultimately, as far as match-day revenue is concerned, retaining the current capacity limits income to the amount that season ticket holders and others are prepared to pay. By increasing capacity, prices can be retained, yet match-day income would increase.

FOCUS ON UNDERSTANDING FINANCIAL OBJECTIVES

MINDMAPS

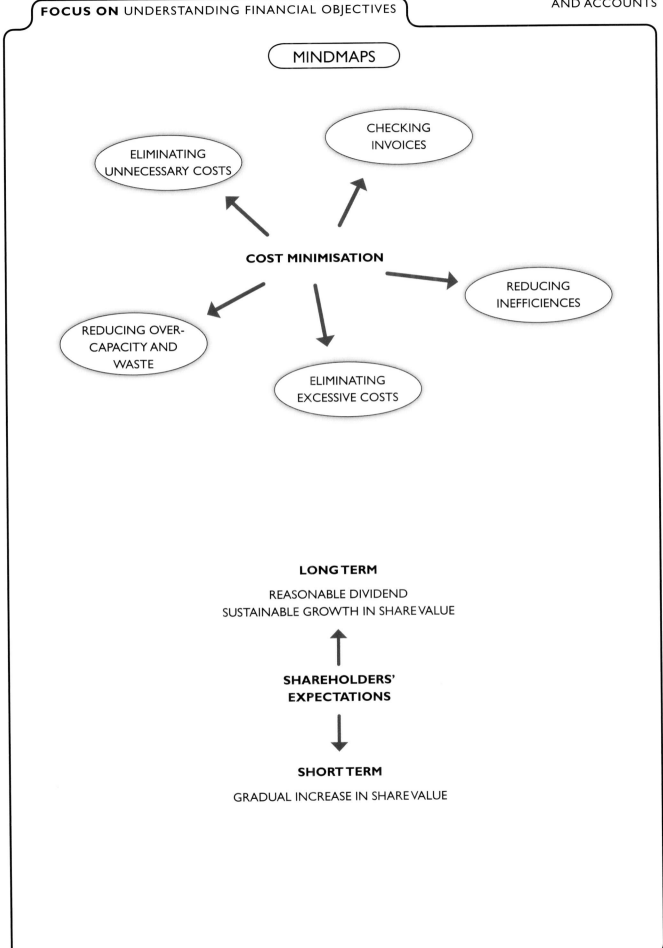

FOCUS ON UNDERSTANDING FINANCIAL OBJECTIVES

MINDMAPS

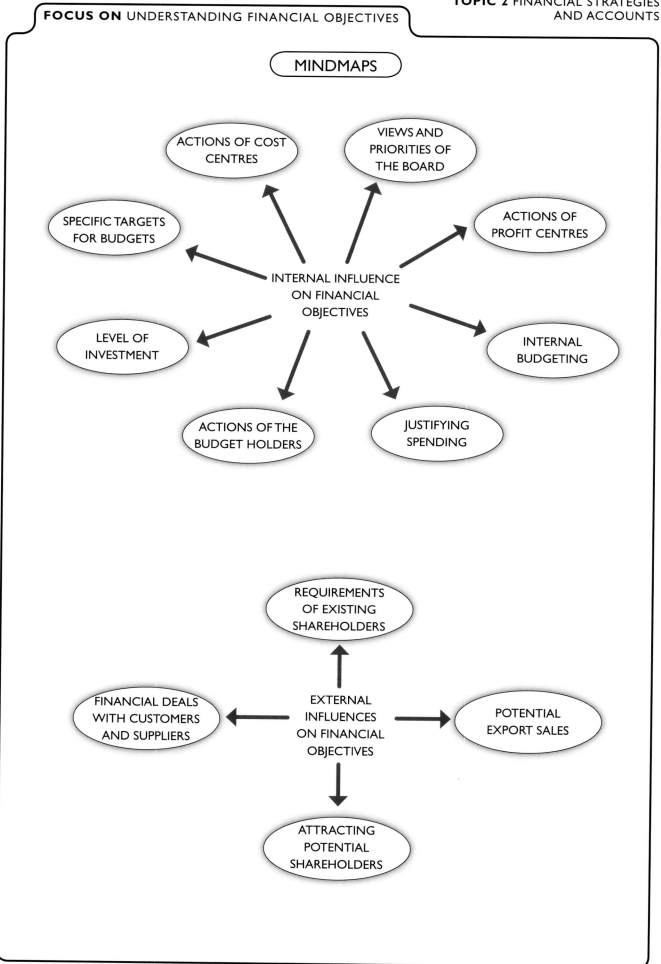

FOCUS ON UNDERSTANDING FINANCIAL OBJECTIVES

WORKSHEET

1 What are the TWO tasks involved in setting cash-flow targets?

2 Identify FIVE potential areas where a business could make savings at very little risk.

3 Briefly identify and explain the key external influences on a business's financial objectives.

Answers ▶ page 221

FOCUS ON USING FINANCIAL DATA
TO MEASURE AND ASSESS PERFORMANCE

Analysing balance sheets ▶ textbook pages 18–19

CASE STUDY – FYFFES PLC

1 What has happened to the total asset value in the two years? Which components of the current and non-current assets are responsible for the changes? (*8 marks*)

The total asset value has fallen. The principle changes have been in the current assets, where trade and other receivables have dropped considerably, indicating that the amount of income that the business has received has fallen. There have been less significant changes in the non-current assets.

2 The business's total liabilities have fallen. Which parts of its liabilities have changed, and how does this affect the financial position of the business? (*10 marks*)

The business has significantly reduced its loans and borrowings, as well as reducing the amount of trade liabilities and other payables. It also does not have any liabilities in terms of provisions or corporation tax. This has contributed to a drastic fall in the level of liabilities of the organisation. It should mean that the business is more liquid.

Analysing income statementss ▶ textbook pages 20–1

CASE STUDY – GLISTEN PLC

1 Briefly comment on the factors that contributed to the business's operating profits over the two years. (*6 marks*)

The turnover was up even though the cost of sales had increased. Gross profit increased but so did administrative costs. Overall, however, operating profit saw a marginal increase of just over £400,000.

2 Why was there a drop in profit in 2007 and why was there a reduction in the basic earnings per share? (*6 marks*)

The business paid significantly more tax in 2007 than in 2006 – approaching £300,000 more. This marginally reduced net profit, which presumably led to the business deciding to reduce the earnings per share by 0.8p and 0.4p respectively.

FOCUS ON USING FINANCIAL DATA
TO MEASURE AND ASSESS PERFORMANCE

Working capital, depreciation, profit utilisation and profit quality ▶

textbook pages 22–3

QUESTIONS

1 It should be easy for a business to be able to value its assets accurately. Discuss. (*12 marks*)

Depreciation is effectively a non-cash expense because it does not require a business to make any actual payment. Depreciation is not a way of providing cash to replace an asset at the end of its useful life. It is, however, important to be able to value assets accurately and effectively to provide a true and fair assessment, not only of the value of the asset, but also of the overall worth of the business. Making sure that this figure is accurate is vital for both investors and for creditors. Straight-line depreciation is actually approved by the Inland Revenue and it simply means that the business should be able to value its assets by working out the likely lifespan of the asset in years and then allocating a depreciation value equal to 100% divided by the number of years; in other words, 25% per year, if the asset is assumed to be serviceable for a total of four years. In this way the business should be able to accurately give a value to its assets.

2 Businesses pay for their assets when they are acquired, so it does not really matter how depreciation is worked out. Discuss. (*12 marks*)

Fixed assets are items of capital expenditure that will be used for a set period of time. However the reduction in the value of these assets is shown on the profit and loss account. It also affects the balance sheet. But capital expenditure itself has no immediate effect on profits. Capital expenditure is expected to generate long-term profits. Therefore when working out the depreciation there are two key options. The first, the reducing balance method, sees the asset reducing in value by a set percentage each year (for example 10% per year over 10 years). Using this method means that fixed assets depreciate by larger amounts in the early years. Many argue that this is more realistic because many assets do lose a large amount of their value in the first few years. The alternative is using straight-line depreciation. However the major argument for using the reducing balance method is that it gives a more accurate value and can also give the business a more accurate calculation of the cost of using that asset. Linking the purchase to the depreciation method, it is certainly the case that many businesses will not purchase the asset outright, but will probably pay a series of staged payments over a number of months or years in order to obtain outright ownership of the asset. The only danger, of course, is that the outstanding balance on the asset can become greater than the actual depreciated value of that asset.

FOCUS ON USING FINANCIAL DATA
TO MEASURE AND ASSESS PERFORMANCE

Using financial data for comparisons, trend analysis and decision-making

▶ textbook pages 24–5

CASE STUDY – NEW HARDWARE

1 **What is the total cost of the proposed investment?** (*4 marks*)

£114,000

2 **What is the total value of the benefits?** (*2 marks*)

£180,000

3 **What is the payback time for the overall project?** (*4 marks*)

0.63 of a year, or eight months.

4 **This is an example of a cost benefit analysis. What are its key advantages and disadvantages?** (*6 marks*)

The tool allows a business to work out how much the change will cost then calculate the

benefits from it. Costs and benefits can be paid or received over time, so it is important to work out the time it will take for the benefits to repay the costs. The technique can only be used with financial costs and financial benefits. Cost benefit analysis does not include intangible items. If a business estimates a value for intangibles there will be an element of subjectivity in the process. Large projects can be evaluated using this kind of approach, which takes into account the complexities, but it only deals with the financial side. It is important to remember that the payback time can also be referred to as the breakeven point for the project. This is often more important than the overall benefits that a project can deliver.

Assessing strengths and weaknesses of financial data in judging performance

▶ textbook pages 26–7

QUESTIONS

1 **Find out what is meant by the term 'window dressing'. How does this apply to accounts?** (*8 marks*)

Window dressing is a way in which businesses can present their accounts in order to flatter their financial position. In effect this is creative accounting. It can be misleading, particularly to shareholders. Accounts can never be viewed as being 100% accurate, as businesses only need to put down their bank balance details and cash holdings on that particular day. They could easily avoid placing orders or paying bills until after the date of the balance sheet. There may be some fixed assets that have been sold in order to boost income and there is no indication of whether the business is about to make a large investment in new assets after the balance sheet has been completed.

2 **How can a business make a fair stock valuation?** (*8 marks*)

A business is required to carry out a stock check as part of the creation of the final accounts. The stock valuation appears on both the balance sheet and the profit and loss account. It therefore has an impact on profit. It is important to remember that stock is the least liquid of current assets, but the stock check needs to be accurate, and the quantities need to be as close to the actual figures as possible. Slow-selling, outdated or unsaleable stock needs to be properly valued. These will have to be given a scrap value, or a value of zero. Any closing stock is valued at historic cost, or net realisable value. The convention is to use whichever is lower.

FOCUS ON USING FINANCIAL DATA
TO MEASURE AND ASSESS PERFORMANCE

Case studies, questions and exam practice ▶ textbook pages 28–9

CASE STUDY – SCHOOL UNIFORMS

1 What does Sandeep mean by 'we produce a balance sheet as part of our annual accounts and as an internal management exercise'? What is the purpose of doing this? (*10 marks*)

Not only does Sandeep have to produce a balance sheet as a legal requirement, but he also creates one in order to help the business plan for the future, by seeing precisely the state of assets and liabilities. It also alerts the business to any potential problems in the future. The balance sheet enabled the company to secure a bank loan for improvement and expansion. Originally, when it did not have a balance sheet, it could not get a loan because it did not have up-to-date accounts. The business recognised this as a problem and put the accounts together as soon as possible.

2 What does Sandeep mean by saying that he used cash flow rather than a loan to fund the refurbishment? (*6 marks*)

The business had sufficient liquidity to be able to pay for the refurbishment. This means that it had a surplus of income compared to expenditure and that rather than take out a bank loan it used this surplus directly to pay for the refurbishment. There was no need for the business to incur the additional costs of interest payments on the loan when it already had the necessary funds to pay for it. This was despite the fact that the loan had been approved. In his own words, Sandeep has kept money in the business rather than take it all out. The balance sheet has allowed him to identify that the business has significantly more money in it than he is currently taking out as wages for himself.

3 Consider Sandeep's top tips and comment on their value to a business. (*12 marks*)

He is right about creditors, as it gives a more accurate view of the financial position of the business. A supplier is more likely to offer discounts and be more flexible about deliveries if it knows that it can trust a customer to pay promptly or at least in accordance with the invoice terms. What is meant by the second point is that separate agreements can be entered into to acquire assets, rather than listing them as being leased assets on the balance sheet. This will artificially inflate the value of assets on the balance sheet. Payments will still have to be made towards these assets but this will not necessarily appear on the balance sheet. On the last point, being too liquid is not the best idea, as holding money in current accounts does not provide the business with a sufficient return. If the business has sufficient cash that will not be needed as working capital, this could be shifted to a higher interest account, in order to make the money work harder for the business and provide a better rate of return.

FOCUS ON USING FINANCIAL DATA
TO MEASURE AND ASSESS PERFORMANCE

MINDMAPS

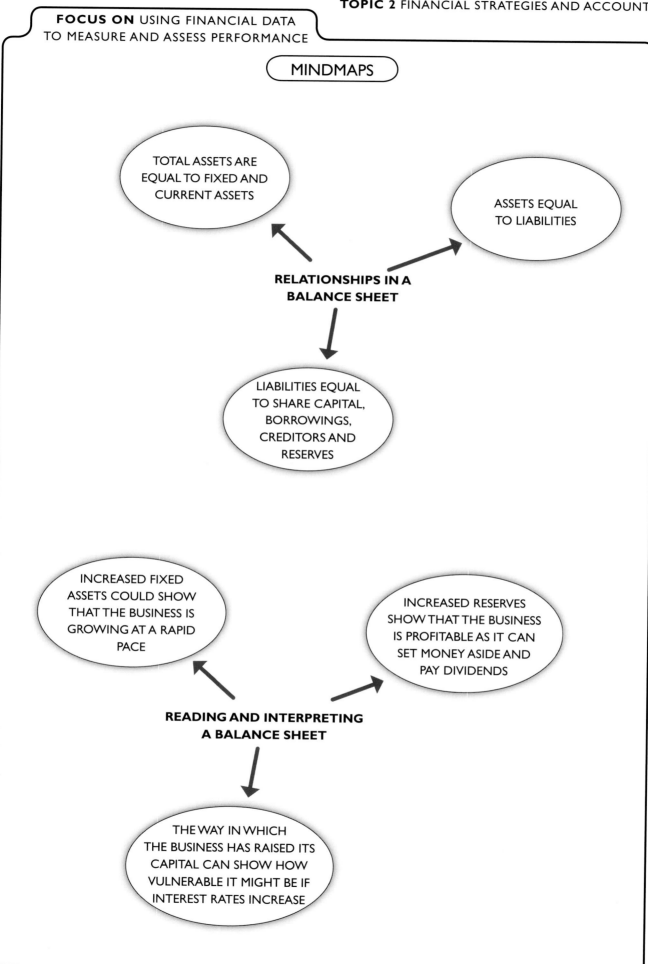

TOTAL ASSETS ARE EQUAL TO FIXED AND CURRENT ASSETS

ASSETS EQUAL TO LIABILITIES

RELATIONSHIPS IN A BALANCE SHEET

LIABILITIES EQUAL TO SHARE CAPITAL, BORROWINGS, CREDITORS AND RESERVES

INCREASED FIXED ASSETS COULD SHOW THAT THE BUSINESS IS GROWING AT A RAPID PACE

INCREASED RESERVES SHOW THAT THE BUSINESS IS PROFITABLE AS IT CAN SET MONEY ASIDE AND PAY DIVIDENDS

READING AND INTERPRETING A BALANCE SHEET

THE WAY IN WHICH THE BUSINESS HAS RAISED ITS CAPITAL CAN SHOW HOW VULNERABLE IT MIGHT BE IF INTEREST RATES INCREASE

FOCUS ON USING FINANCIAL DATA
TO MEASURE AND ASSESS PERFORMANCE

MINDMAPS

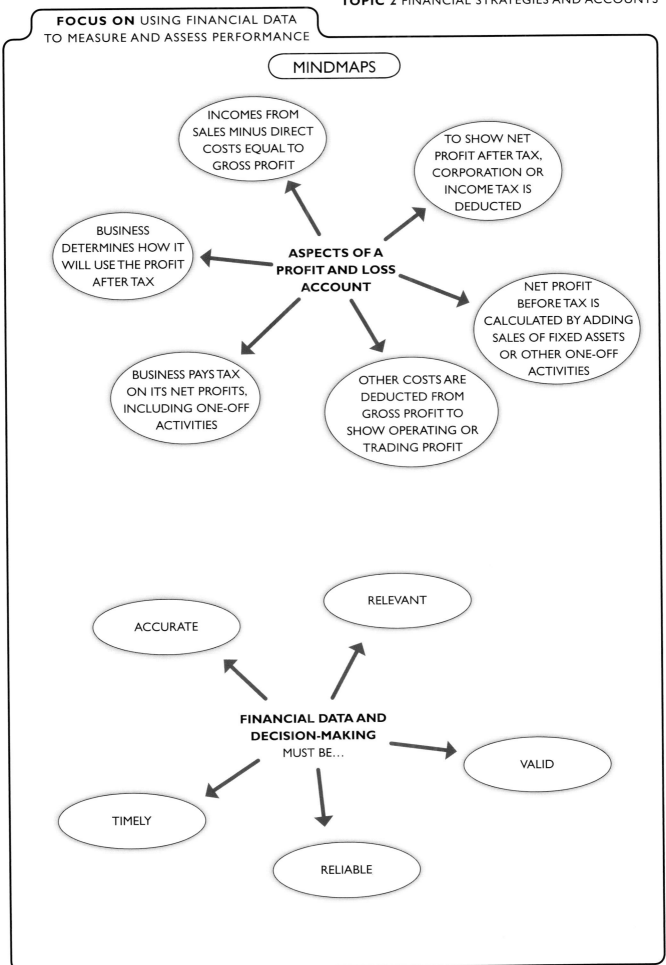

INCOMES FROM
SALES MINUS DIRECT
COSTS EQUAL TO
GROSS PROFIT

TO SHOW NET
PROFIT AFTER TAX,
CORPORATION OR
INCOME TAX IS
DEDUCTED

BUSINESS
DETERMINES HOW IT
WILL USE THE PROFIT
AFTER TAX

**ASPECTS OF A
PROFIT AND LOSS
ACCOUNT**

NET PROFIT
BEFORE TAX IS
CALCULATED BY ADDING
SALES OF FIXED ASSETS
OR OTHER ONE-OFF
ACTIVITIES

BUSINESS PAYS TAX
ON ITS NET PROFITS,
INCLUDING ONE-OFF
ACTIVITIES

OTHER COSTS ARE
DEDUCTED FROM
GROSS PROFIT TO
SHOW OPERATING OR
TRADING PROFIT

RELEVANT

ACCURATE

**FINANCIAL DATA AND
DECISION-MAKING**
MUST BE…

VALID

TIMELY

RELIABLE

FOCUS ON USING FINANCIAL DATA
TO MEASURE AND ASSESS PERFORMANCE

MINDMAPS

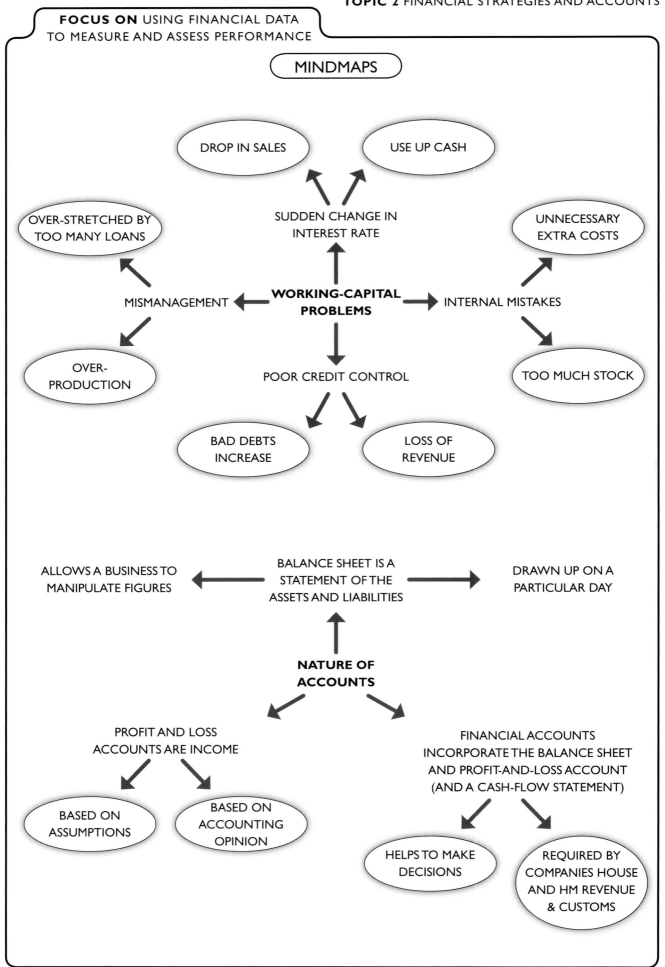

DROP IN SALES

USE UP CASH

OVER-STRETCHED BY
TOO MANY LOANS

SUDDEN CHANGE IN
INTEREST RATE

UNNECESSARY
EXTRA COSTS

MISMANAGEMENT

**WORKING-CAPITAL
PROBLEMS**

INTERNAL MISTAKES

OVER-
PRODUCTION

POOR CREDIT CONTROL

TOO MUCH STOCK

BAD DEBTS
INCREASE

LOSS OF
REVENUE

ALLOWS A BUSINESS TO
MANIPULATE FIGURES

BALANCE SHEET IS A
STATEMENT OF THE
ASSETS AND LIABILITIES

DRAWN UP ON A
PARTICULAR DAY

**NATURE OF
ACCOUNTS**

PROFIT AND LOSS
ACCOUNTS ARE INCOME

FINANCIAL ACCOUNTS
INCORPORATE THE BALANCE SHEET
AND PROFIT-AND-LOSS ACCOUNT
(AND A CASH-FLOW STATEMENT)

BASED ON
ASSUMPTIONS

BASED ON
ACCOUNTING
OPINION

HELPS TO MAKE
DECISIONS

REQUIRED BY
COMPANIES HOUSE
AND HM REVENUE
& CUSTOMS

FOCUS ON USING FINANCIAL DATA
TO MEASURE AND ASSESS PERFORMANCE

MINDMAPS

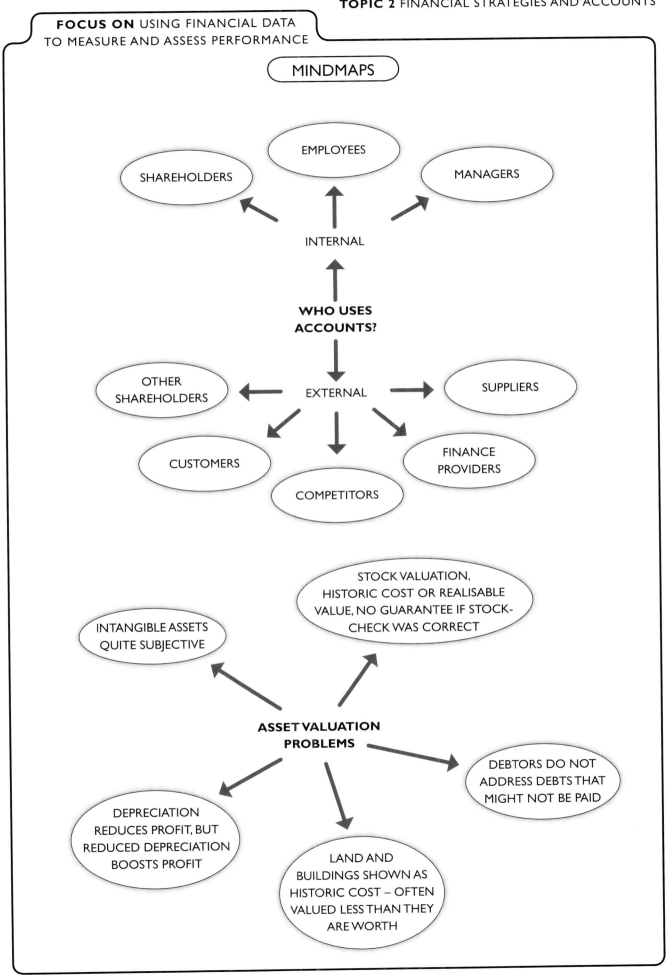

FOCUS ON USING FINANCIAL DATA
TO MEASURE AND ASSESS PERFORMANCE

WORKSHEET

I What are the THREE key relationships on a balance sheet?

2 Why are balance sheets often referred to as snapshots?

3 Briefly explain the important aspects of a profit-and-loss account.

Answers ▶ page 221

A2 ESSENTIAL BUSINESS STUDIES FOR AQA

FOCUS ON USING FINANCIAL DATA
TO MEASURE AND ASSESS PERFORMANCE

WORKSHEET

1　What do you understand by the term 'working capital'?

2　What is the purpose of calculating depreciation?

3　How can financial data provide support to business decision-making?

Answers ▶ page 221

FOCUS ON INTERPRETING
PUBLISHED ACCOUNTS

Conducting ratio analysis (1) ▶ textbook pages 30–1

CASE STUDY – THREE SIMILAR BUSINESSES?

1 Calculate the current ratio, acid test ratio and gearing of Buchan's. (*6 marks*)

Buchan:

Current ratio – 2.1:1
Acid test – 1.5:1
Gearing – 66%

2 Calculate the current ratio, acid test ratio and gearing of Carlisle. (*6 marks*)

Carlisle:

Current ratio – 0.625:1
Acid test – 0.5:1
Gearing – 70%

3 Calculate the current ratio, acid test ratio and gearing of Stimpsons. (*6 marks*)

Stimpsons:

Current ratio – 1.63:1
Acid test – 1.27:1
Gearing – 22%

Conducting ratio analysis (2) ▶ textbook pages 32–3

QUESTION

Which ratio provides a better indication of company performance and why, when comparing dividend yield ratio and dividend per share ratio? (*8 marks*)

The dividend yield really provides a better guide to a business's performance, as it compares the return with the amount that actually needs to be invested to buy the share. It also allows fairer comparisons, taking into account the actual price of the share, rather than simply internal factors, such as the dividend and the number of shares in the dividend per share ratio. The dividend per share ratio does not take into account the actual original investment in the share purchase, so what may appear to be a relatively good dividend per share is in fact relatively poor, as the investment was high to purchase the shares in the first place.

FOCUS ON INTERPRETING PUBLISHED ACCOUNTS

Assessing the value and limitations of ratio analysis ▶ textbook pages 34–5

CASE STUDY – IT FIGURES

1 Outline the key trends in profits over the period 2004–2007. (*6 marks*)

The gross profit margin has significantly increased over the period. The operating profit margin has been relatively stable with a slight upward trend. The pre-tax profit margins peaked in 2005 and since then have fallen back to a figure close to the 2004 level.

2 What other improvements have been made over the same period? Comment on their significance. (*8 marks*)

The business has significantly improved on its ability to recover debts, but has delayed its payments to creditors. Figures were especially good in 2005 as far as return on investment and growth in sales were concerned, although both of these now drop back to relatively modest increases. The ROCE figures are healthy but they again peaked in 2005.

Case studies, questions and exam practices ▶ textbook pages 36–7

CASE STUDY – AVERAGES

1 Comment on how valuable this exercise may be to the business. (*18 marks*)

It is a valuable exercise as it compares like with like. The business is able to compare its own performance figures with those of similar businesses in the same industry. Internally it allows the management to compare its performance and control over the organisation, while allowing potential investors to see that by and large the business is performing far better than the industry average. This would probably only be a significant advantage if the business was performing better than the industry standard: if it had failed in this respect or was considerably lower, then this would highlight deficiencies in the business.

2 Highlight the key relevant comparisons and comment on them. (*16 marks*)

The business's gross profit margin is considerably higher, as are its operating margin and pre-tax profits. The business's return on capital employed is significantly higher than the industry standard, and the return on investment is five times that of the industry standard. The current ratio and debt ratio are broadly in line with the industry standard. The business shows a lower stock turnover than the industry standard and it offers less day's credit to customers, but at the same time it also pays faster. Debtor turnover is faster. The value-added figures are not immediately comparable, but the average sales per employee are considerably lower than the industry standard. The actual growth in sales is significant, as these are far lower than the industry standard.

3 How useful would the second part of the research be and why? (*8 marks*)

By identifying businesses as being part of one of these three groups (and presumably creating a fourth category for businesses that do not fall into any of these three groups) major differences between performances can be explained. For example, larger companies will be enjoying a greater market share, market leadership and economies of scale. Faster growing companies should illustrate that they are retaining profits for reinvestment, rather than distributing them to shareholders. The new entrants to the market will not be expected to be performing as well as more established businesses.

FOCUS ON INTERPRETING
PUBLISHED ACCOUNTS

MINDMAPS

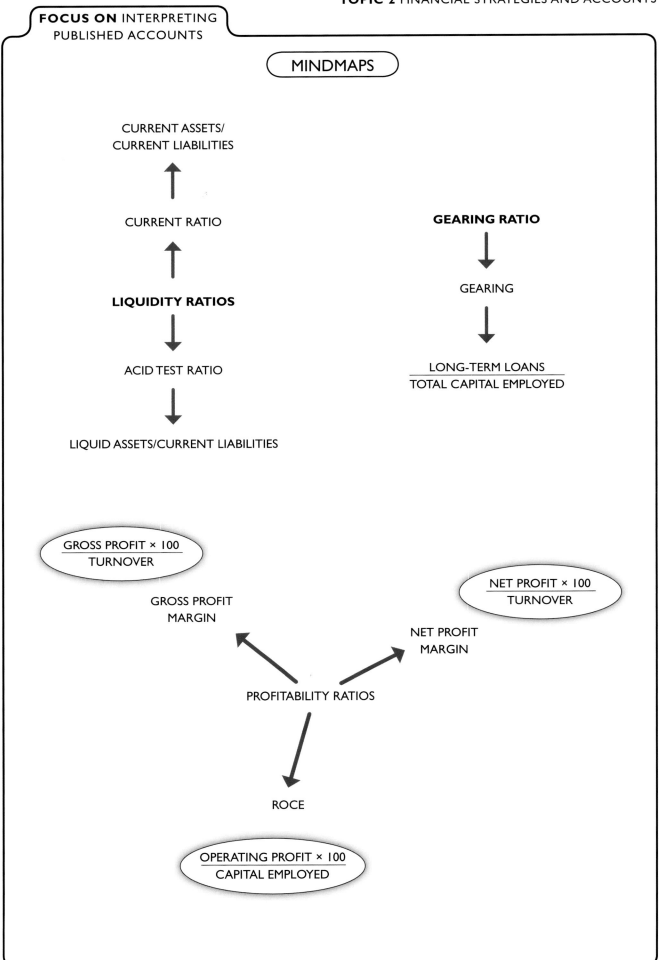

FOCUS ON INTERPRETING
PUBLISHED ACCOUNTS

MINDMAPS

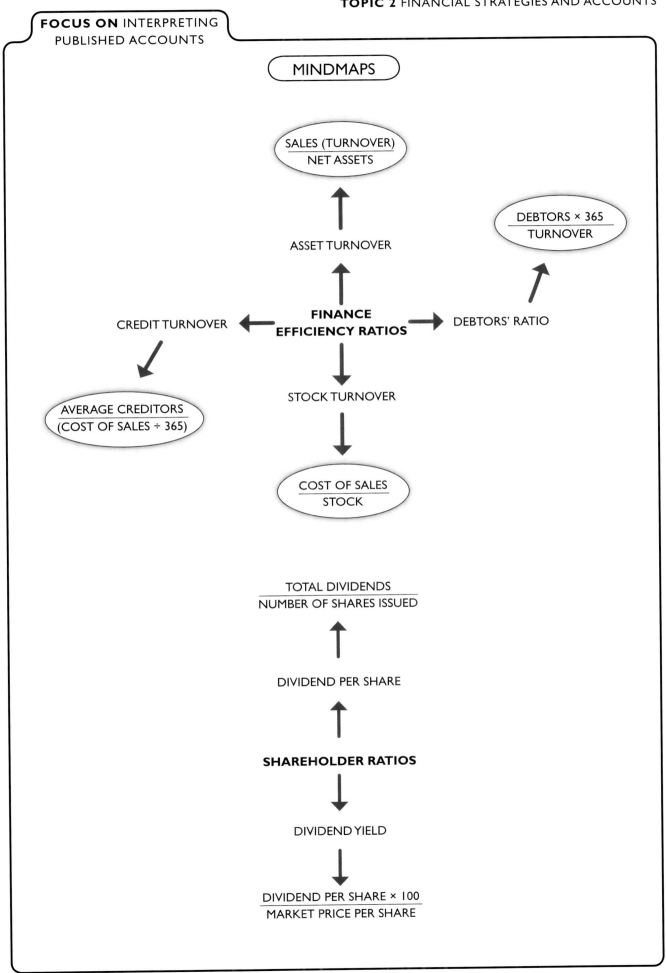

FOCUS ON INTERPRETING
PUBLISHED ACCOUNTS

WORKSHEET

1 What other term is used to describe a liquidity ratio, and what is its purpose?

2 What is meant if a business is described as being 'highly geared'?

3 Briefly explain FOUR limitations of ratio analysis.

FOCUS ON SELECTING FINANCIAL STRATEGIES

Raising finance and implementing profit centres ▶ textbook pages 38–9

QUESTIONS

1 List at least five common direct costs and five common indirect costs. (*10 marks*)

Direct costs – wages of directly engaged employees, materials used, components used, depreciation of machinery and marketing that is specific to that cost or profit centre.

Indirect costs – supervisors or managers' salaries or wages; cross-departmental services, such as human resources, heating and lighting, depreciation of general machinery, administration costs, general marketing costs and running expenses, such as rent and telephone bills.

2 What do you understand by the term 'full costing', and what are the implications for a profit or cost centre? (*6 marks*)

This is a way of allocating indirect overheads between the various cost centres. It is the simplest way of doing it, but possibly the least accurate. An arbitrary method is used to allocate a proportion of the costs that would be allocated to each centre. For example, if one department has 25% of the floor space then it may be allocated 25% of the costs.

Cost minimisation and allocating capital expenditure ▶ textbook pages 40–1

QUESTION

Why might it be unfair to allocate the full costs of overheads to particular cost and profit centres, purely based on the amount of space that they occupy or the number of employees in that centre? (*12 marks*)

The various ways of allocating overheads to cost centres need to be applied with care. Actually determining the full costs are difficult and it is important to include other factors such as marketing and human resources. Costing methods usually simply provide more questions rather than giving answers. If a centre takes up a large share of the physical area of the business is it actually using this area efficiently? If it has large numbers of employees is it an efficient cost centre, or would it actually work far better if it had some capital investment? A broad allocation of costs on a fairly crude basis, such as space or number of employees, does not begin to really address where the costs have been incurred, or to whom they should be charged.

FOCUS ON SELECTING
FINANCIAL STRATEGIES

Case studies, questions and exam practices ▸ textbook pages 42–3

QUESTIONS

1 Explain why the business has decided to set up profit centres. (*8 marks*)

The business describes itself as being entrepreneurial, innovative and customer-focused, so each of the profit centres needs to show skills in selling, buying, promotion and research. It has set up the profit centres so that the teams have a sense of identity and ownership, but each centre recognises that certain services must be provided centrally to enjoy economies of scale.

2 Briefly explain why profit centres might be appropriate to this particular type of business. (*6 marks*)

This is a fast-moving industry and the company is actively seeking out new markets or market niches with high growth potential. It therefore needs to create small and flexible profit-centre teams with experience in these particular markets. It supplies information and services through its publications and in effect each profit centre is a subsidiary product, also providing a series of additional services, such as directories, awards and ceremonies.

3 What is the purpose of the central service teams? (*4 marks*)

Primarily to encourage economies of scale. The creation of a central service infrastructure to provide IT, marketing, human resources and other services, frees up the profit centres so that they can concentrate on specialised work. As new profit centres are added, the central service team can be expanded. It also means that replication is minimised and central costs are more closely monitored and controlled.

MINDMAPS

FOCUS ON SELECTING
FINANCIAL STRATEGIES

MINDMAPS

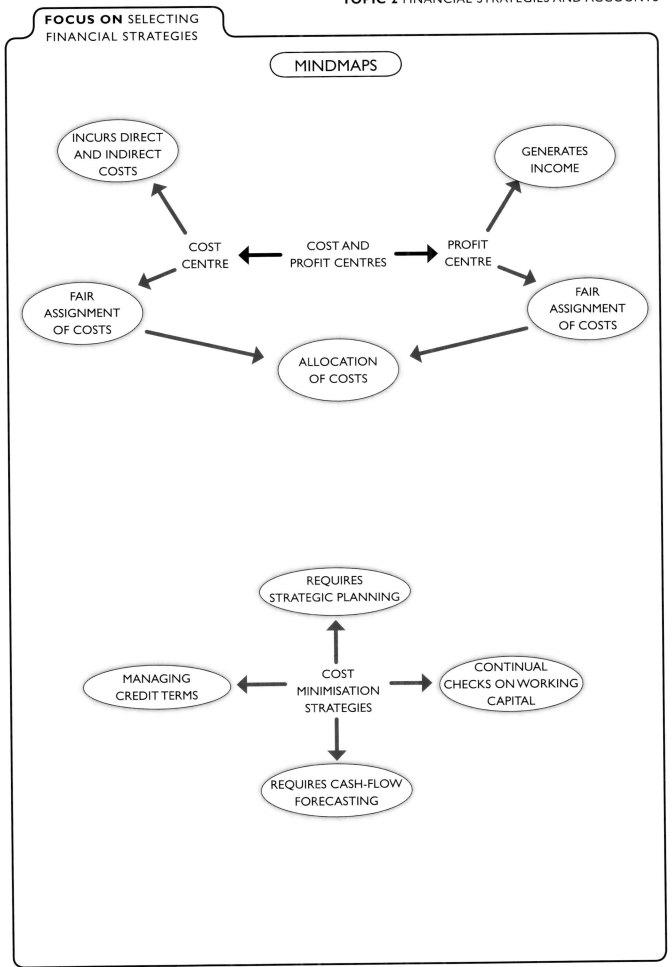

FOCUS ON SELECTING
FINANCIAL STRATEGIES

MINDMAPS

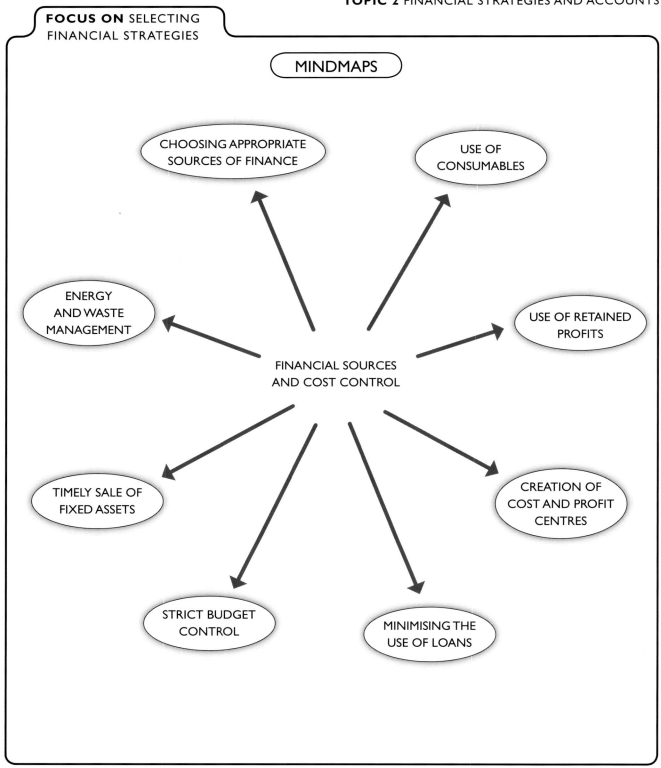

FOCUS ON SELECTING
FINANCIAL STRATEGIES

(WORKSHEET)

I Suggest TWO internal and TWO external sources of finance for a business.

2 Why might a business set up profit or cost centres?

3 Briefly explain how a business might allocate capital expenditure.

Answers ▶ page 222

FOCUS ON MAKING INVESTMENT DECISIONS

Conducting investment appraisal ▶ textbook pages 44–5

CASE STUDY – PROPOSAL

1 **How would you go about considering this investment appraisal?** (*10 marks*)

It would be important for any investment appraisal to incorporate the checking of the figures, to ensure that the capital expenditure estimates are correct. Although the operating costs have been worked out in some detail, there is no clear indication as to how the £50,000 figure has been reached, as income for coaching fees and hire. The initial investment is just £68,000 and almost half of this can be recouped within the first year, with the project more than paying back the initial investment within three years. This does not take into account any possible external factors, particularly the availability of alternatives to this indoor cricket facility. On a non-quantitative basis, one of the purposes is to make use of an unused building and to make the cricketing community more aware of the

business's range of products. This will bring in other benefits (probably financial) that are not directly factored into the proposal itself.

2 **Without carrying out quantitative investment appraisal techniques, would you approve or reject the proposal? Explain your reasons.** (*10 marks*)

Even a quick look at the figures will show that the investment is modest and that the project will pay for itself within about two and three-quarter years. This makes it a very low-risk proposal and in all likelihood it would be approved by the business. Over a period of ten years, for example, assuming no other major investment is necessary, the project will bring in over £250,000 on an initial investment of less than £70,000. While assumptions have been made about the income, which is broadly £1,000 per week, these figures are not excessive and probably realisable.

Investment criteria ▶ textbook pages 46–7

CASE STUDY – THE SOUTH WEST VENTURES FUND

1 **Comment on the implications of South West Ventures Fund's investment criteria as far as a business looking for funding is concerned.** (*8 marks*)

A potential business not only has to fulfil the extensive list of attributes, but also its investment needs must not be in excess of £660,000 in the short-term and £2.1m in the longer-term. It is important to note that the fund seems to reserve the right to bring in other new investors, as well as providing its own funds. The investment criteria does cover businesses that are seeking to expand, either by growing themselves or by acquiring other businesses. This incorporates management buy-outs and management buy-ins, as well as start-up companies. There also appear to be some areas of industry that the fund is not comfortable in dealing with.

2 **What do you think is meant by 'post-investment requirements' and what might be their implications?** (*6 marks*)

In order to oversee and protect the fund's investment, a non-executive director is appointed to the board of the business that has received the funds. On the one hand this individual provides assistance to the business, as they have relevant experience and skills. On the other hand the individual is there to provide the fund with monthly briefing reports and to ensure that the business provides regular financial information to the fund. The implications are that the business will be under greater scrutiny than ever before and it may well have to prepare information and change some of its decisions to fall in line with the fund's advice and requirements.

FOCUS ON MAKING INVESTMENT DECISIONS

Risks and uncertainties of investment decisions ▶ textbook pages 48–9

QUESTION

To what extent does a systematic project appraisal take the risk and uncertainty out of investment decisions? (12 marks)

A systematic approach to project appraisal is absolutely essential, as it should deal with all relevant and non-relevant costs, as well as quantitative and qualitative factors. It will also deal with opportunity costs, and handle the various ways in which a project can be assessed in financial terms using a variety of different techniques. By including as many interested parties as possible in the evaluation process, it would appear that, while not entirely foolproof, the project appraisal system should identify any key concerns and seek to eliminate the majority of the risks. The problem stage arises once authorisation is given, as the project now passes into the hands of a project manager, who must be as diligent in ensuring that the project goes according to plan as those involved in the lead-up to the authorisation.

Evaluating qualitative and quantitative influences on investment decisions

▶ textbook pages 50–1

QUESTIONS

1 What would be the value of a cash flow of £56,000 in four year's time if the interest rate was reckoned to be 8%? (2 marks)

£41,440

2 If a business made an investment of £100,000 and expected £25,000 net inflow per year, what would be the payback period? (2 marks)

Four years

Case studies, questions and exam practices ▶ textbook pages 52–3

CASE STUDY – A TALE OF TWO CITIES

1 Calculate the net present value for each of the projects at the end of year five. Show your workings. (12 marks)

The calculations that should be carried out by the students are summarised in the tables below:

London

YEAR	CASH FLOW	DF	PV
0	(550,000)	1.00	(550,000)
1	88,000	0.91	80,080
2	92,000	0.83	76,360
3	96,000	0.75	72,000
4	94,000	0.68	63,920
5	162,000	0.62	100,440
Net present value = (157,200)			

Norwich

YEAR	CASH FLOW	DF	PV
0	(550,000)	1.00	(550,000)
1	95,000	0.91	86,450
2	95,000	0.83	78,850
3	95,000	0.75	71,250
4	104,000	0.68	70,720
5	95,000	0.62	58,900
Net present value = (183,830)			

2 Which of the two projects would you recommend? Why? (4 marks)

Since neither of the projects will actually go into profit within the first five years, neither of them should be recommended. London is marginally better, but still provides the business with a loss of nearly £160,000.

FOCUS ON MAKING INVESTMENT DECISIONS

MINDMAPS

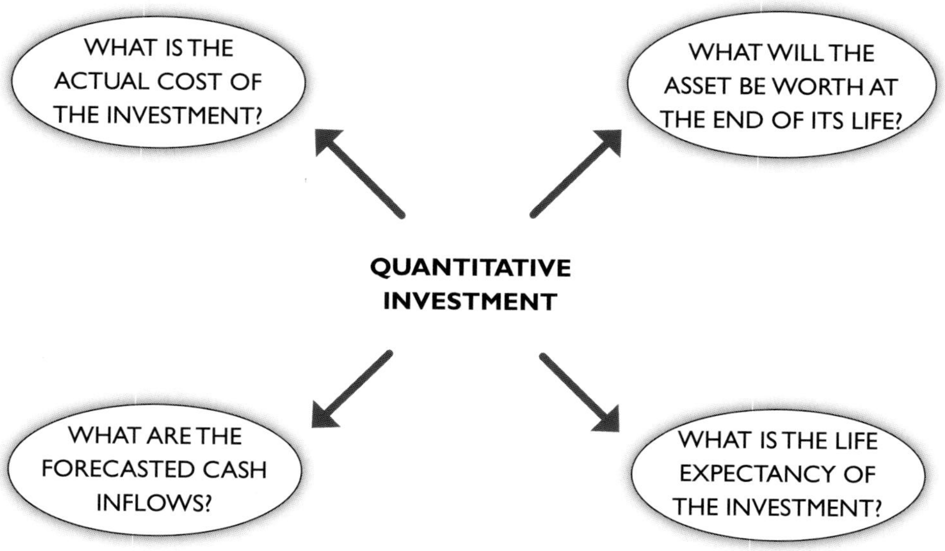

WHAT IS THE
ACTUAL COST OF
THE INVESTMENT?

WHAT WILL THE
ASSET BE WORTH AT
THE END OF ITS LIFE?

**QUANTITATIVE
INVESTMENT**

WHAT ARE THE
FORECASTED CASH
INFLOWS?

WHAT IS THE LIFE
EXPECTANCY OF
THE INVESTMENT?

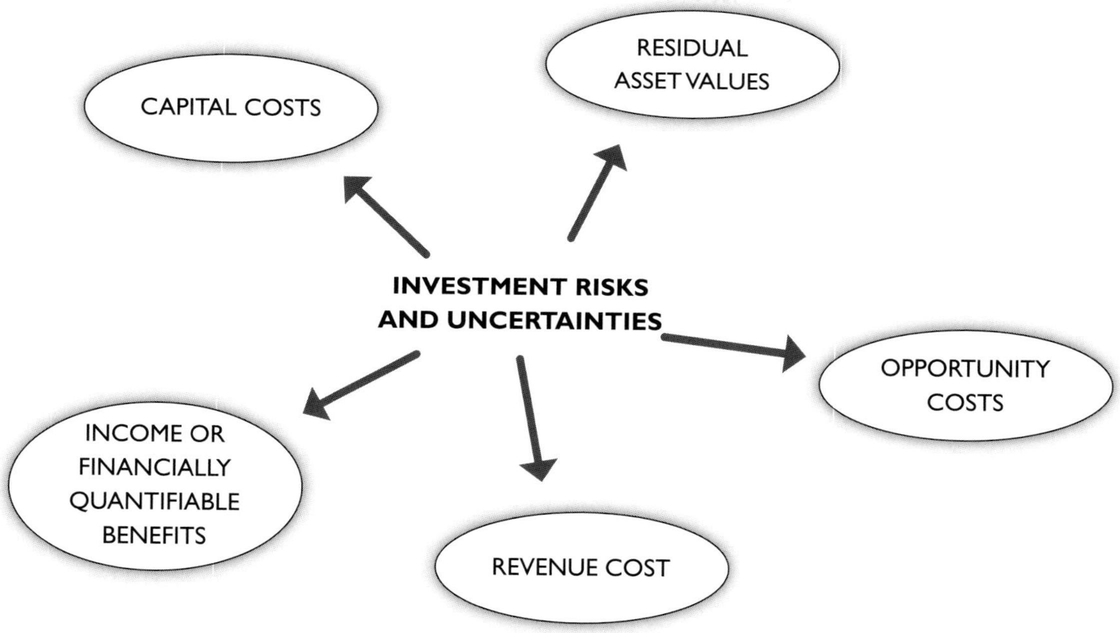

CAPITAL COSTS

RESIDUAL
ASSET VALUES

**INVESTMENT RISKS
AND UNCERTAINTIES**

OPPORTUNITY
COSTS

INCOME OR
FINANCIALLY
QUANTIFIABLE
BENEFITS

REVENUE COST

FOCUS ON MAKING INVESTMENT DECISIONS

MINDMAPS

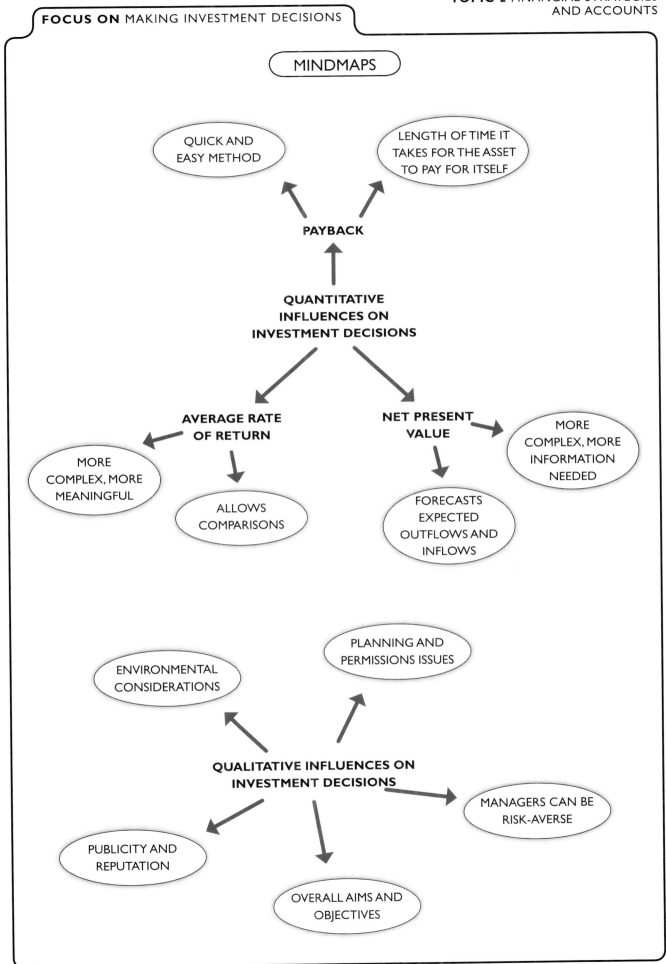

FOCUS ON MAKING INVESTMENT DECISIONS

WORKSHEET

I   What do you understand by the term 'investment appraisal'?

2. Suggest likely areas of investigation that a business might explore before making an investment decision.

3   Distinguish between quantitative and qualitative influences on investment decisions.

Answers ▶ page 222

FOCUS ON UNDERSTANDING MARKETING STRATEGIES

Marketing objectives ▶ textbook pages 56–7

QUESTION

What are the four main types of marketing objective and why do all marketing objectives fit within these four descriptions? (*8 marks*)

The four main objectives are:

- Market penetration – selling more of an existing product or service into an existing market by either increasing consumer demand or by taking customers away from the competitors.

- Market development – selling more of an existing product or service to new customers, perhaps by offering them in a new country or radically changing the advertising or outlets in which the product or service can be purchased.

- Product development – selling a new or improved product to existing customers by encouraging them to upgrade.

- Diversification – moving into a new area of business with new products and services that are targeted at new customers.

All other specific marketing objectives are subsets of these four. Each of the four key objectives deal with market leadership, market share, profitability, issues such as customer service, communication with customers, improving profile and reputation and a host of other key marketing statements.

Internal and external influences on marketing objectives ▶ textbook pages 58–9

CASE STUDY – THE OLYMPIC MOVEMENT'S MARKETING OBJECTIVES

Olympic events are unique, but what do you think are the key marketing objectives of the Olympic Movement? How are these affected by external factors? (*10 marks*)

The Olympic movement wants to ensure that the movement is financially stable, to generate funds for the Olympic movement, ensure that the widest possible range of people can see the games and to preserve the character of the games. In the above example they seem to be successful in almost every aspect, with increased advertising spending, increased awareness, sponsorship and 16,000 hours of coverage. It was also featured extensively on the internet.

Key external influences on their marketing objectives are the relationships between different countries, mainly politically and economically. The Olympic Movement faced enormous challenges in the run-up to the Olympic Games in China in 2008, largely as a result of alleged Chinese human rights abuses and China's continued occupation of Tibet. These are external influences beyond the control of the Olympic Movement.

FOCUS ON UNDERSTANDING MARKETING STRATEGIES

Case studies, questions and exam practice ▶ textbook pages 60–1

THE HOME OF THE OLYMPICS

1 How closely do the events in Athens match the Olympic marketing objectives? (*8 marks*)

The Olympic Games certainly brought in many millions to the Olympic Movement and was a very successful games. The Olympic Movement made sure that the widest possible range of different broadcast media was used to ensure worldwide coverage. As this was a celebration of the return of the Olympics to Greece, it received greater coverage than any other Olympics in history. It could therefore be argued that the Olympic Movement's marketing objectives were fully met by the games.

2 Which new technologies have been embraced by the Olympic Movement to bring the games to a wider audience? (*4 marks*)

Satellite and cable channels provided 24-hour coverage. Many broadcasters used 3G technology to make streaming video and highlight clips available through mobile phones. There was also streaming video via the internet, through various broadcasters, and the Olympic website. The games were also broadcast for the first time in HD TV.

A2 ESSENTIAL BUSINESS STUDIES FOR AQA

MINDMAPS

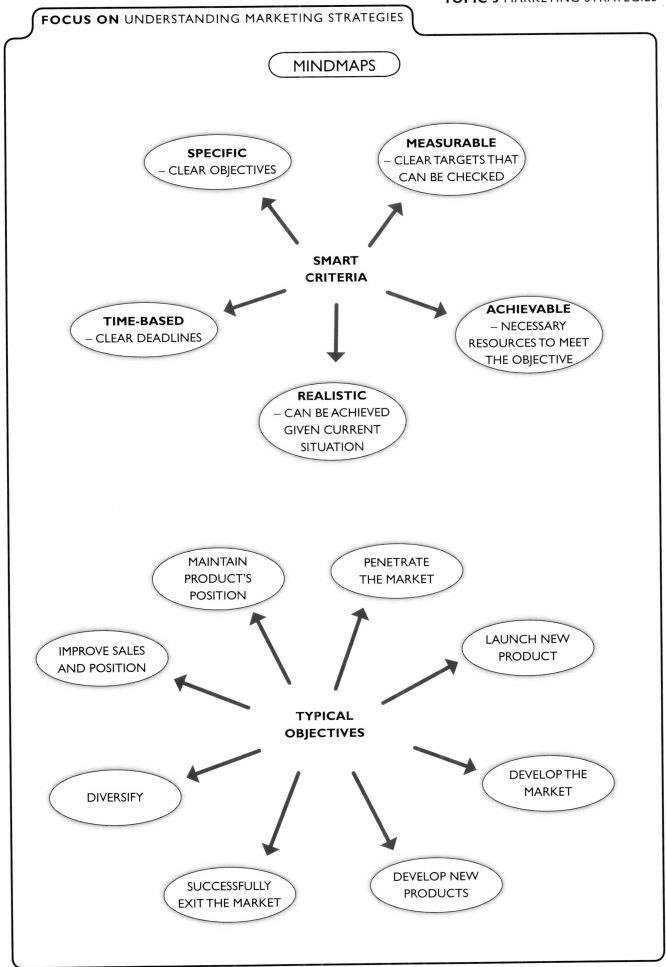

MINDMAPS

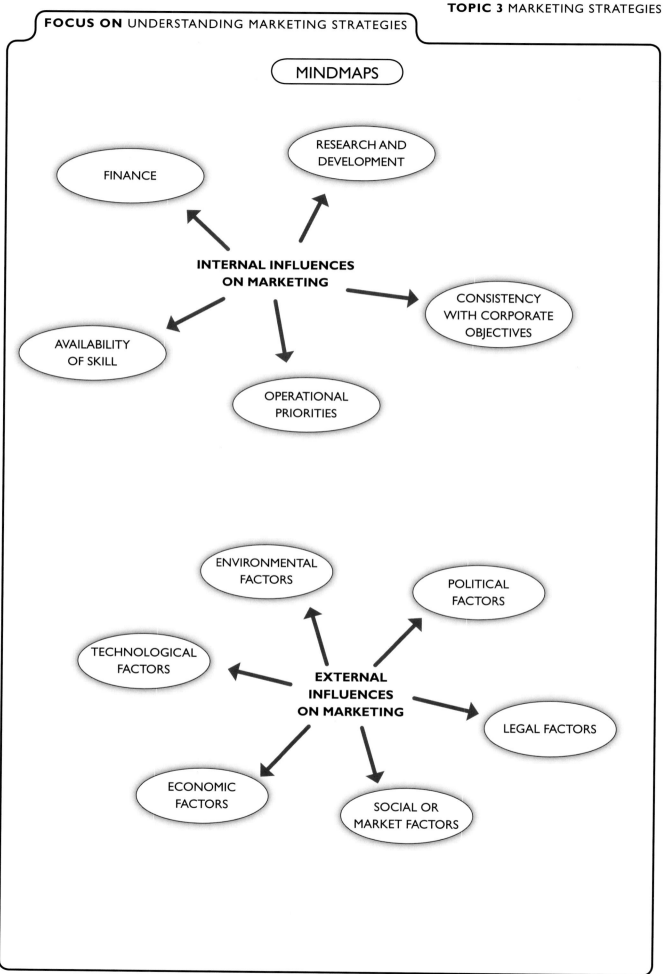

FOCUS ON UNDERSTANDING MARKETING STRATEGIES

WORKSHEET

1 What are the FOUR main types of marketing objective?

2 Briefly explain why businesses should be aware of the nature of a market before becoming involved in it.

3 Briefly explain potential internal influences on a business's marketing objectives.

Answers ▶ page 222

FOCUS ON ANALYSING MARKETS AND MARKETING

Reasons for and the value of market analysis ▶ textbook pages 62–3

QUESTION

For the past five years a business has steadily sold £50 million of products into the market each year. Next year it predicts that this will increase to £60 million as the market is growing. Five years ago the market was worth £550 million and has grown steadily at a rate of 10% each year, but is expected to grow by 20% next year.

What is the market share of the business over this period of time and into next year, and what is the underlying pattern of that market share? (*6 marks*)

In year one the business's market share was 9%. In year two this fell to 8%, in year 3 to 7.5%, in year 4 to 6.8% and in year 5 to 6.2%. By achieving an extra £10m of sales in year 6 the business has only managed to maintain its market share of 6.2%. The underlying trend over the five-year period has been significantly downwards, although if the increase in sales is maintained then this fall can be arrested.

Methods of analysing trends ▶ textbook pages 64–5

QUESTIONS

There is a clear relationship between elasticity and correlation. Price elasticity of demand usually shows a negative correlation because sales fall when prices increase. Price elasticity of demand measures the relationship between price changes and changes in quantity demanded. Income elasticity measures changes in income and quantity demanded.

I   What would normally happen to cheap, own-brand food sales if customers have more disposable income? What type of correlation is likely to be shown? (*4 marks*)

Their sales would fall because customers would switch to branded or more luxurious products. This means that there is a negative correlation.

2   Correlation can help a business to target a specific part of the market. If there is a strong correlation between income levels and demand for its products, what should the business do and what would be the likely outcome? (*4 marks*)

The business should switch to targeting high-income growth markets, as this will mean there will be a faster growth in demand for the products. The stronger the correlation between income and demand, the quicker the growth and the more likely that the business should focus on that type of segment to ensure sustained growth in the future

FOCUS ON ANALYSING MARKETS AND MARKETING

The use of technology in analysing markets ▶ textbook pages 66–7

CASE STUDY – PDSA AND TECHNOLOGY

I   What is the principal reason why the PDSA is using this software? (*4 marks*)

The software is used to drive the organisation's campaigns and to enable it to get the information it needs. It holds the records of its supporters, transactional records and mailing history.

2   What do you understand by the term 'direct marketing'? (*2 marks*)

It is when a business makes direct contact with the customer or consumer (in this case the supporter), rather than using an intermediary to make that contact. It is designed to build a personal relationship between the business and the end-user.

Difficulties in analysing marketing data ▶ textbook pages 68–9

CASE STUDY – DESTINATION FAILURE

I   When carrying out a market analysis for a destination such as those in the case study, is competitor analysis really important? (*4 marks*)

Yes, because it is important to look at the nearby attractions as competitors. There may be a local market of 1.5m but if an existing attraction already pulls in 1m will this necessarily mean that the remaining 500,000 will go to the other attraction? Possibly not. Competitor analysis is vital to any market analysis, but only when comparing like with like and with usage. Are customers likely to go to the same attraction week after week?

2   Given the choice, would a visitor go to a new museum or an existing museum? Give reasons for your answer. (*4 marks*)

They would probably go to the new museum, as they are likely to have already visited the existing one, and even if they haven't, the new one has novelty value. However, it may not necessarily be as popular as, say, a theme park.

3   Suggest how a market analysis could be carried out for the sighting of an attraction. (*10 marks*)

Analysis of the concept, product and visitor experience; analysis of the location and development, including the capacity and access and an investigation into national trends and performance of comparable destinations. Identification of target market segments, both existing and potential, examination of price, value for money, seasonality and repeat visits, visitor admission forecasts and a market segment analysis.

FOCUS ON ANALYSING MARKETS AND MARKETING

Case studies, questions and exam practice ▶ textbook pages 70–1

CASE STUDY – PACKAGING MARKET ANALYSIS

1 Looking at the regional breakdown, which markets appear to be the most attractive and why? (*4 marks*)

Germany, UK, France and then other parts of Western Europe.

2 Having considered which regional markets are the most attractive, which packaging material and sector would provide a business with the most potential for success? (*2 marks*)

It would be paper products for the food and beverage market.

3 Using a three-year moving average, with 2006 as the centre point, what is the moving average for that year? (*2 marks*)

$128bn.

MINDMAPS

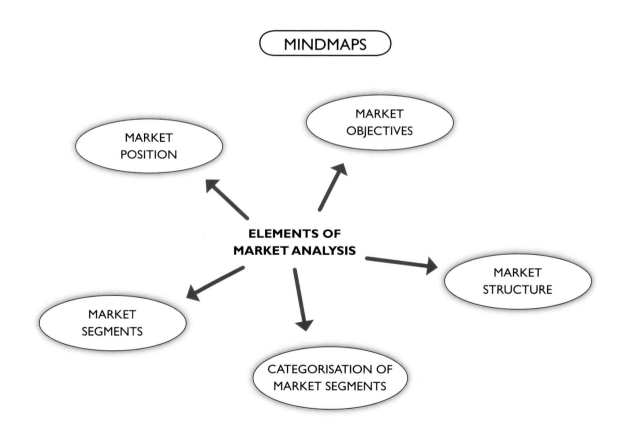

A2 ESSENTIAL BUSINESS STUDIES FOR AQA

MINDMAPS

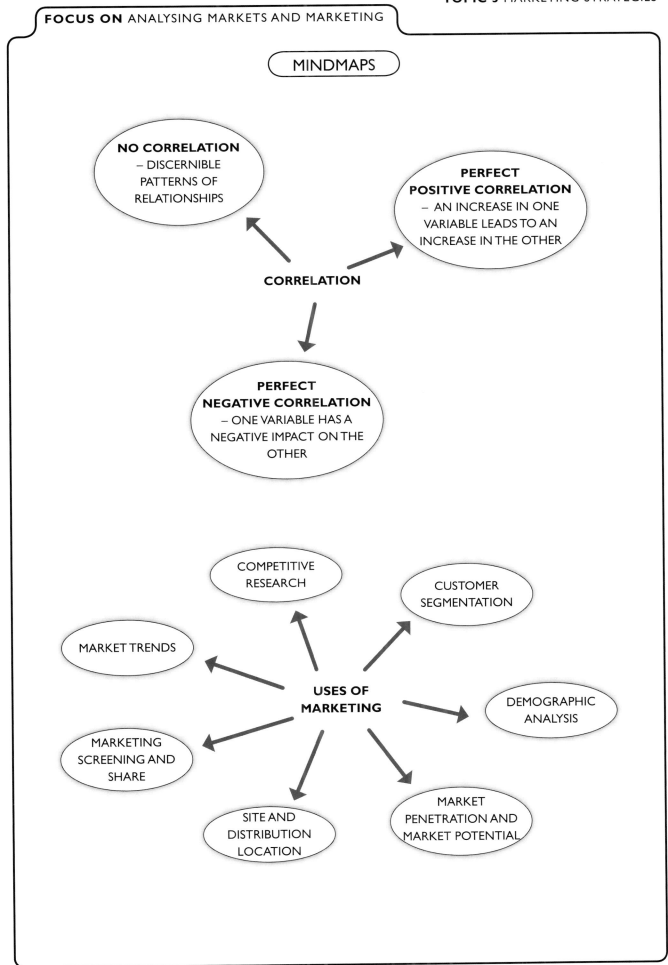

NO CORRELATION
– DISCERNIBLE PATTERNS OF RELATIONSHIPS

PERFECT POSITIVE CORRELATION
– AN INCREASE IN ONE VARIABLE LEADS TO AN INCREASE IN THE OTHER

CORRELATION

PERFECT NEGATIVE CORRELATION
– ONE VARIABLE HAS A NEGATIVE IMPACT ON THE OTHER

COMPETITIVE RESEARCH

CUSTOMER SEGMENTATION

MARKET TRENDS

USES OF MARKETING

DEMOGRAPHIC ANALYSIS

MARKETING SCREENING AND SHARE

SITE AND DISTRIBUTION LOCATION

MARKET PENETRATION AND MARKET POTENTIAL

FOCUS ON ANALYSING MARKETS AND MARKETING

MINDMAPS

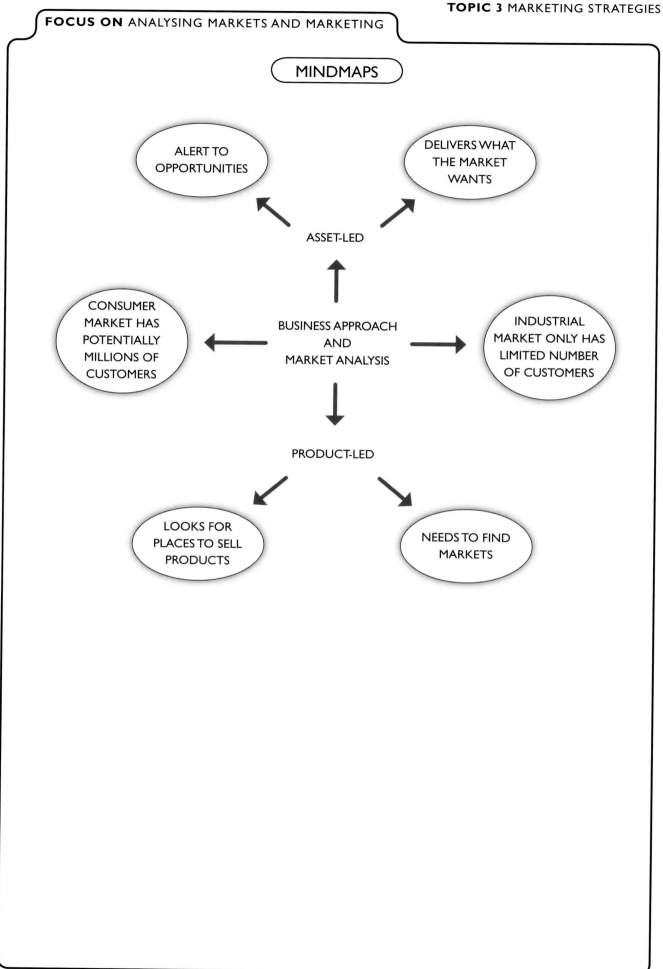

FOCUS ON ANALYSING MARKETS AND MARKETING

WORKSHEET

1 Briefly explain what is meant by a business's market position.

2 How might a business categorise market segments?

3 What is the purpose of attempting to identify patterns in sales?

Answers ▶ page 222

FOCUS ON ANALYSING MARKETS AND MARKETING

WORKSHEET

I What is 'extrapolation'?

2 Explain how a business might use market analysis software.

3 What is the purpose of a test market?

FOCUS ON ANALYSING MARKETS AND MARKETING

WORKSHEET

1 What is MIS?

2 Why do businesses collect secondary data?

3 If a business is said to be asset-led, what does this term mean?

Answers ▶ page 222

FOCUS ON SELECTING MARKETING STRATEGIES

Low cost versus differentiation ▶ textbook pages 72–3

CASE STUDY – EUROPEAN ORGANIC FRUIT JUICES – THE OPTIONS

1 Comment on the advice given to organic juice companies in relation to Porter's four generic strategies. (*8 marks*)

Cost leadership is suggested if businesses have economies of scale in production and marketing due to buying their raw materials in bulk. This has been the way in which British and French companies have managed to gain market leadership. Differentiation requires the producer to make a distinct product, which is not always possible. Cost focus is really only applicable for businesses that produce a wide range of specialised juices. Differentiation focus is perfectly possible, as some unique products can be produced for specific target segments of the market. This seems to be relatively common in Germany, for example.

2 Why is there a suggestion that there should be a different strategy adopted for large and small producers? (*4 marks*)

Cost leadership strategy is recommended for businesses particularly in Britain and Italy where the companies are fairly conventional and larger in scale. For smaller businesses a focus strategy is suggested, as they do not have the key internal and external advantages enjoyed by their larger rivals. They have to target specific segments of the market in order to achieve success.

Market penetration ▶ textbook pages 74–5

CASE STUDY – CROCS

1 What is the development of bags and t-shirts an example of in relation to the Ansoff matrix? (*2 marks*)

Diversification

2 Crocs has recently announced that it is about to launch a line of clothing featuring a form of the plastic resin that is used in its shoes. It has also bought Bite Footwear; the clothing company, Ocean Minded; and the sports company, Fury. Explain how these acquisitions also relate to Ansoff's matrix. (*12 marks*)

This is also an example of diversification and product development. The business hopes to use its name, reputation and skills to sell a broader range of products to its existing customer base. It can utilise its contacts and approach to boost the sales the businesses has acquired.

FOCUS ON SELECTING MARKETING STRATEGIES

Product development and market development strategies ▶ textbook pages 76–7

CASE STUDY – FIREANGEL

1 Explain how the business carried out its research to determine whether there was a market for the new product. (*8 marks*)

The business consulted the government and the fire brigade and found market research reports. It also canvassed individuals in the street and showed them a prototype. It looked extensively at the competition and customers, eventually working out how to go about marketing and selling the product.

2 Setting the price is a difficult task initially. How did the business go about setting a price? (*6 marks*)

Fire Angel looked at the competitors' pricing, but knew it could not charge a premium price because it would sell a limited amount. In any case it wished to sell through supermarkets to gain maximum market penetration. It could charge a slightly higher price than most other competitors because of the simplicity of the product. It, however, took some time to convince high-street retailers to stock the alarm.

Diversification ▶ textbook pages 78–9

CASE STUDY – MITCHELL CHARLESWORTH

Using this business as an example, explain how it is possible for even a relatively small business to successfully achieve diversification. (*12 marks*)

To begin with, the business offered the standard kind of service that a chartered accountant would offer. It then consulted its existing clients to see what other services they might be interested in, and also looked at what the competitors were doing. The company focused on generic business development, but with accountancy behind it. It traded heavily on its quality assurance and began diversification by offering it to the existing customer base as a natural extension. Although the business has found new customers, more than three-quarters of new work is from existing clients.

FOCUS ON SELECTING MARKETING STRATEGIES

Assessing effectiveness of marketing strategies ▶ textbook pages 80–1

CASE STUDY – THE REAL THING REALLY

It would seem from the response of customers that the market research was a waste of time. Comment on this view. (8 marks)

The main problem was that Coca-Cola did not ask the crucial question – did customers actually want a new Coke? Clearly they did not. What is more, Coca-Cola did not understand the deep emotions of many people with regard to their product. Public reaction was overwhelmingly negative. The

organisation had carried out two years of taste tests and research in great secrecy. However, the market research must have been fundamentally flawed. Strangely enough, in blind tests, new Coke continued to win taste tests. This may say far more about messing around with brands that have established themselves in the market and have a strong customer loyalty than the accuracy of market research.

Case studies, questions and exam practice ▶ textbook pages 82–3

CASE STUDY – ANSOFF AND APPLE

1 Explain how Apple has been able to use all four of Ansoff's key sets of marketing strategies. (12 marks)

Apple was already an existing player in the marketplace, but it took the decision to create a new product that would appeal to its present market. It rested on its innovation and product design to initially encourage Mac users to purchase the iPod. It had already established itself as a relatively strong player in the computer market, with its present products selling to the current and dedicated customer base. But by redesigning its computers it was able to expand its customer base. Simultaneously, new markets were developed through the new designs of both the computer and the new product itself, the iPod, leading to market development that many other businesses tried to copy. This then allowed diversification into the digital entertainment market, attracting new users who were encouraged by their experience to purchase other, existing, Mac products. It gives the business access to a whole range of potential customers that otherwise it would find impossible to target.

2 Outline how a retailer such as Marks and Spencer or Tesco might also have used all four strategies. (16 marks)

Both of these retail organisations are ideal examples of commercial businesses that have been able to create marketing strategies addressing all four of Ansoff's suggestions. Both companies have established themselves as market leaders with a range of existing products in existing markets. They have also tried and succeeded in introducing a whole range of new products to their existing markets by simply expanding the current range of products available. Tesco, for example, is no longer simply a food retailer. It sells durable goods in-store, including clothes, consumer electronics and a range of other products and services. In terms of market development Tesco is a prime example. The company has sought to increase its market penetration by establishing a range of express stores, which are smaller and slightly more expensive versions of its larger superstores and it has also invested heavily in developing its Internet shopping facilities, including home delivery and a rival brand to Argos, using a traditional catalogue order and pick-up, or order and deliver service. It has also diversified into insurance, banking, holidays and other financial services.

MINDMAPS

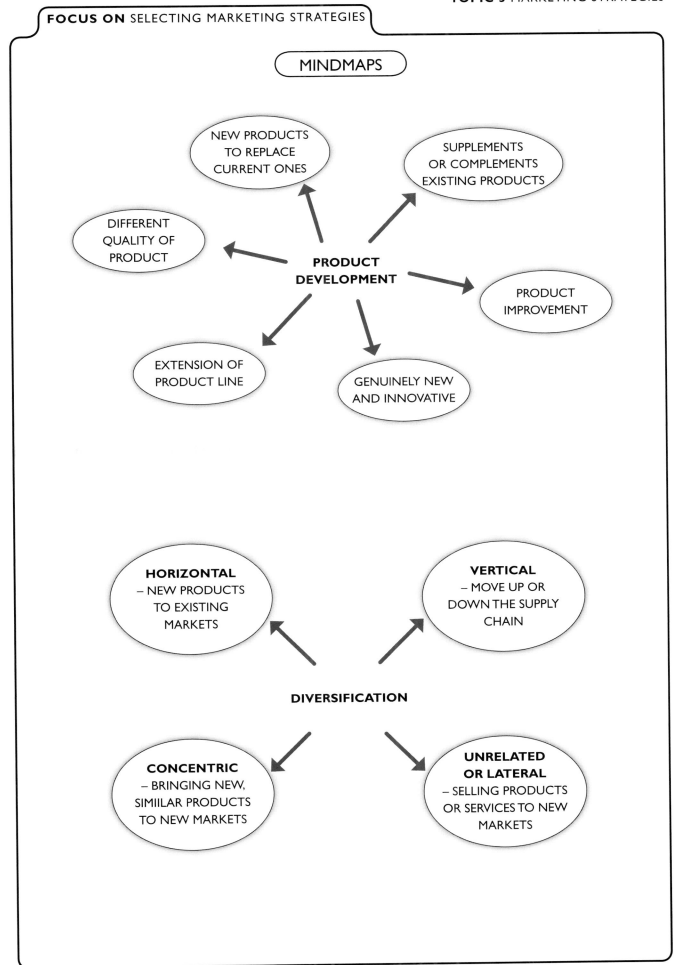

NEW PRODUCTS
TO REPLACE
CURRENT ONES

SUPPLEMENTS
OR COMPLEMENTS
EXISTING PRODUCTS

DIFFERENT
QUALITY OF
PRODUCT

**PRODUCT
DEVELOPMENT**

PRODUCT
IMPROVEMENT

EXTENSION OF
PRODUCT LINE

GENUINELY NEW
AND INNOVATIVE

HORIZONTAL
– NEW PRODUCTS
TO EXISTING
MARKETS

VERTICAL
– MOVE UP OR
DOWN THE SUPPLY
CHAIN

DIVERSIFICATION

CONCENTRIC
– BRINGING NEW,
SIMIILAR PRODUCTS
TO NEW MARKETS

**UNRELATED
OR LATERAL**
– SELLING PRODUCTS
OR SERVICES TO NEW
MARKETS

FOCUS ON SELECTING MARKETING STRATEGIES

MINDMAPS

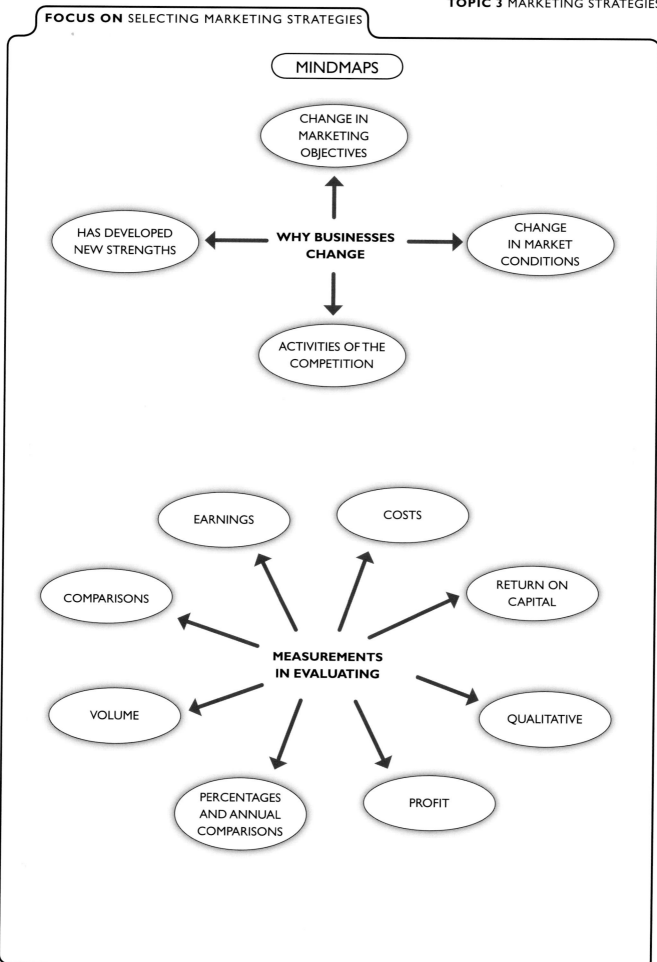

FOCUS ON SELECTING MARKETING STRATEGIES

WORKSHEET

I What is meant by 'cost leadership strategy'?

2 What are the FOUR essential elements of a low-cost strategy?

3 What is differentiation strategy? Give TWO examples.

Answers ▶ page 223

FOCUS ON SELECTING MARKETING STRATEGIES

(WORKSHEET)

1 What are the FOUR elements of Ansoff's Matrix?

2 Briefly explain how market penetration can be successful.

3 Why is it NOT necessary for new products to be genuinely new or innovative?

Answers ▶ page 223

FOCUS ON SELECTING MARKETING STRATEGIES

WORKSHEET

I   What is 'diversification'? Give ONE example of how it works.

2   Distinguish between horizontal diversification and vertical diversification.

3   Why might a business choose to change its marketing strategy?

Answers ▶ page 223

FOCUS ON DEVELOPING AND
IMPLEMENTING MARKETING PLANS

Components of marketing plans ▶ textbook pages 84–5

QUESTIONS

1 What is gap analysis? (*2 marks*)

It is the process of investigating the difference between forecast performance and actual performance.

2 Why are contingency plans important? (*6 marks*)

They are important for a number of reasons. Firstly they illustrate the fact that the business has already considered what actions it will take if the marketing plan does not go according to the forecast. Secondly that it has in place a number of alternative actions to remedy difficulties. Thirdly that it has the capacity to respond in a timely manner to take corrective action.

Assessing internal and external influences on marketing plans

▶ textbook pages 86–7

CASE STUDY – SHOCKVERTISING

Using the Internet, find out more about this style of advertising, whether it works and how people respond to it.

Most of the major newspapers and the BBC have articles about Benetton's use of photo journalism in their advertisements. They provide a useful background for discussions about the ethics of particular marketing campaigns. Benetton deliberately tries to be controversial, both to make a social point and to receive an enormous amount of free publicity.

Issues in implementing marketing plans ▶ textbook pages 88–9

CASE STUDY – FACEBOOK

1 How would Facebook find out whether this is a problem of their making or an industry-wide problem? (*6 marks*)

Facebook would have to carry out a fairly extensive market analysis and try to discover the numbers of users of its major competitors. The loss of customers and the arrival of new customers, or the turnover of customers is often referred to as the churn rate. The higher the churn rate, the more effort the business needs to put into replacing lost customers, otherwise its overall customer numbers will fall.

2 Microsoft invested $240 million for a 1.6% share of Facebook. How might they view their investment now? (*6 marks*)

It very much depends how Microsoft views its investment in Facebook. If it was looking at a short-term investment then it would probably be very disappointed, as the value of shares is likely to have fallen, particularly because the reported net cash flow of Facebook was $150m in 2007. It is certainly valued at less than the $15bn. However it is more likely that Microsoft has invested for the longer-term, so it may not be overly concerned.

FOCUS ON DEVELOPING AND
IMPLEMENTING MARKETING PLANS

Case studies, questions and exam practice ▶ textbook pages 90–1

CASE STUDY – SPY AND CHIPS

1 How might a business justify the use of a new product development such as this and why might customers be reluctant to accept its introduction? (*8 marks*)

It would seem that any future attempt to introduce technology as contentious as RFID chips will require consideration of basic change management principles. There will need to be genuine openness and consultation with consumers. The benefits of the technology must be properly identified and the highest level of persuasion and influencing skills will need to be applied to achieve successful acceptance.

Originally RFID tags were used in closed systems such as the supply chains of individual companies. However, as the cost of tags decreases and worldwide industry-accepted standards become available, individual item tagging will become more widespread. This has led some consumer and civil liberties groups to raise privacy issues. The main concerns are:

- Use of the data by a third party
- An increase in targeted direct marketing
- The ability to track individuals

Even if tags contain only a number and not personal data, they can still be linked to personal information, e.g. through the use of loyalty cards. Privacy groups argue that although linking personal data to products is already possible with bar codes, there is increased potential for direct marketing with item-level tagging, as consumers could be recognised on entering a store and their habits in-store monitored. Technologists state that tracking of individuals through RFID is difficult because of the large amount of power that would be required to read RFID tags at a distance. The statutory limitations on power are fixed on safety grounds. However privacy groups point out that technological development may increase the potential for privacy infringements in the future, for example by placing readers in floor tiles or in mobile phones. It is unclear whether legislation, such as the Human Rights Act, would protect individual privacy in these cases.

2 Radio frequency identification (RFID) technology provides a means of automatic identification. It is already widely used in animal tagging and electronic payment, such as Transport for London's Oyster cards. Many other potential applications such as improving supply chain efficiency and reducing crime are being investigated. Why might this be an ideal solution for businesses such as transport providers? (*4 marks*)

All over the world, smart cards based on RFID technology are becoming more common in transport. Hong Kong introduced the 'Octopus' system in 1997, which is now used by over 95% of the population. The Oyster card, a Transport for London (TfL) contactless ticketing scheme, is a smart card. TfL estimates that one million fewer transactions per week are made at ticket offices and that there is a 30% improvement in the speed of passengers passing through the ticket gates. It is more difficult to copy Oyster cards than the magnetic stripe cards and, as each card contains a unique ID number, it can be immediately cancelled if the card is reported lost or stolen.

FOCUS ON DEVELOPING AND
IMPLEMENTING MARKETING PLANS

MINDMAPS

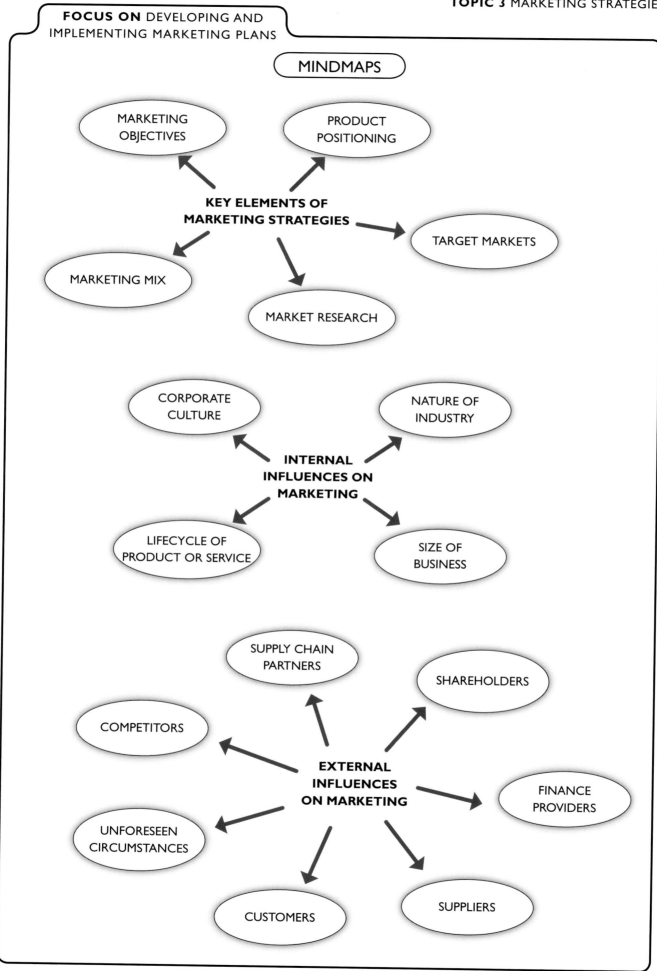

FOCUS ON DEVELOPING AND
IMPLEMENTING MARKETING PLANS

MINDMAPS

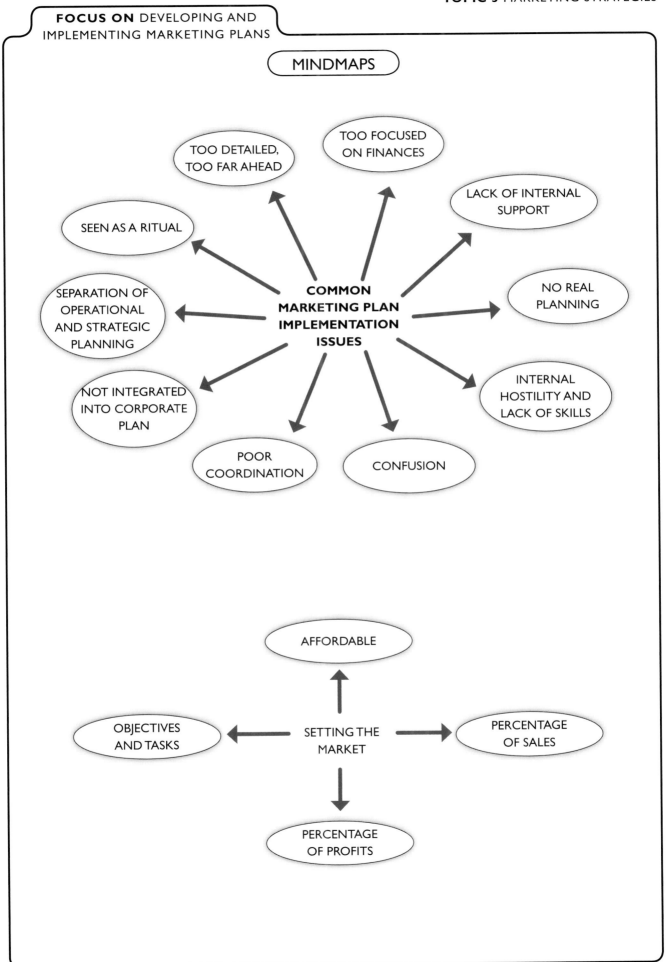

TOO DETAILED,
TOO FAR AHEAD

TOO FOCUSED
ON FINANCES

LACK OF INTERNAL
SUPPORT

SEEN AS A RITUAL

NO REAL
PLANNING

SEPARATION OF
OPERATIONAL
AND STRATEGIC
PLANNING

**COMMON
MARKETING PLAN
IMPLEMENTATION
ISSUES**

INTERNAL
HOSTILITY AND
LACK OF SKILLS

NOT INTEGRATED
INTO CORPORATE
PLAN

POOR
COORDINATION

CONFUSION

AFFORDABLE

OBJECTIVES
AND TASKS

SETTING THE
MARKET

PERCENTAGE
OF SALES

PERCENTAGE
OF PROFITS

FOCUS ON DEVELOPING AND IMPLEMENTING MARKETING PLANS

WORKSHEET

I   What are the FOUR key building blocks of a marketing plan?

2   Identify FOUR common implementation problems for a marketing plan.

3   Briefly identify the FOUR ways in which a marketing budget is determined.

Answers ▶ page 223

Operations objectives ▸ textbook pages 94–5

QUESTIONS

1 What do you understand by the term 'operations management'? (*2 marks*)

It involves the planning, organising and coordination of activities, usually directly related to the production and delivery of products and services within a business.

2 In an organisation that does not have a distinct operations management team, where would the responsibilities lie in meeting operations objectives? (*8 marks*)

All functional parts of the business organisation could be considered to be involved in operations management. Students should specifically mention departments such as sales, marketing, accounts, purchasing and production and note their overall operations responsibilities, as well as the fact that individually and collectively they all contribute towards meeting the operations objectives of the organisation.

Assessing internal and external influences on operational objectives

▸ textbook pages 96–7

QUESTIONS

1 How might the nature of a product have an impact on the business's operational objectives? (*4 marks*)

Students should focus on the handling requirements of the product or service, particularly in terms of timescales involved and whether production or creation is capital-intensive or labour-intensive. Also, mention of perishability and tangible and intangible products and services would be valuable.

2 How might a business compare itself to a competitor's performance? (*4 marks*)

The business could compare itself to competitors in a number of different ways, including gross and net profit, turnover (sales revenue), costs, overall expenditure, earnings per share, share value, value of fixed assets and market share. On a qualitative basis it could compare on the basis of image, reputation, market leadership and issues such as perceived quality and value.

FOCUS ON UNDERSTANDING
OPERATIONAL OBJECTIVES

Case studies, questions and exam practice ▶ textbook pages 98–9

CASE STUDY – JAGUAR

1 What does quality actually mean for an organisation such as Jaguar? (*7 marks*)

Performance – Capacity for speed, powerful acceleration, responsive handling and so on are generally regarded as the mark of a 'prestige' car.

Aesthetics – The overall appearance of the car should reflect its values. A Jaguar is smooth, luxurious, dashing and sporty! The key question for Jaguar is 'does the overall appearance and shape of the car reflect these values and appeal to its target customers?'

Equipment – Is the car equipped with the type of things one would expect from a luxury car, such as leather seats, global position system equipment, adjustable headlights and so on?

Finish – Are the visible areas of the car free from any marks or blemish-s? This means an absence of scratches or small marks as well as an appropriate surface finish to all visible surfaces.

Build quality – This normally refers to how the car feels as doors open and close, windows are raised and lowered and so on. Is there a satisfying 'solidity' about the feel of the car?

Reliability – When in use does the car (or some part of the car) break down? Do things go wrong?

After sales service – Should the owner have any problems or wish to know something more about the car, is it easy for him or her to find out?

2 How did the changes that Jaguar made to its operations affect the quality of its products? (*6 marks*)

Training would equip operators with the skills to assemble the car in the correct manner without making mistakes.

Statistical Process Control would enable the operators to make sure that shop-floor processes are operating as they should be and preferably improving.

Changing the payment system both encouraged operators to learn more skills and prevented them sacrificing quality in order to earn higher wages in the short term.

Multi-skilled teams would allow any absent workers to be covered for by people with equivalent skills and, more importantly, encourage continuous improvement to production processes.

Totally productive maintenance, improvement teams and benchmarking would likewise allow everyone working at the company to contribute to the general improvement effort.

All these changes were important but it is also vital to realise that, without the necessary investment, the changes in Jaguar would have been difficult or even impossible. Yet these issues are connected. It was the success of the company's management in starting these changes which encouraged the parent group (Ford) to invest considerable sums of money in the company, which in turn allowed the changes described above to have a real impact.

FOCUS ON UNDERSTANDING
OPERATIONAL OBJECTIVES

MINDMAPS

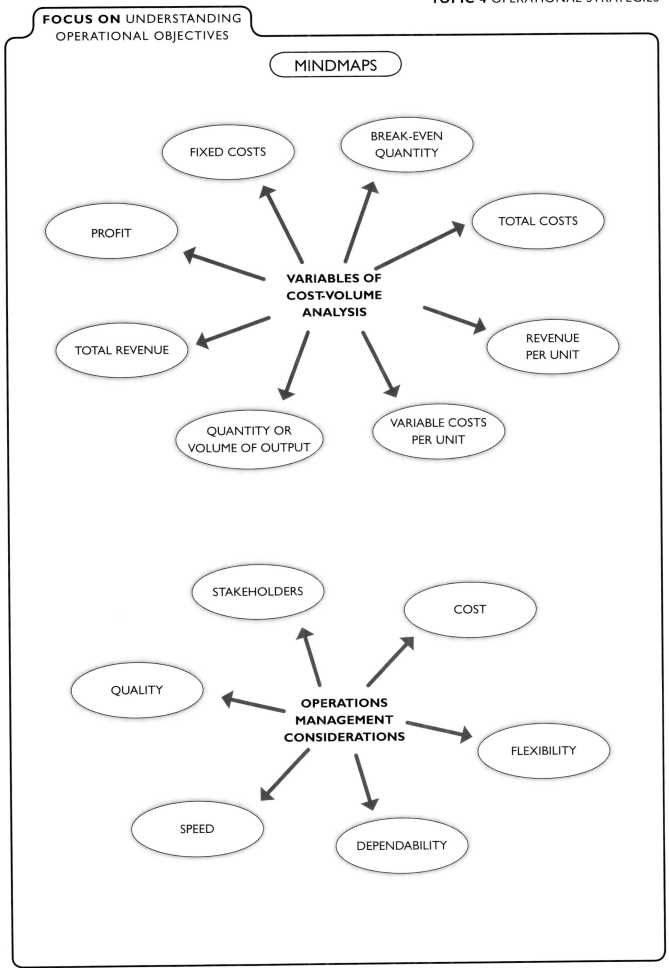

FOCUS ON UNDERSTANDING
OPERATIONAL OBJECTIVES

MINDMAPS

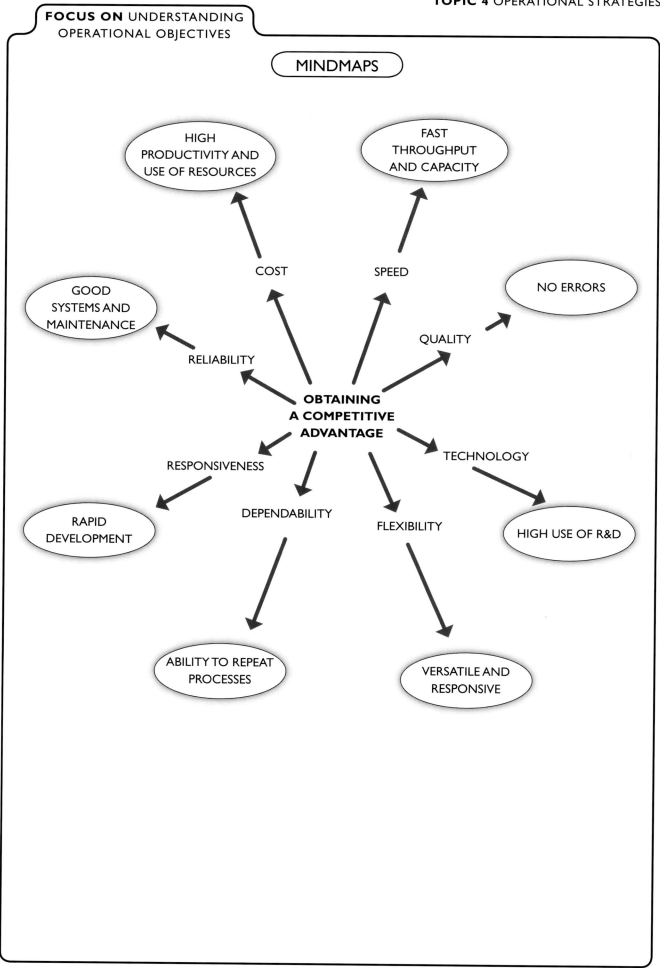

FOCUS ON UNDERSTANDING
OPERATIONAL OBJECTIVES

WORKSHEET

1 What do you understand by the term 'conformance'?

2 Identify FIVE operational objectives or policies common to businesses.

3 Why is demand often referred to as the ultimate determinant of an operational objective?

Answers ▶ page 223

FOCUS ON OPERATIONAL STRATEGIES:
SCALE AND RESOURCE MIX

Choosing the right scale of production ▶ textbook pages 100–1

QUESTIONS

1 Why might many businesses fall into the trap of creating diseconomies of scale even though they have been successful in growing? (*10 marks*)

The simple answer to this question is that they have probably grown too quickly through mergers and takeovers rather than organic growth. Though being successful and profitable has allowed them to grow, they have not taken into consideration the effect of rapid growth

and how it impacts on the workings of the organisation itself. Organic growth should bring with it a gradual development in the way in which the internal communications and coordination works within the business.

2 At which point will a business be able to enjoy the lowest cost of production? (*2 marks*)

Theoretically, when the economies of scale outweigh the diseconomies. This will be at close to maximum output.

Choosing the optimal mix of resources ▶ textbook pages 102–3

QUESTIONS

1 How can capacity be calculated? (*4 marks*)

It can be calculated per minute, hour, day or shift. It is a theoretical capacity, as it usually aims to identify the optimum or maximum capacity.

2 What do you understand by the term 'capacity cushion'? (*2 marks*)

It is the amount of capacity that a business has in excess of expected demand.

Case studies, questions and exam practice ▶ textbook pages 104–5

CASE STUDY – BROWN SUGAR

1 Identify which of the sugar production processes are capital-intensive or labour-intensive, and explain why. (*10 marks*)

Broadly, the smaller-scale production techniques tend to be labour-intensive with the medium scale either labour or capital intensive. The larger-scale refining is exclusively capital intensive. The production and quality of the sugar is also related to the markets in which it is sold. Although some small-scale factories do have limited scales of production, they tend to still be labour-intensive rather than relying on machinery.

2 Why might certain types of production not be appropriate or possible in under-developed countries? (*6 marks*)

It is often a question of available investment with the underdeveloped countries tending to produce sugar only for the domestic market. The quality of the sugar is variable, and in the smaller-scale production there is a considerable amount of contaminant in the sugar which would not be acceptable for exports. With little investment, the domestic production cannot be stepped up or improved, making long-term investment difficult to obtain. In any case, the smaller-scale production facilities would find it difficult to compete with the larger refineries.

FOCUS ON OPERATIONAL STRATEGIES:
SCALE AND RESOURCE MIX

MINDMAPS

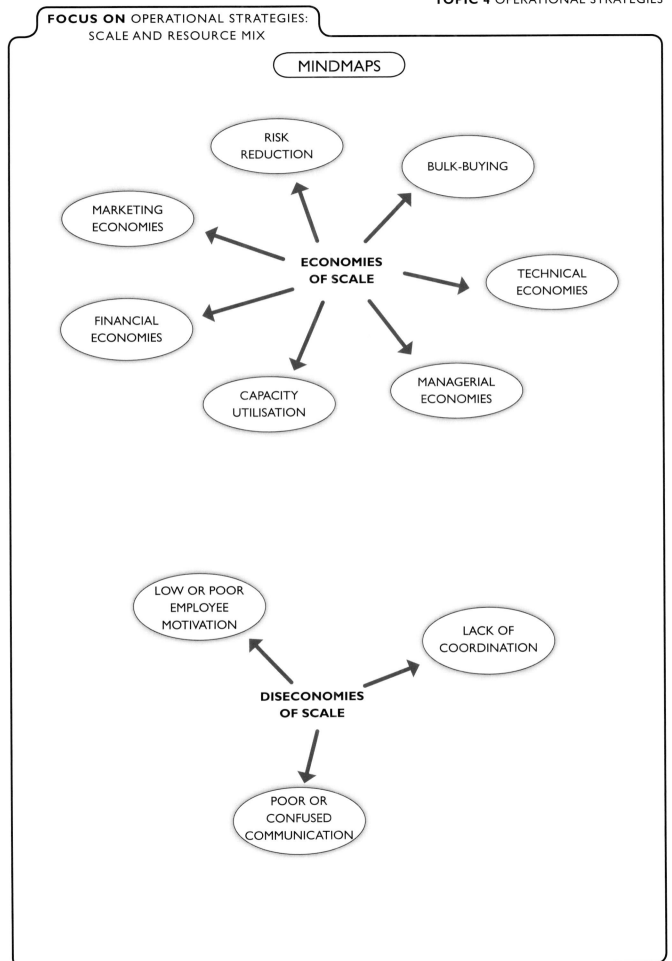

FOCUS ON OPERATIONAL STRATEGIES:
SCALE AND RESOURCE MIX

MINDMAPS

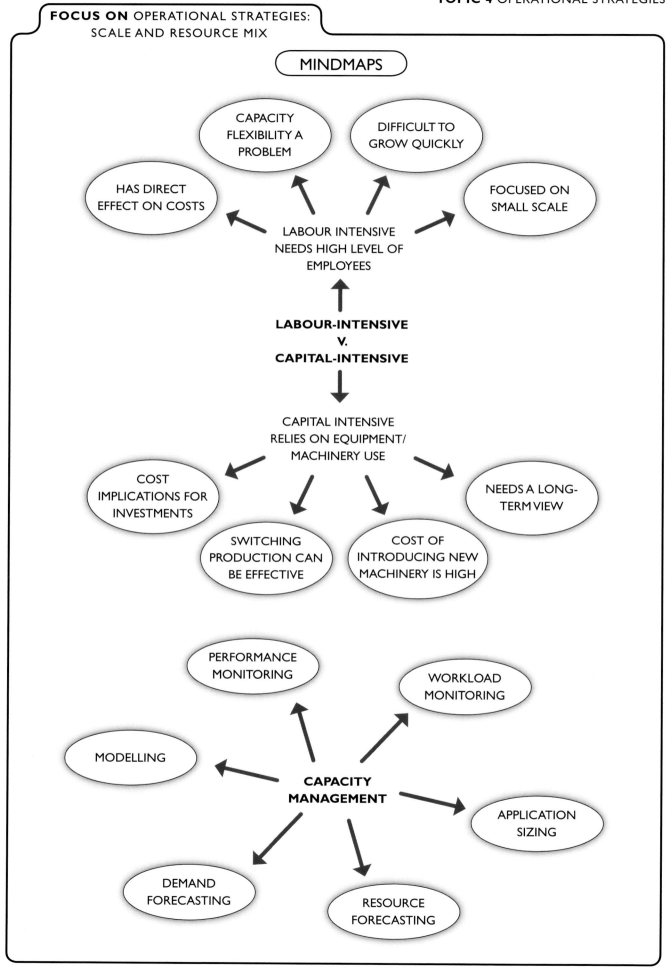

FOCUS ON OPERATIONAL STRATEGIES:
SCALE AND RESOURCE MIX

WORKSHEET

I List FIVE key economies of scale that can be enjoyed by a business of a sufficiently large size.

2 Explain what is meant by the term 'diseconomies of scale'.

3 Distinguish between a labour-intensive business and a capital-intensive business.

Answers ▶ page 223

FOCUS ON OPERATIONAL STRATIES: INNOVATION

Innovation research and development ▶ textbook pages 106–7

CASE STUDY – DIRECT AIR DRIERS

I The product is not only an innovative one, but it is also environmentally friendly. How might this be the case? (*4 marks*)

It not only returns the home or business back to use far quicker, but it also reduces the carbon footprint and is therefore more environmentally friendly than conventional ways of drying out buildings.

2 Up to 27,000 homes and 5,000 businesses are affected by flooding each year. How might this product be of benefit to the general economy? (*6 marks*)

By cutting both the direct and the indirect costs of having to relocate home owners and businesses, the product inevitably saves money. Also businesses can be back in production far faster using this product.

Purpose, costs, benefits and risks of innovation ▶ textbook pages 108–9

CASE STUDY – APPLE

Why would losing this court battle be disastrous for an organisation such as Apple? (*6 marks*)

Because they actually have a patent themselves for this technology, which they would defend at

all costs. If they were to lose the patent then other mobile phone producers would be able to use it. Their reputation for innovation would be jeopardised if they were to lose the court case.

Case studies, questions and exam practice ▶ textbook pages 110–11

CASE STUDY – FREEMINER BREWERY

I What were the problems facing the brewery and how were they overcome? (*10 marks*)

Small local breweries were losing ground to the larger premium brands and were closing. The way to compete was to concentrate on the distinctive nature of the beers. Don did this by repacking the beer and redesigning the bottle and the label. He also approached local and regional supermarket stockists. The foot and mouth epidemic had nearly killed off all local trade and the brewery was disrupted by a change in location. Don's main goal was to re-educate the public about the beers and offer them as a main alternative to wine.

2 How would you describe Don's mission? (*6 marks*)

Central to Don's mission was 'to get quality beers onto the dining table and on a level playing field with wine'. The key to this mission was 'a high-quality naturally-conditioned beer in an elegant bottle that would be attractive on a supermarket shelf and not look out of place on the dining table'. In other words, Don wanted to transform the perception of beer into an acceptable and preferred alternative to wine.

FOCUS ON OPERATIONAL STRATIES: INNOVATION

MINDMAPS

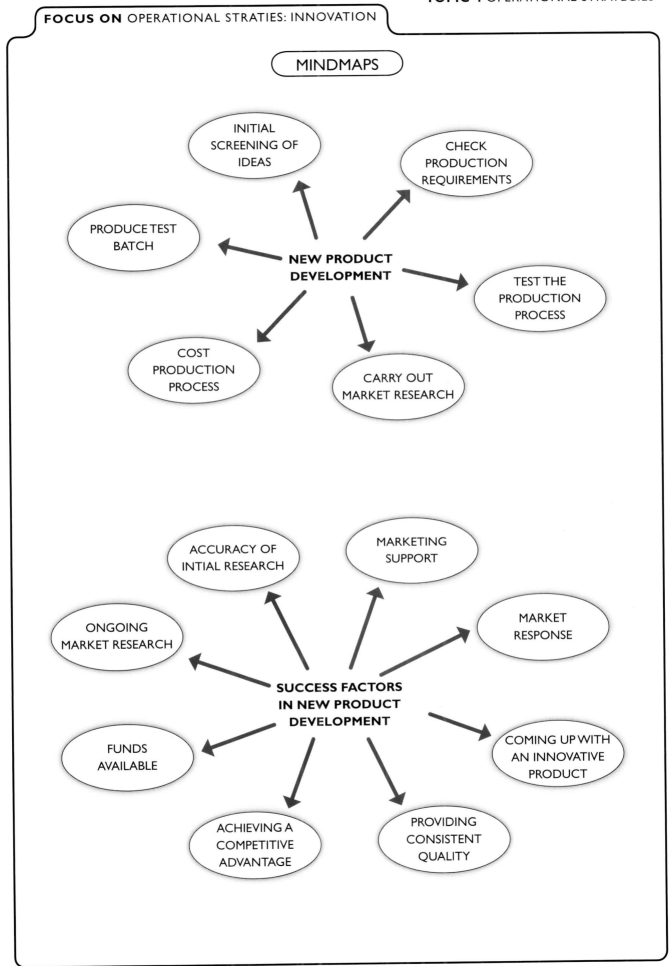

FOCUS ON OPERATIONAL STRATIES: INNOVATION

MINDMAPS

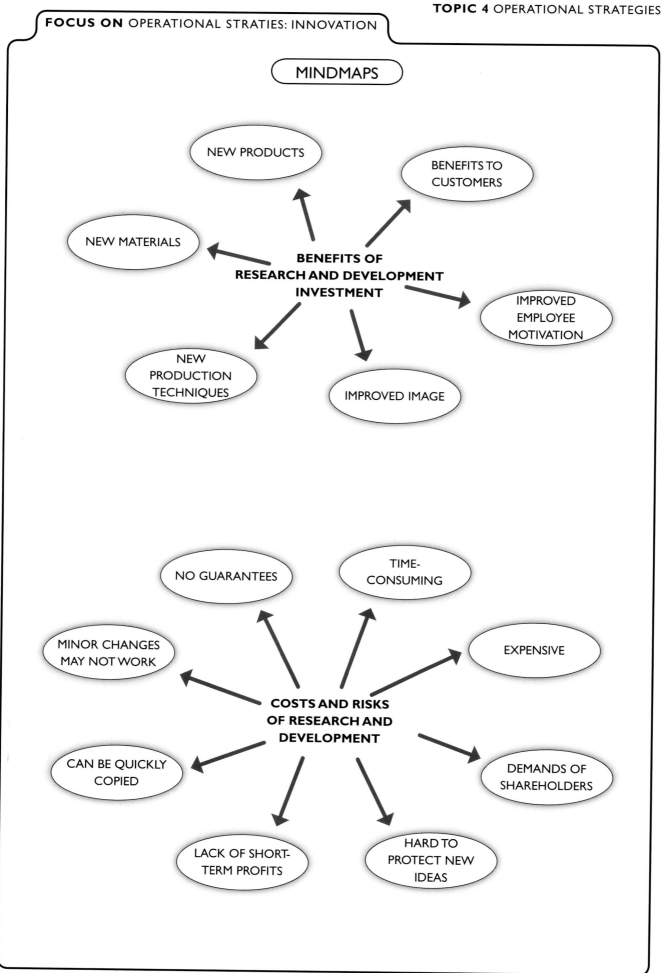

FOCUS ON OPERATIONAL STRATIES: INNOVATION

WORKSHEET

I   Briefly outline the key planning steps in new product development.

2   Why might a business such as Dyson be able to charge a premium price for its products?

3   How can a business's level of innovation be measured?

Answers ▶ page 224

FOCUS ON OPERATIONAL STRATEGIES: LOCATION

Methods of making location decisions ▶ textbook pages 112–13

QUESTION

How important would the location decision be in determining the success of a retail clothes chain? (*15 marks*)

Students should certainly try to focus on as many of the relevant decision factors as possible, including costs, incentives, infrastructure,

location of the market (i.e. proximity to a large enough catchment area), available potential staff resources and significant quantitative factors, which may include break-even analysis and investment appraisal.

Benefits of optimal location ▶ textbook pages 114–15

QUESTION

Is the finance director right? Are there any other factors that the business needs to take into account? (*12 marks*)

Obviously there is no right or wrong answer, but the students should be encouraged to support their opinions by considering a relevant number of qualitative and quantitative factors. Students should consider the complications and impact on the workforce. They should also consider how the business would intend to carry out its operations in the future with production facilities located abroad and presumably the sales and marketing located in Britain. Some key employees will have to be moved to Malaysia in order to oversee the

shift in production operations and to ensure issues such as suppliers, quality of production, recruitment of personnel, and distribution back to the business's main markets. In effect, the business may be better served by considering outsourcing the operation rather than setting up its own production facilities in Malaysia. This too brings with it a number of complications and certainly in terms of the workforce the business will need to considerably downsize. The finance director's opinion is based purely on costs and does not take into account any qualitative factors. The opinion may be at variance with the business's overall aims and objectives.

A2 ESSENTIAL BUSINESS STUDIES FOR AQA

FOCUS ON OPERATIONAL STRATEGIES: LOCATION

Advantages and disadvantages of multi-site locations ▶ textbook pages 116–17

CASE STUDY – FLOWER POWER

1 Outline Halaris's reasoning behind the advantages he enjoys from multiple locations. (*8 marks*)

Primarily he has a larger marketing budget, greater buying power, more access to a wider range of experienced staff and the ability to shift employees from one location to another. An additional consideration is the fact that the business is a franchise, with external support from the franchisor.

2 What disadvantages might there be? (*8 marks*)

Students should certainly recognise the fact that establishing each location has had its usual costs in terms of setting up a retail operation, and also that the owner has presumably had to pay a franchise fee to the franchisor, which makes the expansion of outlets rather more expensive than it would be under normal circumstances. Clearly he wanted control over a particular geographical area by acquiring three franchises rather than one.

International location ▶ textbook pages 118–19

QUESTIONS

What might be the advantages and disadvantages to an underdeveloped country in attracting a multinational corporation? (*12 marks*)

The listing of potential advantages and disadvantages on the appropriate spread can provide the basis of this answer. However the students should certainly refer to some

positive and negative impacts of multinational organisations around the world. For example Coca-Cola used enormous amounts of water supplies in southern India, causing a negative impact on the environment. Businesses have also set up baby milk manufacturing plants and used lax advertising regulations to convince women not to breastfeed.

Case studies, questions and exam practice ▶ textbook pages 120–1

CASE STUDY – HOW I CHOOSE MY BUSINESS LOCATION

1 Explain why the restaurant site in Kennington was an optimal one? (*10 marks*)

It was up and coming. It was close to the cricket stadium, the Oval, where there would be a regular customer base. It was opposite a tube station, on an A road, and had free parking. It was also a high-visibility site with good access for suppliers and customers. All these factors helped, as the restaurant would be relying on passing trade.

2 Different criteria were used to choose the Peterborough site. Why could they still be considered to be optimal? (*6 marks*)

It is a unique site on a barge. It does not have parking but is in a safe and quiet part of the town. The town is popular for pedestrian traffic and the site is well situated for that. It is not close to the town centre, but in a more picturesque area. The location is where many pedestrians can be found strolling rather than shopping.

FOCUS ON OPERATIONAL STRATEGIES: LOCATION

MINDMAPS

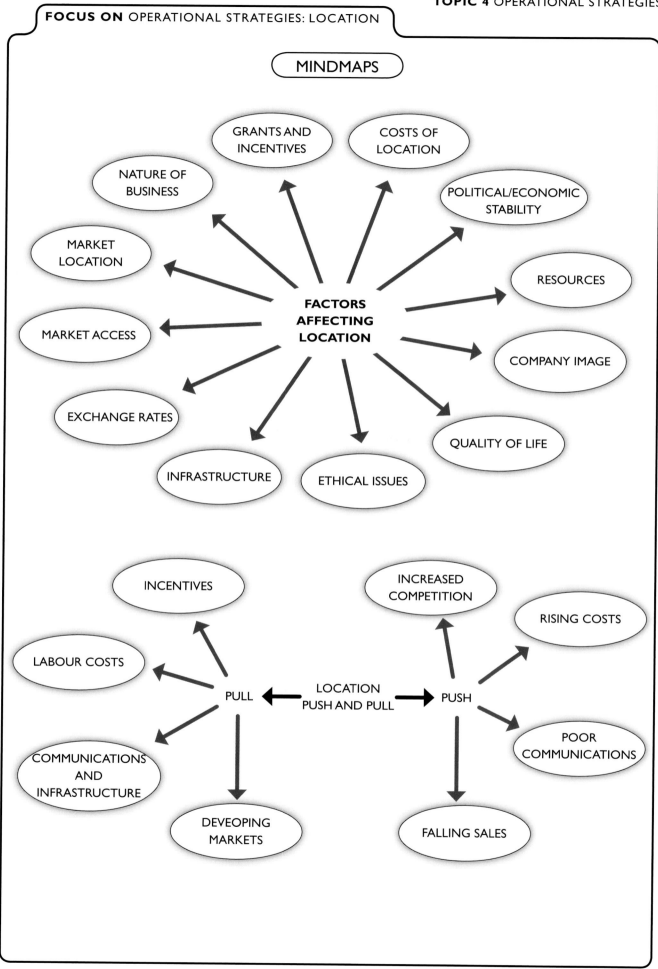

FOCUS ON OPERATIONAL STRATEGIES: LOCATION

MINDMAPS

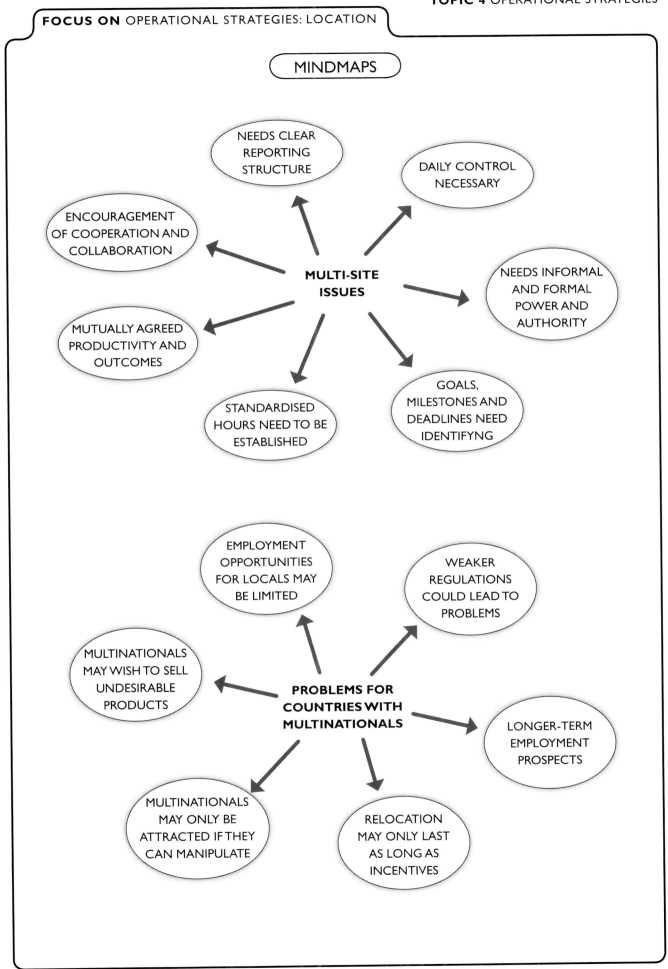

FOCUS ON OPERATIONAL STRATEGIES: LOCATION

WORKSHEET

I Distinguish between quantitative and qualitative location factors.

2 Why is it advisable for a Japanese company to have a production facility within the EU?

3 How might company image be a key consideration for a business choosing its location?

Answers ▶ page 224

FOCUS ON OPERATIONAL STRATEGIES: LOCATION

WORKSHEET

1 Outline FOUR push factors involved in location.

2 What are the potential drawbacks of a low-cost location?

3 Why might a business be tempted to locate in an area that is associated with that type of business or industry?

Answers ▶ page 224

FOCUS ON OPERATIONAL STRATEGIES: LOCATION

WORKSHEET

1 Why is it important for multi-site organisations to establish standardised hours?

2 Why do many remote locations feel that a multinational's headquarters interfere with their decision-making?

3 In terms of subsidiary locations, what is meant by 'autonomy' and 'empowerment'?

Answers ▶ page 224

FOCUS ON OPERATIONAL STRATEGIES: LOCATION

WORKSHEET

I   Why might a business choose to become a multinational?

2   What are the advantages to a country of attracting a multinational?

3   What are the downsides of multinationals operating in a particular country?

Answers ▶ page 224

FOCUS ON OPERATIONAL
STRATEGIES: LEAN PRODUCTION

Time management ▶ textbook pages 122–3

Using the Internet, find out ways in which you could manage your own time more effectively throughout your course of study. How transferable are these skills to business situations?

There is an enormous number of generic time management sites and portals, offering advice from goal setting, decision-making and specific information for students. Many of the universities also have specific time management sections on their websites. Many of the lessons that can be learned from student time management are immediately adaptable to business situations.

Critical path analysis ▶ textbook pages 124–5

What do you think are the key advantages and disadvantages of critical path analysis? *(6 marks)*

Advantages could include reduced lost time between tasks, ensuring the smooth running of projects, identifying projects that can be carried out at the same time, and identifying resources needed and when they should be ordered. This would reduce cash outflows and ensure working capital is not being tied up. It should assist JIT and if the project is likely to be delayed then a network is a good way to look at the implications. Disadvantages include the fact that complex tasks can make the process unmanageable and that a critical path network is only as effective as the user's commitment to it.

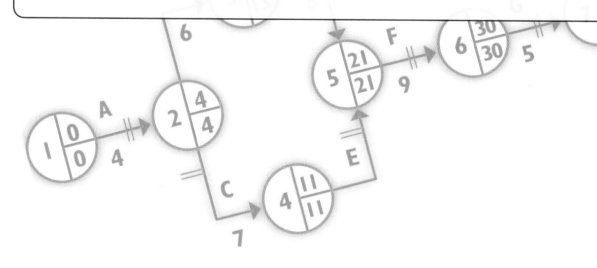

FOCUS ON OPERATIONAL
STRATEGIES: LEAN PRODUCTION

Time management of resources ▶ textbook pages 126–7

CASE STUDY – THE RISE OF LEAN PRODUCTION

1 In a lean production factory how are the workers organised? (*4 marks*)

Workers on the assembly line are organised into teams, which gives them individual responsibility to correct mistakes before the vehicle reaches the end of the production line.

2 Why is it important for a lean production factory to have long-term relationships with its suppliers? (*4 marks*)

Building long-term relationships with suppliers is essential as it ensures quality and the facility to automatically re-order parts as they are used up on the factory floor.

Case studies, questions and exam practice ▶ textbook pages 128–9

CASE STUDY – ROJEE TASHA STAMPINGS LTD

1 How was the business able to introduce lean manufacturing without any real capital investment? (*12 marks*)

Primarily through introducing initiatives such as single minute exchange of die (SMED); 5S activities (Sort – Straighten – Sweep – Standardise – Self-discipline); variations of the Kanban system and other recognised methods of generating productivity gains.

2 What is meant by 'takt time' and 'kanban'? (*4 marks*)

Takt time is the daily rate of demand divided by the number of available working hours over a given period (invariably a day). Takt time is used by an organisation to estimate its cycle time (how long it will take to meet the level of demand). Kanban is a Japanese word meaning signal. In effect this is exactly what the system does by sending a signal to employees to perform a particular action related to the process or work station in which they are involved.

FOCUS ON OPERATIONAL STRATEGIES: LEAN PRODUCTION

MINDMAPS

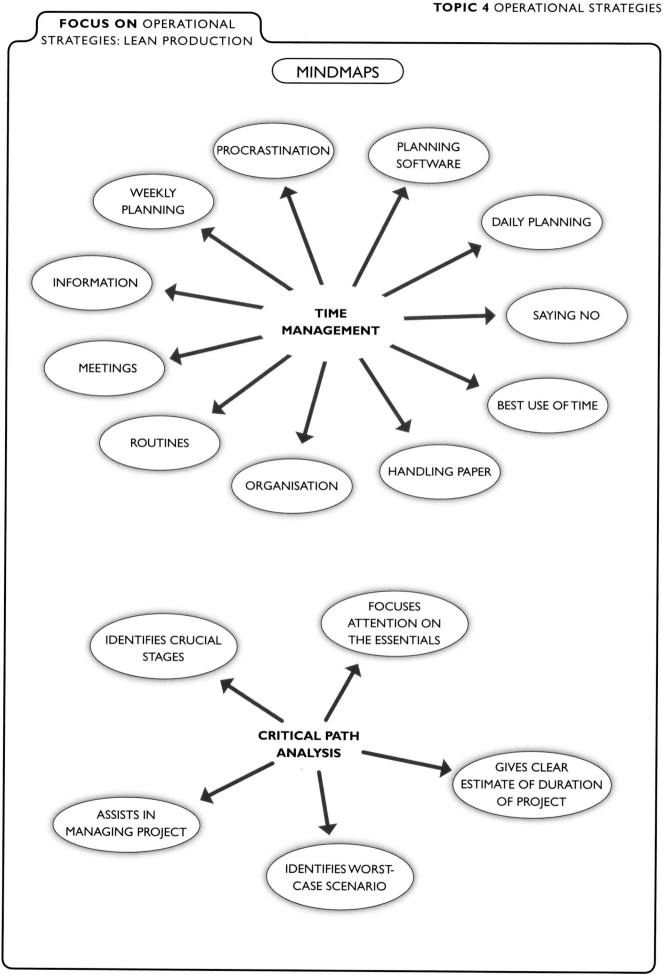

FOCUS ON OPERATIONAL
STRATEGIES: LEAN PRODUCTION

MINDMAPS

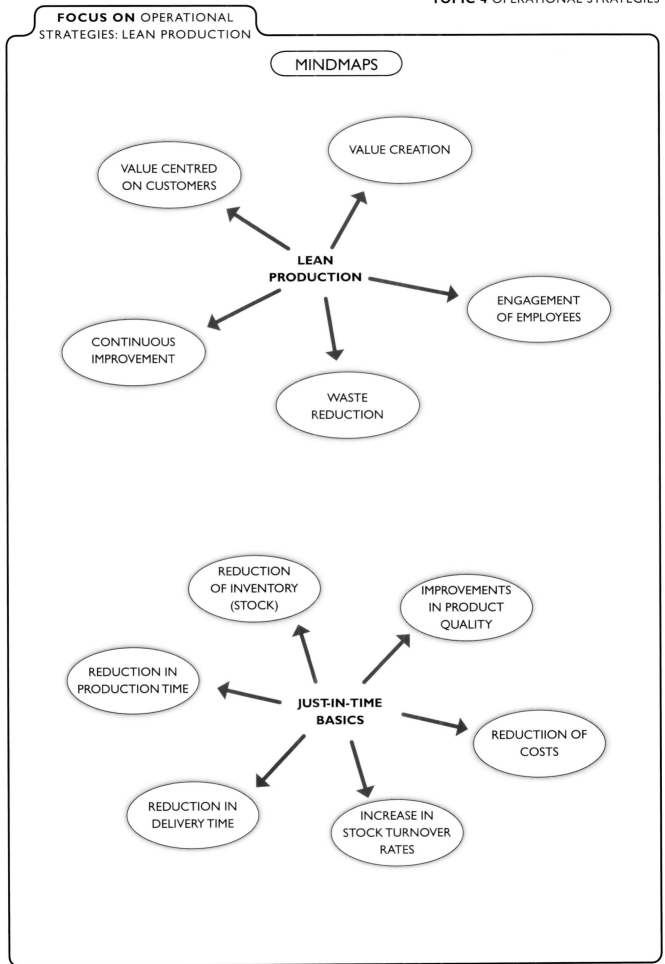

FOCUS ON OPERATIONAL
STRATEGIES: LEAN PRODUCTION

WORKSHEET

I   What do you understand by the term 'time study'?

2   What is the purpose of critical path analysis?

3   Distinguish between lean production, JIT and Kaizen.

Answers ▶ page 224

FOCUS ON HR OBJECTIVES AND STRATEGIES

HR objectives ► textbook pages 132–3

QUESTIONS

Using the Internet, find out about initiatives by the government to develop workforce skills in Britain. The Confederation of British Industry and the Trade Union Congress found that businesses lose up to £10 billion each year due to basic skills shortages, and that eight million members of the workforce have skills below the equivalent of five GCSEs. What steps are being taken to remedy this situation?

Initiatives began back in 2002 with the suggestion to bring in the National Modern Apprenticeships to fund employer training pilots and other measures to improve the workforce skills. Information can be found at www.hm-treasury.gov.uk; www.cwdcouncil.org.uk; and www.ogc.gov.uk.

Internal and external influences on HR objectives ► textbook pages 134–5

QUESTIONS

I Why might larger businesses find it more difficult to recruit than smaller ones? (*6 marks*)

As the case study suggests, the larger businesses were cutting down on their recruitment costs, but generally, larger businesses find it more difficult to recruit, as employees are less likely to be willing to fit into a large organisation often adopting rigid processes and working practices.

2 What do you think is meant by the term 'absence management'? (*4 marks*)

Absence management refers to dealing with unexplained or periodic absences by particular members of staff, which may display a pattern unrelated to illness or external commitments.

FOCUS ON HR OBJECTIVES AND STRATEGIES

HR strategies ▶ textbook pages 136–7

QUESTIONS

How might a human resource plan ensure that HR objectives are met? (*12 marks*)

A human resource plan will outline the key HR objectives and will look at needs and programmes that will have to be set up in order to achieve those objectives. This will include recruitment, redundancy, training, professional development, costs, productivity targets and the allocation of resources. Integral to an HR plan are the organisation's objectives, the utilisation of human resources, the internal and external environments and the potential supply of labour. This should allow the business to develop ways in which to manage employees and ensure that duplication of effort and resources is minimised.

	Poor	Good	Excellent
Quality of Work	☐	☐	☑
Quantity of Work	☐	☐	☑
Dependability	☐	☑	☐
Communication Skills	☐	☐	☑
Supervision	☐	☐	☑
Leadership Skills	☐	☐	☐
Initiative	☐	☐	☐
Cooperation	☐	☐	☐
Relations	☐	☐	☐
Adaptability	☐	☐	☐

Case studies, questions and exam practice ▶ textbook pages 138–9

CASE STUDY – HR AND MERGERS

1 What is meant by 'find ways to deliver head-count reduction, and higher productivity through synergy, while ensuring that the company has the right skills to take the new organisation forward'? Is this a hard or soft HR job? (*8 marks*)

Synergy in this context refers to the potential duplication of activities undertaken by the two merged businesses (e.g. duplicate sales and marketing, accounts etc.) It is about bringing the duplicate activities together and then trimming off any excess capacity by reducing staff numbers. It also means choosing the right balance of staff numbers to ensure that savings are made without compromising efficiency. In this respect, it would be a hard HR decision that takes into account the needs of the merged business and not the individual needs of the employees.

2 Why might employees be more concerned with job security in situations such as this rather than the reorganisation of the business itself? (*4 marks*)

Largely because of the rationalisation processes that are inevitable in situations such as this, employees' positions are under threat as they may well do exactly the same job as someone who is joining the business from the merger company. Equally, the likelihood that their jobs will change is high, as the needs of the new business are likely to be different from the original business.

FOCUS ON HR OBJECTIVES AND STRATEGIES

MINDMAPS

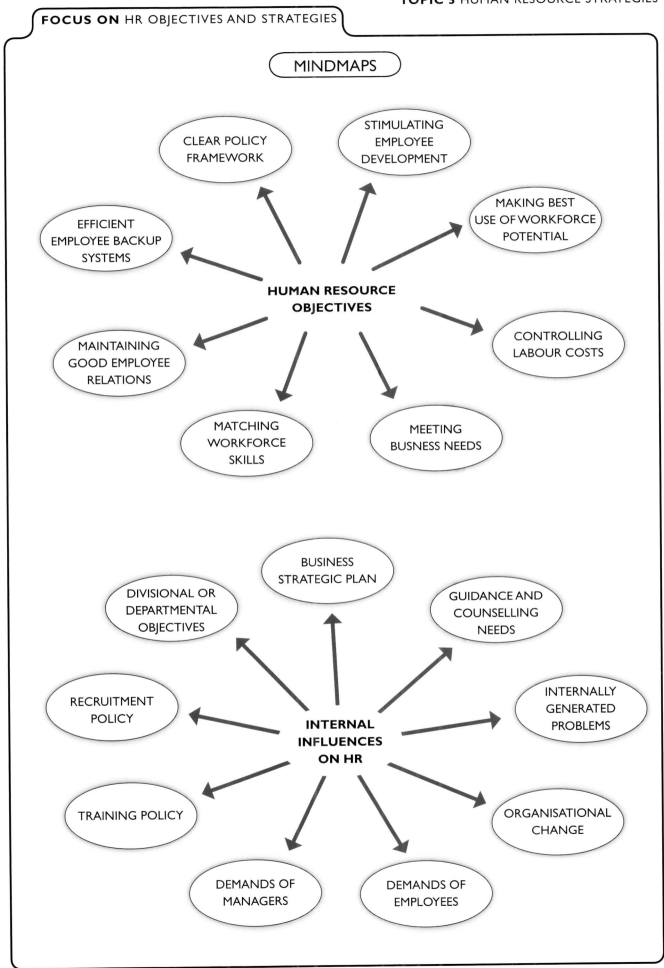

FOCUS ON HR OBJECTIVES AND STRATEGIES

MINDMAPS

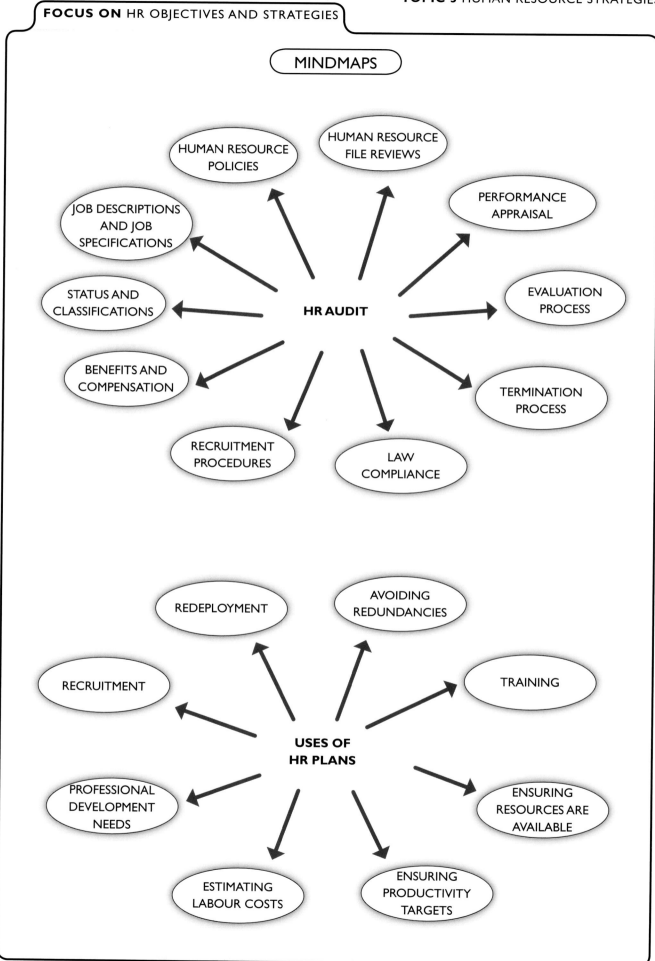

HUMAN RESOURCE POLICIES

HUMAN RESOURCE FILE REVIEWS

JOB DESCRIPTIONS AND JOB SPECIFICATIONS

PERFORMANCE APPRAISAL

STATUS AND CLASSIFICATIONS

HR AUDIT

EVALUATION PROCESS

BENEFITS AND COMPENSATION

TERMINATION PROCESS

RECRUITMENT PROCEDURES

LAW COMPLIANCE

REDEPLOYMENT

AVOIDING REDUNDANCIES

RECRUITMENT

TRAINING

USES OF HR PLANS

PROFESSIONAL DEVELOPMENT NEEDS

ENSURING RESOURCES ARE AVAILABLE

ESTIMATING LABOUR COSTS

ENSURING PRODUCTIVITY TARGETS

FOCUS ON HR OBJECTIVES AND STRATEGIES

WORKSHEET

1   What do you understand by the term 'hard HRM'?

2   Briefly identify and explain THREE key HR objectives.

3   What is the purpose of a human resource plan?

Answers ▶ page 225

FOCUS ON DEVELOPING AND IMPLEMENTING WORKFORCE PLANS

Components of workforce plans ▶ textbook pages 140–1

QUESTION

An organisation's vision, mission, and measurable goals and objectives drive the identification of future functional requirements. In turn, those requirements drive the analysis and elements of the workforce plan. Discuss. (*18 marks*)

Workforce planning naturally complements and is a follow-up to strategic planning. Just as strategic planning helps organisations map where they are, where they are going, and how they plan to get there, a workforce plan lays out the specific tasks and actions needed to ensure that an agency has the resources to accomplish its mission. One of the main purposes of workforce planning is to ensure that an organisation has the necessary workers to support its mission and strategic plan. In Phase I, those responsible for workforce planning should identify the organisation's mission and the key goals and objectives of its strategic plan.

A strategic plan charts the future with broad mission-related targets and milestones. An organisation's vision, mission, and measurable goals and objectives drive the identification of what type of work needs to be accomplished. A workforce plan translates strategic thinking into concrete action in the area of workforce staffing and training needs. It attempts to answer the following questions:

- How many and what types of jobs are needed to meet the performance objectives of the organisation?
- How will the organisation develop worker skills?
- What strategies should the organisation use to retain these skills?
- How have retirements, reductions in force, and/or hiring freezes affected the organisation's ability to get the work done?

Assessing internal and external influences on workforce plans

▶ textbook pages 142–3

QUESTION

Suggest four ways in which a business could forecast future workforce demands. (*8 marks*)

Any reasonable answer including:

- Demand for existing and new products
- Business disposals and product closures
- Introduction of new technology (e.g. new production equipment)

- Cost reduction programmes (most usually involve a reduction in staff numbers somewhere within the business)
- Changes to the business organisational structure
- Business acquisitions, joint ventures, strategic partnerships

FOCUS ON DEVELOPING AND IMPLEMENTING WORKFORCE PLANS

Issues in implementing workforce plans ▶ textbook pages 144–5

CASE STUDY – NO HR?

Why might it be the case that HR is not as closely involved in workforce planning as we would imagine? (*10 marks*)

The reason behind this appears to be that business owners do not consider that HR has a broad enough understanding of the demands on an organisation beyond their specialised area. However there is a major discrepancy between the figures, as Human Resources claim to be more involved in creating workforce plans than business owners state. Human Resources personnel accept that they have gaps in their understanding of broader business issues. The net result is that by not involving HR in workforce planning, the business itself is losing out from its expertise, and HR is missing an opportunity to broaden its understanding of business issues.

The value of workforce planning ▶ textbook pages 146–7

CASE STUDY – POOR PLANNING

How might the fact that the workforce planning is affected by an external finance provider (in this case the government) make the planning process far more complicated? (*12 marks*)

This is a significant problem for the human resources departments within the NHS. The NHS is a multi-tiered organisation with trusts being funded directly or indirectly by the government. The government has primary responsibility for the strategic workforce planning, while the NHS trusts have to make their own strategic plans and work out their own workforce planning requirements and forecasts. However the two elements do not seem to be communicating with one another in an efficient manner. The forward planning part is the government's responsibility and they seem to have failed to have communicated their strategic requirements for the future, which has led to a disparity between the work of the HR departments in the trusts and the specific demands and financial constraints of the government. It inevitably makes the planning process far more complicated and it would be advisable for representatives of the NHS trusts to have some input into the strategic planning process.

FOCUS ON DEVELOPING AND IMPLEMENTING WORKFORCE PLANS

Case studies, questions and exam practice ▶ textbook pages 148–9

CASE STUDY – WORKFORCE ANALYSIS

1 Suggest SIX ways in which an organisation could analyse its existing workforce. (*6 marks*)

Analysis of the current workforce can include:
- Number of employees and contracted workers
- Skill assessment of employees
- Salary and contract workforce expenditure data
- Workforce diversity (age, gender, and race)
- Retirement eligibility statistics
- Location

2 What is meant by environmental scanning and organisational analysis? (*4 marks*)

Environmental scanning is the process of examining external trends to obtain a better understanding of what is happening in the environment in which the organisation operates. There are several approaches to environmental scanning. The scan should include trends and issues in the economic, social, technological, legal, and political areas. An organisational analysis should include internal factors such as strategic objectives, business functions, and technology.

3 Explain the two possible outcomes of gap analysis. (*8 marks*)

A gap (when projected supply is less than forecast demand), which indicates a future shortage of needed workers or skills. A surplus (when projected supply is greater than forecast demand), which indicates a future excess in some categories of workers and may require action. The surplus data may represent occupations or skills that will not be needed in the future or at least not needed to the same extent.

4 Suggest FOUR factors that could influence or have an impact on strategy. (*8 marks*)

Time – Is there enough time to develop staff internally for anticipated vacancies or new skill needs, or is special, fast-paced recruitment the best approach? Resources – What resources (for example, technology, websites, structured templates, and sample plans) are currently available to provide assistance, or must resources be developed? Internal depth – Do existing staff demonstrate the potential or interest to develop new skills and assume new or modified positions, or is external recruitment needed? 'In-demand' skills – What competition exists for future skills that are needed? Will the agency need to recruit for these skills or develop them internally? Job classification – Do presently used job classifications and position descriptions reflect future functional requirements and skills? Reorganisation – Will some divisions need to be reorganised to meet business needs and strategic objectives?

FOCUS ON DEVELOPING AND
IMPLEMENTING WORKFORCE PLANS

MINDMAPS

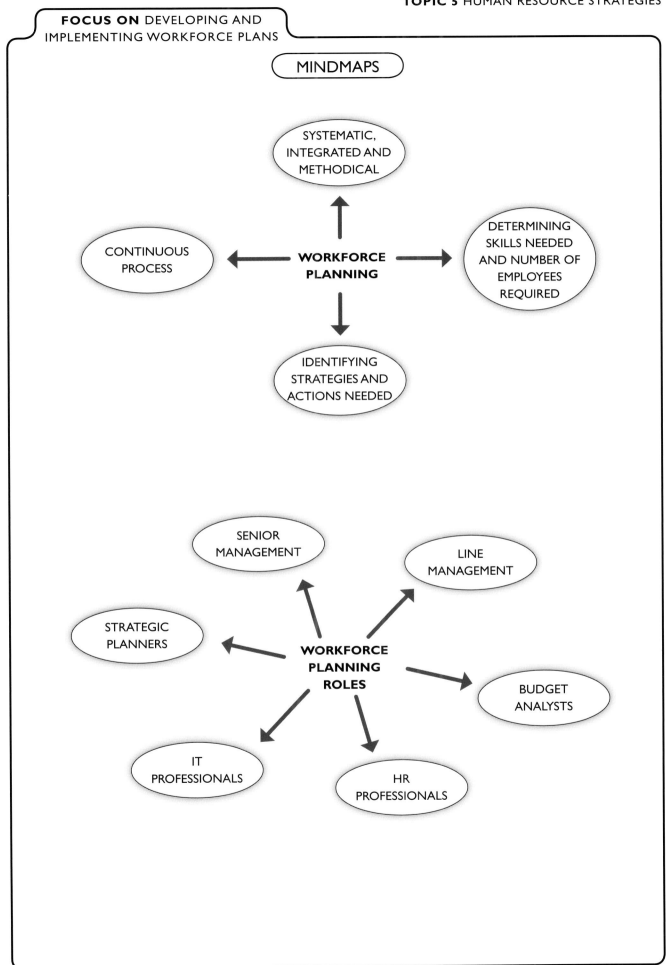

FOCUS ON DEVELOPING AND IMPLEMENTING WORKFORCE PLANS

MINDMAPS

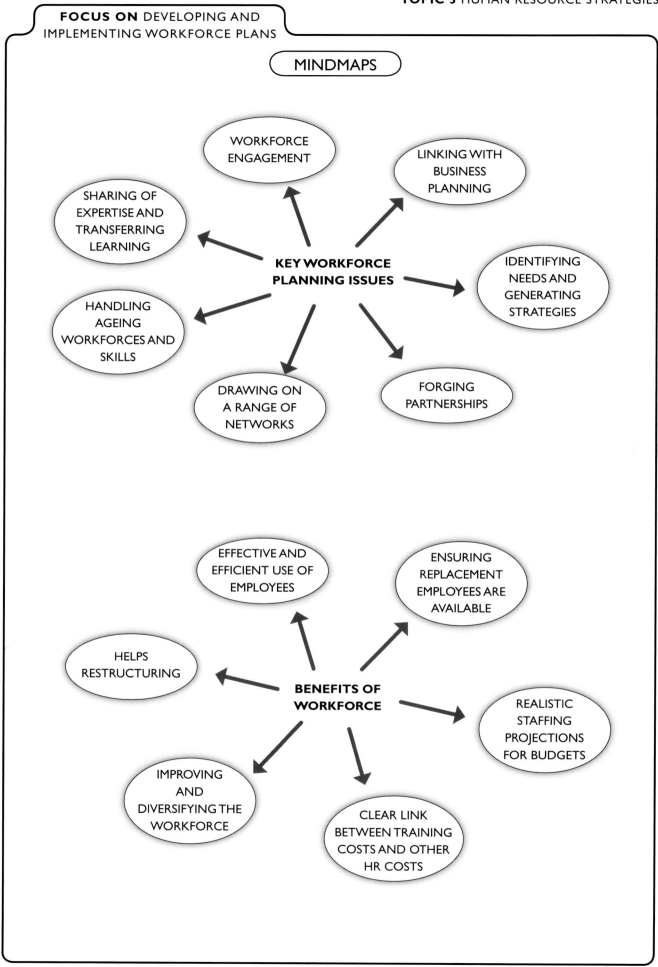

WORKFORCE ENGAGEMENT

LINKING WITH BUSINESS PLANNING

SHARING OF EXPERTISE AND TRANSFERRING LEARNING

KEY WORKFORCE PLANNING ISSUES

IDENTIFYING NEEDS AND GENERATING STRATEGIES

HANDLING AGEING WORKFORCES AND SKILLS

DRAWING ON A RANGE OF NETWORKS

FORGING PARTNERSHIPS

EFFECTIVE AND EFFICIENT USE OF EMPLOYEES

ENSURING REPLACEMENT EMPLOYEES ARE AVAILABLE

HELPS RESTRUCTURING

BENEFITS OF WORKFORCE

REALISTIC STAFFING PROJECTIONS FOR BUDGETS

IMPROVING AND DIVERSIFYING THE WORKFORCE

CLEAR LINK BETWEEN TRAINING COSTS AND OTHER HR COSTS

FOCUS ON DEVELOPING AND
IMPLEMENTING WORKFORCE PLANS

WORKSHEET

1 What do you understand by the term 'workforce planning'?

2 Why is Phase IV of a workforce plan so crucial?

3 Identify and explain the role of THREE different groups or individuals within a business that have an involvement in the workforce planning process.

Answers ▶ page 225

FOCUS ON DEVELOPING AND
IMPLEMENTING WORKFORCE PLANS

WORKSHEET

1 What is gap analysis, as applied to workforce planning?

2 How might a business handle an ageing workforce coupled with a skills gap?

3 Briefly identify FOUR drivers of change that would impact on the number of employees needed due to change in workloads.

Answers ▶ page 225

FOCUS ON DEVELOPING AND
IMPLEMENTING WORKFORCE PLANS

WORKSHEET

I   Briefly identify and explain THREE key benefits of workforce planning.

2   Briefly identify THREE key advantages of workforce planning.

3   Explain how new roles and working practices may affect a workforce plan.

Answers ▶ page 225

FOCUS ON COMPETITIVE ORGANISATIONAL STRUCTURES

Factors determining choice of organisational structures ▸ textbook pages 150–1

QUESTIONS

To what extent does Charles Handy's theory explain how organisations choose to structure themselves? (*12 marks*)

Handy actually suggests four different types of organisational culture, all of which seek to explain the differing needs of an organisation and how the culture determines the structure. Power culture infers that there will be bureaucratic procedures and that the organisation will tend to have a hierarchical structure. Role culture is also bureaucratic, with rules and procedures and

again quite a hierarchical structure. Task-based cultures have flexible organisational structures as they rely on employee expertise and the need to change fast to accommodate fluctuations in their environment. A person-based culture is the most flexible and flat of all of the organisational structures, as each individual has their own set of responsibilities, yet there is a coordinating branch of the organisation to ensure that information is exchanged between its different parts.

Adapting structures to improve competitiveness (1) ▸ textbook pages 152–3

QUESTION

Why has the National Trust chosen to centralise in this way? What degree of autonomy has remained and why? (*12 marks*)

The National Trust needed to coordinate its supplies and to collate information to help its catering function become more profitable. The business wanted to be able to easily record stock usage, purchase invoices and sales data. However, it did not wish to prevent each of the

catering outlets from sourcing local food products and arriving at their own pricing structure. Hence they chose a management system that centralised some of the processes while retaining a degree of flexibility for local managers. The process of centralisation was also aimed at trying to encourage the sharing of best practice and to illustrate to some restaurants that a higher margin on certain products could be achieved.

Adapting structures to improve competitiveness (2) ▸ textbook pages 154–5

QUESTIONS

Explain how Fayol's theory could help explain how an organisation chooses to structure itself. (*15 marks*)

Firstly Fayol suggested that organisational structure needs to be imposed by senior management, rather than developed in an organic way. He identified six main categories of activity and then superimposed on these his fourteen elements and principles of management. By combining coverage of the six categories of activity with the fourteen appropriate principles of management he suggests a clear

division of work; a system by which authority gives instructions; a rigid discipline; a unity of command and direction; the requirement to subordinate personal interests in the interests of the organisation; centralised services to ensure that tasks are concentrated and not duplicated; a clear scalar chain; internal order; equality; stability; fair remuneration and the ability for employees to use their initiative. Taken together, these suggest a hierarchical structure in which there are various layers of management that aim to ensure the activities are delivered within the fourteen principles of management.

FOCUS ON COMPETITIVE
ORGANISATIONAL STRUCTURES

Adapting structures to improve competitiveness (3) ▶ textbook pages 156–7

QUESTIONS

A compressed working week should work for almost any organisation. Discuss. (*12 marks*)

The compressed working week is relatively popular and successful in a number of businesses around the world. It is ideal for businesses that want to achieve full staffing on a daily basis, to ensure seamless production and manning levels. It avoids having to pay overtime and allows the business to deploy employees at crucial times, lowering staffing levels when demand for staff is lower. The system has built into it a flexibility that allows the compressed working week to be adjusted according to changes in demand. Another key advantage is that it actually improves recruitment and retention because it provides employees with guaranteed flexibility to cover their domestic requirements. On the down side, however, research has shown that it does place a physical strain on employees who have shorter breaks between blocks of work. In order for the system to work effectively negotiation methods need to be put in place in order for employees to reschedule their other commitments.

Case studies, questions and exam practice ▶ textbook pages 158–9

CASE STUDY – A NEW WORKING ENVIRONMENT

1   **What were the main reasons why the two organisations wanted to introduce flexible working?** (*6 marks*)

Slough Borough Council was finding it difficult to recruit and retain employees, as they were being attracted by better paid jobs with other councils. It chose to offer flexible home-working as an alternative to financial incentives in order to attract employees. Staff output has improved and labour turnover reduced. Digital Steps also wanted to attract qualified specialists, particularly more female staff, and wanted this to become a major selling point for the organisation in terms of recruitment.

2   **What were the outcomes for the two organisations?** (*6 marks*)

For Slough Borough Council it was an ideal match for the particular job, where most of the work is carried out outside the office. Team leaders were helped to trust their staff more. The Council has been able to retain staff by offering flexible home-working, reducing employee turnover and making savings in office space, with the result that the output of the staff has increased considerably. Digital Steps wanted to encourage a work-life balance. It introduced flexitime and has seen no downturn in output, even though its work system has changed entirely.

FOCUS ON COMPETITIVE
ORGANISATIONAL STRUCTURES

MINDMAPS

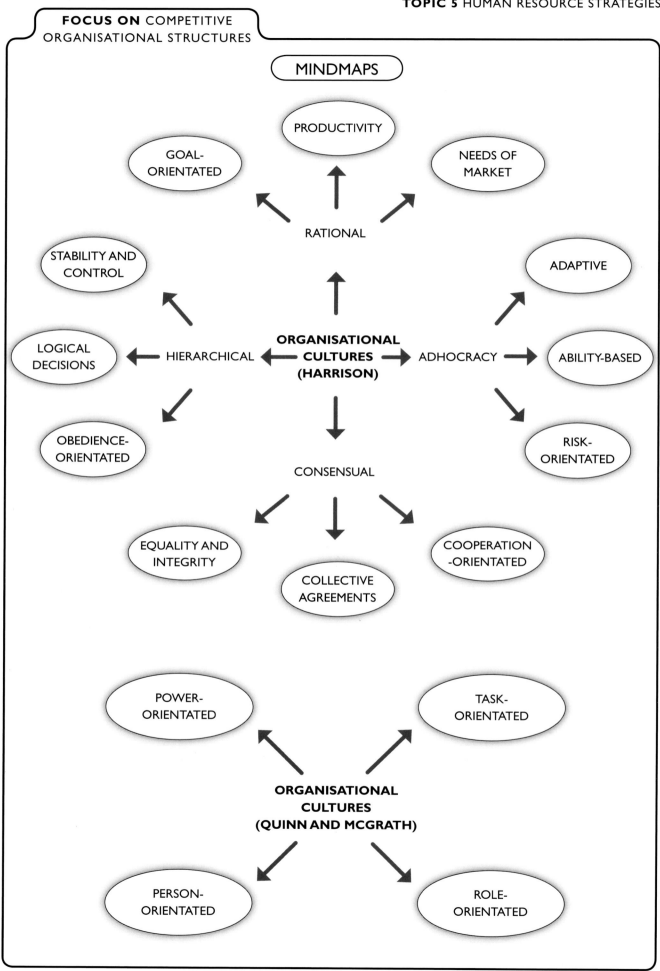

FOCUS ON COMPETITIVE
ORGANISATIONAL STRUCTURES

MINDMAPS

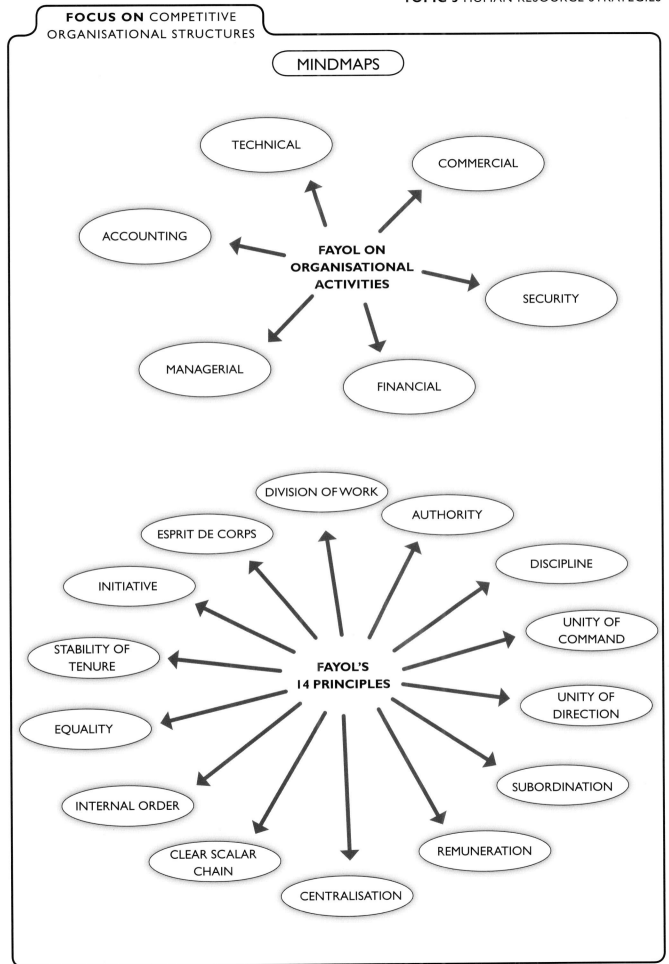

FOCUS ON COMPETITIVE
ORGANISATIONAL STRUCTURES

WORKSHEET

1   In terms of organisational culture, what is an adhocracy?

2   What is meant, according to Harrison, by a business whose culture is based on tasks?

3   What is a matrix organisational structure, and what is its purpose?

Answers ▶ page 225

FOCUS ON COMPETITIVE
ORGANISATIONAL STRUCTURES

WORKSHEET

1 Outline THREE key advantages of a decentralised structure.

2 Distinguish between empowerment and autonomy.

3 Why are flat organisational structures often referred to as de-layered structures?

Answers ▶ page 226

FOCUS ON COMPETITIVE
ORGANISATIONAL STRUCTURES

WORKSHEET

1 Distinguish between a chain of command and a span of control.

2 What do you understand by the term 'flexi place'?

3 Why might a business be prepared to bring in a compressed working week?

Answers ▶ page 226

FOCUS ON EFFECTIVE
EMPLOYER/EMPLOYEE RELATIONS

Managing communications with employees ▶ textbook pages 160–1

CASE STUDY – ROTHERHAM METROPOLITAN BOROUGH COUNCIL

Explain how the HEART approach had an impact on the council. (*10 marks*)

By improving its communication with employees, the council was able to systematically tackle the five aspects of the HEART approach. It engendered greater understanding, communication, coordination and contribution throughout the organisation. The net impact on the council was to significantly reduce staff turnover, reduce sickness and absence rates, drastically improve its status in terms of independent, external rating, and significantly improve the motivation and work ethic of the employees. It also allowed Rotherham Council to win a runner-up prize in a management award.

Methods of employee representation ▶ textbook pages 162–3

QUESTION

Distinguish between works councils and trade unions. (*12 marks*)

Works councils are not independent of the employer; rather they are set up by, and supported and funded by the employer. They are designed to primarily operate as a way in which the employees can be represented at decision-making level within a business, rather than representing themselves independently via industrial disputes and grievances. Trade unions, on the other hand, are fully independent of the employer. They are separated both legally and fundamentally from the employer, as their sole purpose is to protect the interests of their members. Representatives are elected and they are involved in collective agreements, bargaining and dispute resolution. They are also involved in dealing with disciplinary and grievance matters.

FOCUS ON EFFECTIVE EMPLOYER/EMPLOYEE RELATIONS

Avoiding and resolving industrial disputes ▶ textbook pages 164–5

QUESTION

Distinguish between the work of industrial tribunals and ACAS. (12 marks)

Industrial tribunals are usually the result of European-wide employment law. They are legalistic and formal and act as a means by which issues such as unfair dismissal, discrimination, disciplinary issues and breaches of employment law can be resolved. Both sides present their evidence and judgement is passed by the tribunal itself. The two parties are at liberty to appeal against any decision that is made. ACAS, on the other hand, acts as an arbitrator between employers and employees. It aims to encourage a good working relationship and a practical way of settling disputes. Both sides need to agree to abide by the decision of ACAS and only a quarter of cases referred to them are actually referred to an employment tribunal.

Case studies, questions and exam practice ▶ textbook pages 166–7

CASE STUDY – NATIONWIDE COMMUNICATIONS

Suggest the different types of internal communications that could be used in an organisation like Nationwide, and why the nature of the business and its structure requires a range of types to be used. (12 marks)

Students could suggest a wide range of different internal communication techniques. Obviously the most significant one is the one mentioned in the case study – the use of the house magazine. However the case study also suggests that the intranet, email, audio-visual and face-to-face communications are used. In fact, students should focus primarily on Tom Harvey's desire to use new technology, but to continue to keep the messages straightforward and easy to understand, so that they are effective. An organisation like Nationwide has a distinct internal communication set-up, as it has numerous offices and outlets scattered around the country. It is difficult for such an organisation to make valuable use of mass staff meetings and it might rely instead on disseminating information indirectly from the main office. This makes the challenge of internal communication all the more complex, as to a large extent the organisation will be reliant upon local management to ensure that important communications are delivered and understood.

FOCUS ON EFFECTIVE
EMPLOYER/EMPLOYEE RELATIONS

MINDMAPS

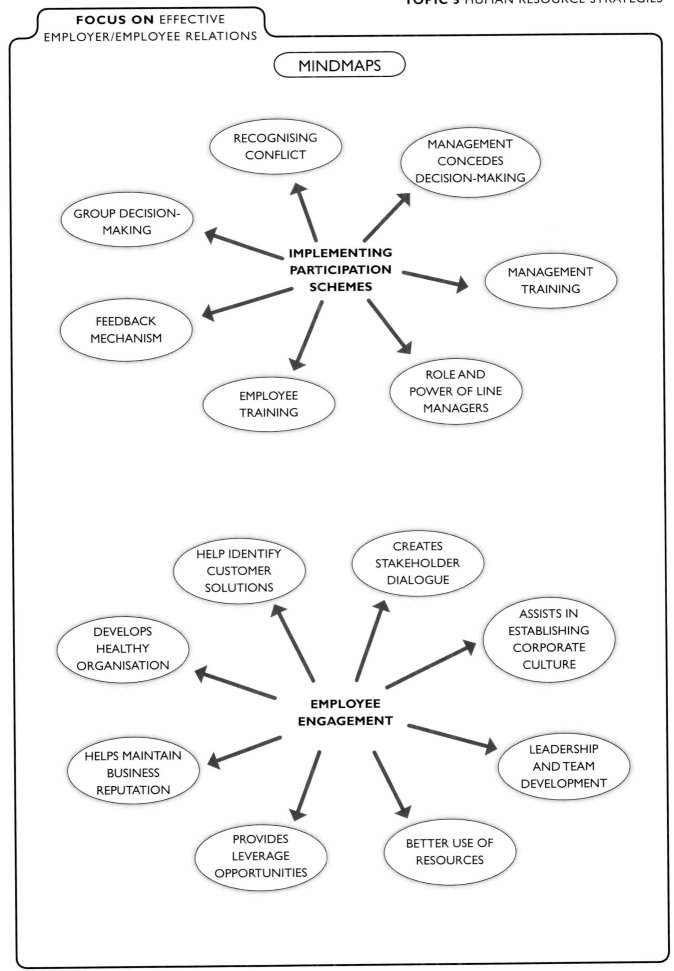

RECOGNISING
CONFLICT

MANAGEMENT
CONCEDES
DECISION-MAKING

GROUP DECISION-
MAKING

**IMPLEMENTING
PARTICIPATION
SCHEMES**

MANAGEMENT
TRAINING

FEEDBACK
MECHANISM

EMPLOYEE
TRAINING

ROLE AND
POWER OF LINE
MANAGERS

HELP IDENTIFY
CUSTOMER
SOLUTIONS

CREATES
STAKEHOLDER
DIALOGUE

DEVELOPS
HEALTHY
ORGANISATION

ASSISTS IN
ESTABLISHING
CORPORATE
CULTURE

**EMPLOYEE
ENGAGEMENT**

HELPS MAINTAIN
BUSINESS
REPUTATION

LEADERSHIP
AND TEAM
DEVELOPMENT

PROVIDES
LEVERAGE
OPPORTUNITIES

BETTER USE OF
RESOURCES

FOCUS ON EFFECTIVE
EMPLOYER/EMPLOYEE RELATIONS

MINDMAPS

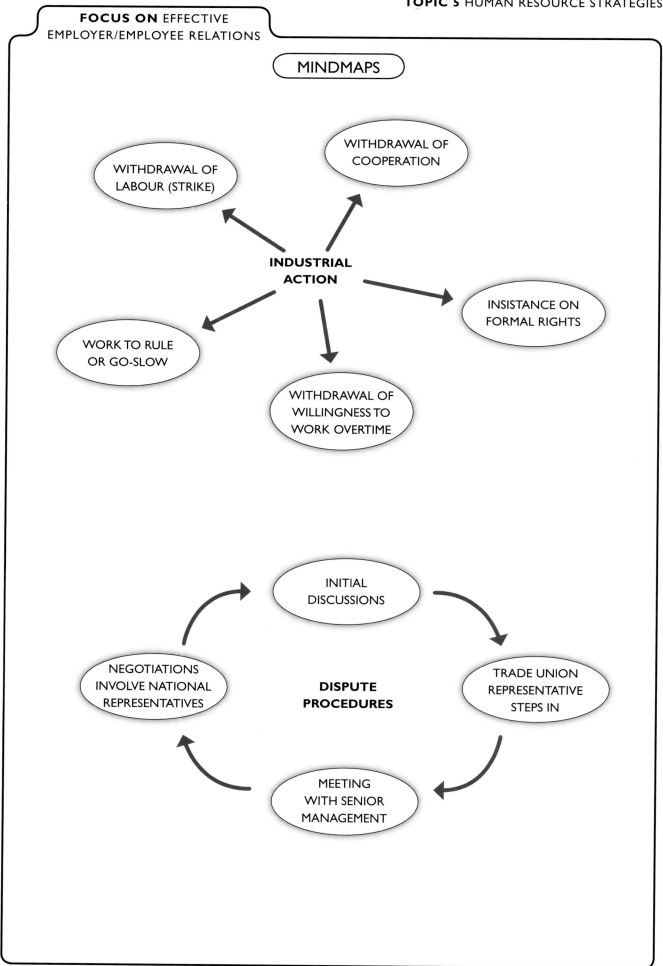

FOCUS ON EFFECTIVE
EMPLOYER/EMPLOYEE RELATIONS

WORKSHEET

1   What is the purpose of a works council?

2   What is the role of ACAS?

3   Why is it important for a business to take employee engagement seriously?

Answers ▶ page226

Mock exam ▶ textbook pages 168–9

INVESTMENT CHOICES

1 Calculate the ROCE and the net profit margin of the two businesses and compare them with the industry averages. On these figures, suggest which would be the better investment and why. Assume that the purchase price is £490,000 in each case. (*10 marks*)

The ROCE on option one is £22,000/£490,000 × 100 = 4.48%. The net profit margin on this investment is £22,000/£156,000 × 100 = 14.10%. For the second investment, the ROCE is £29,000/£490,000 × 100 = 5.91% and the net profit margin is £29,000/£233,000 × 100 = 12.44%. The ROCE is poorer for the first investment and considerably lower than the industry standard. The net profit margin is, however, considerably higher. The second investment exceeds the ROCE of the industry average and the net profit margin is also much better. Taking these calculations only into account, the consultants are likely to suggest that Option 2 is the better investment opportunity. This would be in line with the requirements of the investors.

2 Analyse the market using the data from Appendix B in relation to market potential for the two different businesses. (*30 marks*)

Market analsis should focus on the potential catchment area for the two businesses. It should also note the employment situation and average wage, and there should be an indication as to the possible level of competition (as shown by the number of workers in the industry). The market analysis needs to combine the data that looks at the immediate catchment areas for the businesses as well as the broader catchment area. Note that those working in the city are far in excess of those actually living and working in the city. The two businesses have slightly different potential customer bases. The pub/restaurant and guest house would have a different customer profile from the night club.

3 Identify areas of market research that may be missing but necessary to complete the market analysis, and make a decision about the optimal location for the two businesses. Also use Appendix C for this question. (*15 marks*)

What is conspicuously absent is the breakdown of the population by age, the number of tourists visiting the city and the average disposable income of the local population. It would also have been valuable to have compiled a listing of main competitors in the immediate area and across the city. Numbers of competitors, outlet closures, and the number sold in the past months would also have been useful. Future infrastructure plans would be valuable to get a fuller picture of the direction in which the city is moving. Some indication of future investment in the city with regard to employment, retail facilities and potential new competition could add to the information.

4 Comment on the current employee relations in the two businesses and suggest how they might be resolved under new ownership. (*15 marks*)

The pub's main problem with staff is one of high turnover and a reliance on teenagers who are being paid low wages with little incentive. The pub needs to build up a reliable employee base and pay employees an incentive or better base rate in order to ensure that the better staff remain with the business. Staff turnover does tend to be high in catering, but this seems particularly high. The night club's main problems are the daytime operations and the attitude of the DJs. The business could consider partitioning off part of the building so that only a selected part is accessible and could be handled by fewer staff, to bring down the wage bill. The contracts with the DJs may have to be renegotiated, or at least the DJs could be offered an incentive if they manage to attract a certain number of customers to the nightclub or the nightclub turns over a certain level in cash sales. Otherwise, the club needs to change the DJs and negotiate the termination of the contracts.

Mock exam

Surname		Other names	

UNIT 3   **STRATEGIES FOR SUCCESS**
MOCK EXAMINATION PAPER

ASSESSMENT

WRITTEN PAPER: **1 HOUR AND 45 MINUTES**

INFORMATION

THE MAXIMUM MARK FOR THIS MOCK PAPER IS 80.

WEIGHTING IS 25% OF TOTAL A-LEVEL MARK

THE MARKS FOR QUESTIONS ARE SHOWN IN BRACKETS.

THE QUESTIONS WILL REQUIRE EXTENDED ANSWERS THAT DRAW ON AS MATERIALS. THE FOCUS IS ON MEASURING BUSINESS PERFORMANCE AND ASSESSING APPROPRIATE FUNCTIONAL STRATEGIES TO ACHIEVE SUCCESS. YOU WILL BE PRESENTED WITH AN UNSEEN CASE STUDY THAT INCORPORATES A RANGE OF NUMERICAL DATA.

FOR EXAMINER'S USE			
Question	Mark	Question	Mark
1		3	
2		4	
Total column 1			
Total column 2			
TOTAL			
Signature			

TOPIC LIST

- *Functional objectives and strategies* – examining their appropriateness in the context of corporate objectives
- *Financial strategies and accounts* – making investment decisions, measuring performance, financial decisions
- *Marketing strategies* – analysing markets, and selecting successful marketing strategies, developing marketing plans
- *Operations strategies* – operational issues, location, innovation, improving operational efficiency
- *Human resource strategies* – workforce planning, adapting organisational structures, successful employee relations

Answers ▶ page 231

Mock exam (continued)

Answer all questions in the spaces provided.

Read the case study below and then answer the questions that follow.

EAST ANGLIAN HEALTHCARE SOLUTIONS LTD

East Anglian Healthcare Solutions Ltd is an eco-friendly business that focuses on creating waste-disposal solutions for the healthcare industry. It is based in Ipswich, Suffolk. The company's products are primarily designed to reduce costs and CO_2 emissions when hospitals, laboratories and dental surgeries dispose of infectious waste.

The business has 440 employees in Britain and has recently released a super-absorbent mat, which uses thousands of tiny crystals that can absorb many hundreds of times their own weight in liquid. The business has recently acquired a new warehouse with attached research-and-development facilities to ensure the company's continued growth. It also wishes to minimise shipping time involved in bringing the products from China, where they are manufactured, to the European market. The business has chosen to lease this new warehouse site.

The business's products are already being used in many hospitals all over Britain. In recent years, after appearing at a number of healthcare exhibitions and events, they have attracted significant interest from abroad. Many hospitals and other healthcare institutions are very interested in the fact that the business's products can help reduce their carbon footprint, which is caused by incinerating plastic materials. The business has therefore set up a number of subsidiary operations across the world and now has a global workforce of 3,700.

Appendix A East Anglian Healthcare Solutions Ltd Key Financials

	2008	2007	2006	2005	2004	2003	2002	Compound annual growth rate
Turnover (£m)	225.0	152.6	116.9	71.9	32.4	27.1	12.7	61.6%
Operating profit (£m)	32.7	18.8	13.1	9.8	4.1	2.6	1.6	65.4%
Profit before tax (£m)	24.9	16.9	12.7	9.6	4.2	2.6	1.6	59.5%
Adjusted basic earnings per share (pence)	35.5	29.2	23.8	20.4	12.8	9.9	7.9	28.6%
Operating cash flow	48.7	33.1	27.6	21.1	6.9	6.3	3.1	58.5%
Dividend per share	10.1	8.4	7.0	6.0	3.8	2.9	2.4	27.1%

Mock exam (continued)

EAST ANGLIAN HEALTHCARE SOLUTIONS LTD

Appendix B Chairman's statement

Employees

Our workforce has continued to grow in line with the business and we now employ more than 3,700 people in Europe, Asia and South Africa. We are seeking to differentiate the business through the quality of our people and we therefore actively promote extensive investment in training, development and talent management programmes for our employees.

The Board recognises the professionalism of our team and the important contribution it makes to the success of the business, and I would like to thank them for their efforts this year.

Outlook

The global market for healthcare continues to expand, driven by demographic trends and increased prosperity in developing countries, and our business is well placed to capitalise on this macro trend. The Company has completed another successful year with a strong financial performance and good progression towards a number of strategic objectives centred on the internationalisation of the business, particularly in China.

We have a strong business model providing essential services with substantial barriers to entry and a forward order book of over £800 million. With several new contracts started during the new financial year, as well as the additional capacity coming on-stream, we are confident that the business will enjoy another successful year.

It has been almost seven years since we were first listed on AIM as a small UK-based healthcare company. During this period, we have performed impressively, extending our operations to 11 countries and resulting in compound-growth rates of 61.6%, 59.5% and 28.6% for revenue, profit before tax, amortisation of intangibles, and non-recurring items and adjusted EPS respectively.

The order book has increased from £40 million at the date of admission to AIM in 2001 to over £800 million today. This dramatic growth is reflected in an increased market capitalisation from £12.5 million to approximately £365 million today.

The business operates subsidiaries in the United Kingdom, Ireland, the Netherlands, France, Germany, South Africa, Malaysia and Thailand. Regional offices have recently been opened in China and Dubai, and our distributor network has now grown to over 60 countries.

Mock exam (continued)

EAST ANGLIAN HEALTHCARE SOLUTIONS LTD

Appendix B Chief executive's statement on strategy

We have a clear strategy to expand the business internationally over the coming three to five years. Most of our recent investment has been targeted at China, where we are building a new sterilisation centre to support the expansion of our commercial and hospital sterilisation services. Given the potential of this market, with approximately 14,000 hospitals, and the very clear intentions of our large multinational medical device customers to invest in China, we have given this opportunity a high degree of priority. As a consequence, until our Chinese investments have achieved a degree of scale, our developments in other parts of Asia – such as our proposed development office in Singapore – will be deferred.

In Europe we continue to expand the business organically with the opening of our commercial sterilisation facility in the Netherlands near the German border, and with two new contracts for hospital sterilisation services, one in the Netherlands and the other in Belgium. We continue to develop our revenue and marketing infrastructure primarily in Europe to support our organic objectives.

Recently we have opened an office in Dubai as part of a plan to extend our hospital services in the Emirates. With this investment we are expecting to see strong growth in the region over the coming years.

Both the North and South American markets are attractive opportunities for Synergy in the medium term, while our priorities are Europe, the Middle East and Asia, as a strategic partner to a number of multinational medical device manufacturers,

The business will evaluate opportunities to expand organically in the Americas when there is sufficiently strong demand.

Mock exam (continued)

Question One

Calculate the gross profit percentage over the seven years and comment on the results of your calculations. *(16 marks)*

2002 gross profit percentage

_____

_____

2003 gross profit percentage

_____

_____

2004 gross profit percentage

_____

_____

2005 gross profit percentage

_____

_____

2006 gross profit percentage

_____

_____

2007 gross profit percentage

_____

_____

2008 gross profit percentage

_____

_____

Mock exam (continued)

Question Two

In the last quarter of reported results the business showed sales in Britain worth £38.4 million, compared to £34.6 million pounds in the same quarter of the previous year. The figures for the rest of Europe were £27.5 million compared to £22.6 million and for Asia and South Africa £2 million compared to £1.6 million. Calculate the growth in sales and comment on the business's decision to focus on Asia as a key growth market. *(24 marks)*

Mock exam (continued)

Question Three

Comment on the corporate strategy of the business and how the statements by both the Chairman and the Chief Executive would encourage or discourage potential investors.

(20 marks)

Mock exam (continued)

Question Four

Comment on the business's human resource strategy. Suggest what types of HR initiatives may be in place in a business such as this and comment on whether they are likely to be applicable across the whole of the organisation. *(20 marks)*

FOCUS ON UNDERSTANDING
MISSION AIMS AND OBJECTIVES

Functional and corporate objectives ▶ textbook pages 174–5

QUESTION

How might this view of the way in which mission statements are created and written be useful to businesses? *(10 marks)*

The case study suggests that many businesses will automatically use left-brain thinking when creating a mission statement, indicated by the familiar phrases such as 'easier', 'safe' and 'proven'. This suggests a logical and analytical approach to the creation of mission statements. It also means, however, that the mission statements have a limited perspective and may actually fail to engage those who are expected to either respond to or adhere to them. The right-hand side of the brain is far more visual and creative and capable of using emotive language. This produces an altogether more engaging mission statement, incorporating words such as exciting, challenging, creative or innovative, which should be more aspirational, both for employees and management, as well as customers.

Corporate aims and objectives ▶ textbook pages 176–7

QUESTION

Explain the criteria that should be applied to all organisational goals. *(18 marks)*

Students should focus on the eight key criteria and explain why it is important to include them, and the consequences of either not including them or choosing to change them. Goals need to be stable to be attained. They also need to be unambiguous and realistic. They should cover the entire organisation, aim to be unique and designed to differentiate the organisation and its products and services from the competition. They should be linked to actions at both management and employee level, and in order to show forward-thinking and innovation they should indicate where the business wishes to be at some point in the future.

Corporate strategies ▶ textbook pages 178–9

QUESTION

Using the model of a planning process, how might a mission statement outlining plans to increase a business's commitment to first-class customer service, be translated into reality? *(12 marks)*

The business will begin with a mission statement, from which it will carry out an environmental analysis. This will help senior management make decisions on how to implement the objectives derived from the mission statement. There would then be a period where the objectives were implemented and the results ultimately evaluated. The results of the performance are then fed back to senior management, who will undertake a revision of policies and plans. This could ultimately lead to new decisions being made to adapt objectives to meet the requirements of the mission statement. In effect it is a circular process, which should also incorporate periodic re-examination of the environment.

FOCUS ON UNDERSTANDING
MISSION AIMS AND OBJECTIVES

Differing stakeholder perspectives ▶ textbook pages 180–1

QUESTION

How might a business go about identifying its stakeholders, their influence and their attitude to future plans? *(18 marks)*

A business should begin by looking for individuals and groups that may have a vested interest in the business or may be affected directly or indirectly by its actions. Usually a business will begin with a comprehensive list of all possible stakeholders and then eliminate those that may be only marginally affected by the actions of the organisation. The business will also need to appreciate that by categorising potential stakeholders into large groups, such as

central or local government, there may actually be differing perspectives within that stakeholder group. In other words, the perspective of central government may be markedly different from that of local government. It is a complex process, not only in initially identifying the stakeholders but also determining their degree of influence and their current attitude to the organisation. Broadly, those that can have a direct impact on the activities of the organisation will have a high level of influence, while those only marginally concerned may be allocated a low level of influence.

Case studies, questions and exam practice ▶ textbook pages 182–3

CASE STUDY – TOTALLY GREENWICH CAR FREE WEEKEND

Identify the stakeholders in this case study and comment on their likely perspectives. *(12 marks)*

The primary stakeholders are visitors, residents and businesses, although clearly there are many other organisations, agencies and groups directly or indirectly affected by this project and that influence it in some way. The key stakeholder perspectives and the stakeholders' relative influence should be considered in relation to the main objectives of the event. On the first issue, traffic and pollution are directly related to both policing and environmental health, as well as

broader environmental groups. Increasing visitor spend is primarily related to the local businesses. Attractions and tourist organisations have a hand in targeting new visitor audiences. The phrase 'promote shoulder seasons' suggests that Greenwich wants to attract more visitors to the area out of high-peak periods, which could impact on a number of different stakeholder groups. Customers are the main stakeholders, as are the owners of the attractions, with regard to repeat visits and the council itself. Environmental groups and bodies are related to the environmental improvements.

FOCUS ON UNDERSTANDING
MISSION AIMS AND OBJECTIVES

MINDMAPS

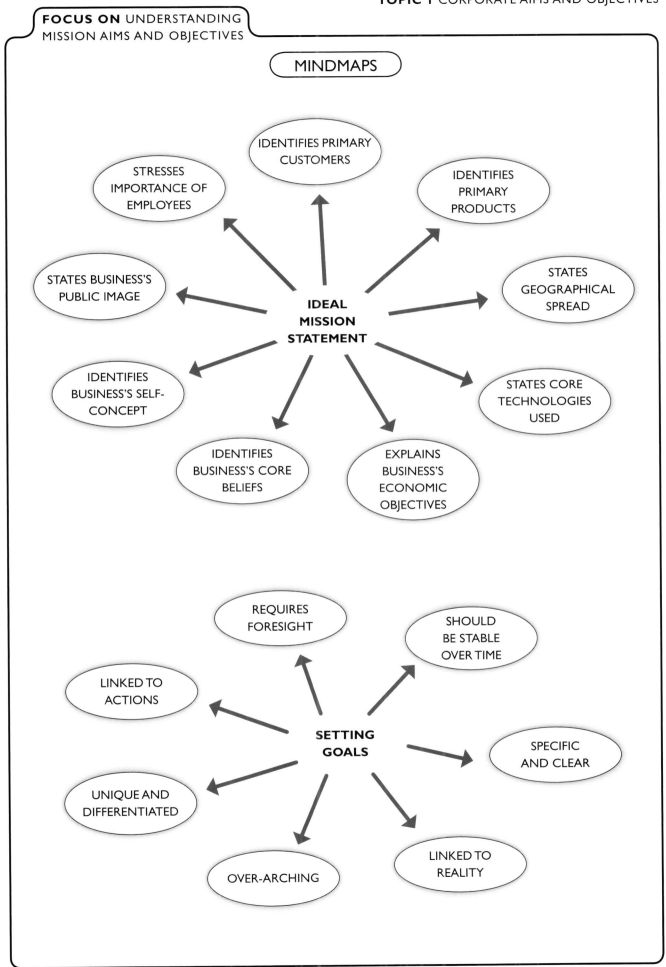

STRESSES IMPORTANCE OF EMPLOYEES

IDENTIFIES PRIMARY CUSTOMERS

IDENTIFIES PRIMARY PRODUCTS

STATES BUSINESS'S PUBLIC IMAGE

IDEAL MISSION STATEMENT

STATES GEOGRAPHICAL SPREAD

IDENTIFIES BUSINESS'S SELF-CONCEPT

STATES CORE TECHNOLOGIES USED

IDENTIFIES BUSINESS'S CORE BELIEFS

EXPLAINS BUSINESS'S ECONOMIC OBJECTIVES

REQUIRES FORESIGHT

SHOULD BE STABLE OVER TIME

LINKED TO ACTIONS

SETTING GOALS

SPECIFIC AND CLEAR

UNIQUE AND DIFFERENTIATED

OVER-ARCHING

LINKED TO REALITY

FOCUS ON UNDERSTANDING
MISSION AIMS AND OBJECTIVES

MINDMAPS

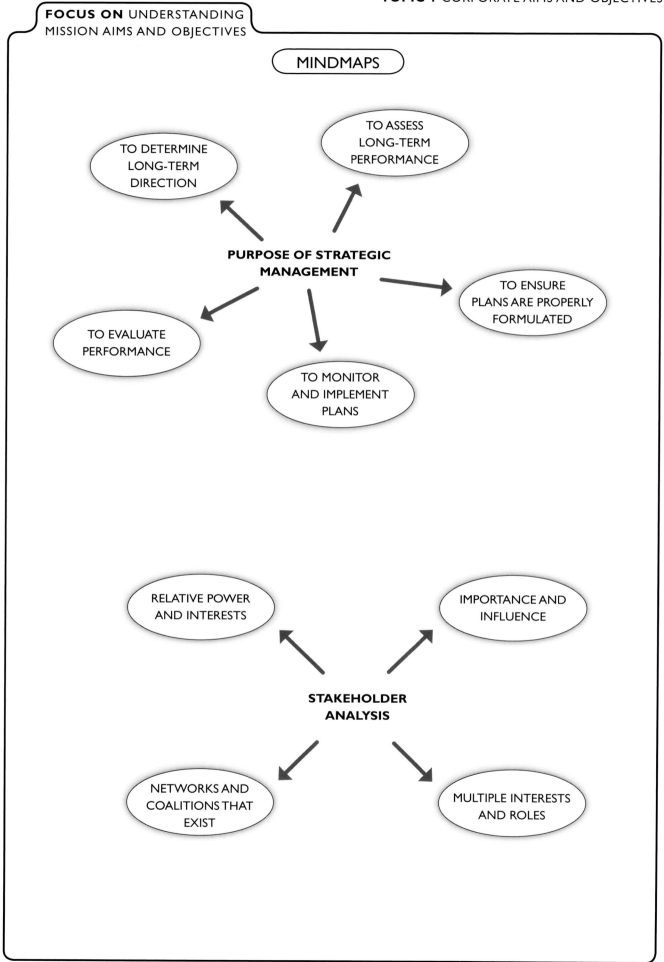

FOCUS ON UNDERSTANDING
MISSION AIMS AND OBJECTIVES

WORKSHEET

1   Outline FOUR key features of a mission statement.

2   Identify and explain the THREE different levels at which strategic formulation takes place within a business.

3   Explain the purpose of stakeholder analysis.

Answers ▶ page 226

FOCUS ON THE ECONOMIC ENVIRONMENT

Impact of the competitive environment ▶ textbook pages 186–7

QUESTION

To what extent does Porter's Five Forces model explain the nature of a competitive market? *(18 marks)*

Porter's five forces aims to explain the circumstances that create competitive rivalry in a specific market. It measures relative power and also addresses the fact that businesses and their products and services may be more or less exposed to the prospect of being overtaken by newer, better products or more aggressive businesses. The model is useful in examining the two key factors that may be out of the control of most businesses: the relative power of the supplier and the relative power of the buyer. Collectively, the model allows a business to address its capability of dealing with these potential threats and how vulnerable it is to the threats of substitution and new entry.

The structures of markets and industries

▶ textbook pages 188–9

CASE STUDY – SUPERMARKET PRICE FIXING

Find out what the allegations were that were made against supermarkets regarding dairy price fixing. What was the outcome? *(12 marks)*

Six firms, including Sainsbury's and Asda, have admitted colluding to fix the price of dairy products following an investigation by the Office of Fair Trading. Now they have each agreed to pay fines – totalling more than £116 million. The OFT probe relates to claims of price-fixing of dairy products in 2002 and 2003. Asda, Morrisons, Safeway, Sainsbury's and Tesco were each accused of colluding with other retailers on the price they charged for milk. It was always alleged that Asda, Safeway, Sainsbury's and Tesco also fixed the price of cheese, while Safeway and Tesco were accused of colluding on the price of some brands of butter. Meanwhile, dairy processors Arla, Dairy Crest, Wiseman Dairies, The Cheese Company and Lactalis McLelland were accused of helping the retailers share information. Sainsbury's, Asda and Safeway (operating before it was bought by Morrisons) have admitted anti-competitive behaviour. So too have Dairy Crest, Wiseman Dairies and The Cheese Company. Arla has been given immunity from financial penalty on the condition that it continues to co-operate having applied for leniency. All the firms have agreed fines – which they say are smaller than if they had not admitted their involvement at this stage. Tesco, Morrisons and dairy processor Lactalis McLelland have not accepted liability. They must now make representations on the OFT's provisional findings which will then be considered before a final decision is made. All those involved who have admitted liability say that their actions were motivated by trying to help British farmers. The OFT has said that as a result of the price fixing, an extra £270 million was spent by UK consumers. It estimates that the collusion saw shoppers pay 3p extra for a pint of milk, and 15p extra per quarter-pound of butter. The overcharging also led to customers being allegedly overcharged by 15p per half-pound of cheese.

FOCUS ON THE ECONOMIC ENVIRONMENT

The business cycle ▶ textbook pages 190–1

QUESTION

What is the role of investment in the business cycle? *(12 marks)*

Investment tends to fluctuate more than consumption. If the economy is weak it will lead to a fall in interest rates, making businesses more likely to borrow money to fund investments. The increased spending produces rising incomes for certain individuals and businesses. Their increased spending generates further increases in incomes. As a result, aggregate demand continues to rise and businesses are more optimistic. At the end of a boom, however, rising costs and rising interest rates make businesses less optimistic. Because it is less profitable to make an investment, businesses tend not to plough money into the future. As a result there is a cumulative fall in income and a slowing down of aggregate demand. If this continues, incomes and outputs continue to fall.

Interest and exchange rates ▶ textbook pages 192–3

CASE STUDY – EXCHANGE RATE WINNERS AND LOSERS

How can the weak pound give British businesses opportunities in the Euro zone? *(8 marks)*

Because the Euro is strong compared to sterling, British products abroad are comparatively cheap. It would be attractive for Euro zone businesses to purchase British-made products and services, as these will be comparatively less expensive than in other Euro zone countries, or countries outside the Euro zone. The weak pound and the strong Euro offer British manufacturers the best opportunities, assuming of course that there is no rapid and immediate change in the exchange rates between the two currencies.

FOCUS ON THE ECONOMIC ENVIRONMENT

Inflation and unemployment ▸ textbook pages 194–5

QUESTION

What particular problems might be encountered when using the Phillips Curve? *(12 marks)*

The Phillips Curve is not even theoretically perfect. In fact, there are many problems with it if it is taken as denoting anything more than a general relationship between unemployment and inflation. In particular, the Phillips curve does a terrible job of explaining the relationship between inflation and unemployment from 1970 to 1984. Inflation in these years was much higher than would have been expected given the unemployment for these years.

Such a situation of high inflation and high unemployment is called stagflation. The phenomenon of stagflation is something of a mystery, though many economists believe that it results from changes in the error term of

the previously stated Phillips curve equation. These errors can include things like energy cost increases and food price increases. But no matter what its source, stagflation of the 1970s and early 1980s seems to refute the general applicability of the Phillips Curve.

The Phillips Curve must not be looked at as an exact set of points that the economy can reach and then remain at in equilibrium. Instead, the curve describes a historical picture of where the inflation rate has tended to be in relation to the unemployment rate. When the relationship is understood in this way, it becomes evident that the Phillips Curve is useful not as a means of picking an unemployment and inflation rate pair, but rather as a means of understanding how unemployment and inflation might move given historical data.

Economic growth ▸ textbook pages 196–7

QUESTION

How useful is GDP per capita as a measure of economic growth? *(12 marks)*

There is a scientific way of measuring prosperity that, while not fully descriptive, is useful in comparing the standard of living across countries. This is called the GDP per capita measure. This is simply calculated by dividing the nominal GDP in a common currency, say US dollars, by the total number of people in the country. This gives the average amount of income that each member of the population potentially has access to. In other words, the more money each individual is able to access, the higher the potential standard of living.

This is a useful means of comparing economic wellbeing – that is, prosperity – across countries. For instance, the GDP per capita in the US is around $25,000 while in Mexico it is around $7000. It stands to reason that by and

large, the standard of living in the US is higher than the standard of living in Mexico. This same logic can be used to compare the standard of living between any countries.

As mentioned earlier, the GDP per capita measure is the nominal GDP divided by the population. Thus, for a given amount of output, a country with a smaller population will have a higher standard of living than a country with a larger population. This is a problem often encountered in countries with very low GDP per capita measures of the standard of living. When GDP grows slowly and the population increases rapidly, the GDP per capita, and thus the standard of living tends to decline over time. Thus, a major way of increasing the standard of living in a country is to control the population growth rate and thus increase the GDP per capita.

FOCUS ON THE ECONOMIC ENVIRONMENT

Growth of global markets ▶ textbook pages 198–9

QUESTION

To what extent is McDonaldisation just a feature of globalisation? *(18 marks)*

Central to this answer are the three key characteristics: efficiency, control and predictability. There is also the enormous impact of standardisation, in that products offered across the world do not differ in any significant way. It has meant that a broader range, albeit of standardised products, is available to larger sections of the world population. Coupled with this are convenience and uniform quality standards. The spread of businesses adopting this approach had a marked impact on smaller and longer-established businesses, as can be seen by the rise of supermarket giants such as Tesco in Britain. McDonaldisation itself originally referred to technological advances and the growing ownership of cars, added to which there was the development of the suburbs in the US. This too has been replicated in many countries, although McDonaldisation itself as a term is now a far broader one that implies the provision of stable and safe ranges of products.

Evaluating strategies to respond to change ▶ textbook pages 200–1

QUESTION

Rapid rates of economic growth bring very few benefits to a business and an enormous number of problems. Discuss. *(15 marks)*

Students should begin by focusing on the benefits, which include higher levels of spending and demand, higher sales, increased profits, expansion, investment and the creation of new markets for products. However, the business will also see increased competition, shortages of labour and other resources, higher wage costs and increased costs from suppliers for raw materials, components and finished goods. The business will have to consider passing on these increases through price increases. Coupled with this is the fact that increasing costs and prices will fuel inflation and create uncertainty. Internally the business will be under considerable pressure with increased workloads and less time to make decisions. The business would run the risk of falling quality levels, poor coordination and the possibility that it would lose its sense of direction.

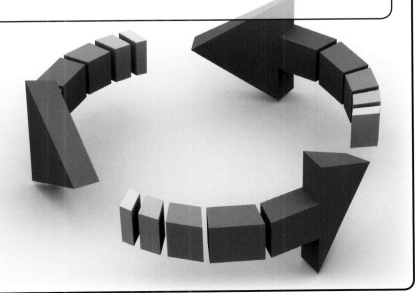

FOCUS ON THE ECONOMIC
ENVIRONMENT

Case studies, questions and exam practice ▶ textbook pages 202–3

CASE STUDY – NIKE

1 **Give reasons why Nike's managers could justify globalisation?** *(15 marks)*

Here are some of the reasons that the managers at Nike may have used to justify their expansion:

Lower input costs: Like any business, Nike aims to buy its products for the lowest possible price, and then sell them for a profit. The higher the margin, the more their wealth will increase with each sale. There is no doubt that in choosing to have their shoes manufactured in other countries Nike has been able to access workers who are paid lower wages than if the company had established its production lines in America. Lowering costs is a key goal for managers in most companies.

Access new markets: While the population of the United States is large, there are even more people in the rest of the world. In choosing to sell its shoes in other countries, Nike was able to gain access to an even greater number of consumers. This allowed the organisation to increase its global sales, which ultimately resulted in an increase in profits.

Access resources: One of the most important inputs used in the production of Nike shoes is rubber. Rubber is not produced in the United States and must be sourced in other countries.

Transportation costs: At first glance it might seem that transport costs for the company would be higher if it adopted a globalised approach. However, with customers all over the world, Nike needed a way to ensure that its transport costs could be minimised to all customers. While it might be cheaper to sell to American customers from a US-based distribution centre, it is far more expensive to sell to other customers from that location.

Economies of scale: We have seen that Nike is keen to expand its customer base, but at the same time would like to minimise transport costs. In order to achieve these joint goals, production has been centralised in certain countries. This has allowed for very high production levels, and as a result of this the company has been able to achieve economies of large-scale production. In other words, producing in this way has enabled it to lower its cost per item.

2 **Nike is committed to making investments in the future of the countries in which it operates. Suggest how it might do this and why.** *(8 marks)*

On many occasions the founding partner, Mr Phil Knight, has stated that the future of the company depends on the growth and productivity of the people who make the products. In this respect, Nike has funded the management training of over 30,000 people every year for at least ten years. In each case, the people receiving the training are those from the countries in which the factories operate. Nike employees are also supported when they choose to upgrade their own skills. On-site training programs are made available to all employees. For example, many people in South East Asia have used this opportunity to upgrade their computer literacy, while others have learned about making budgets and improving their financial skills.

Finally, Nike is also making a significant capital investment in these countries. In the past, multinational companies were criticised for operating with very few capital resources. In this way, companies were able to leave a country quickly when cheaper labour became available elsewhere. This is no longer the case. As workers become more productive, they become more valuable. This means that Nike has been willing to pay these people the higher wages that they demand, rather than move to a new country.

FOCUS ON THE ECONOMIC ENVIRONMENT

MINDMAPS

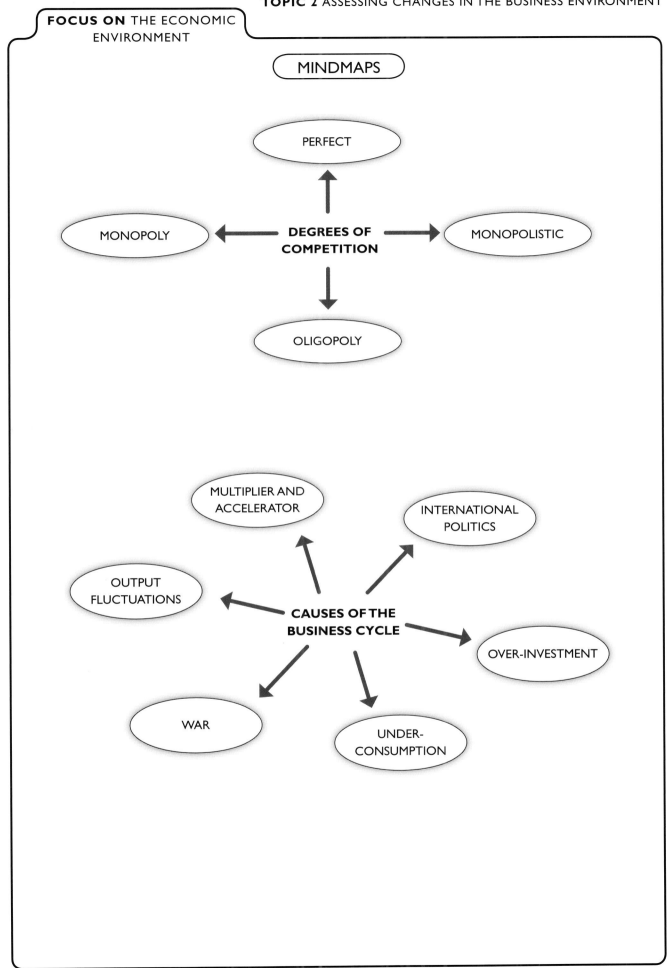

FOCUS ON THE ECONOMIC
ENVIRONMENT

MINDMAPS

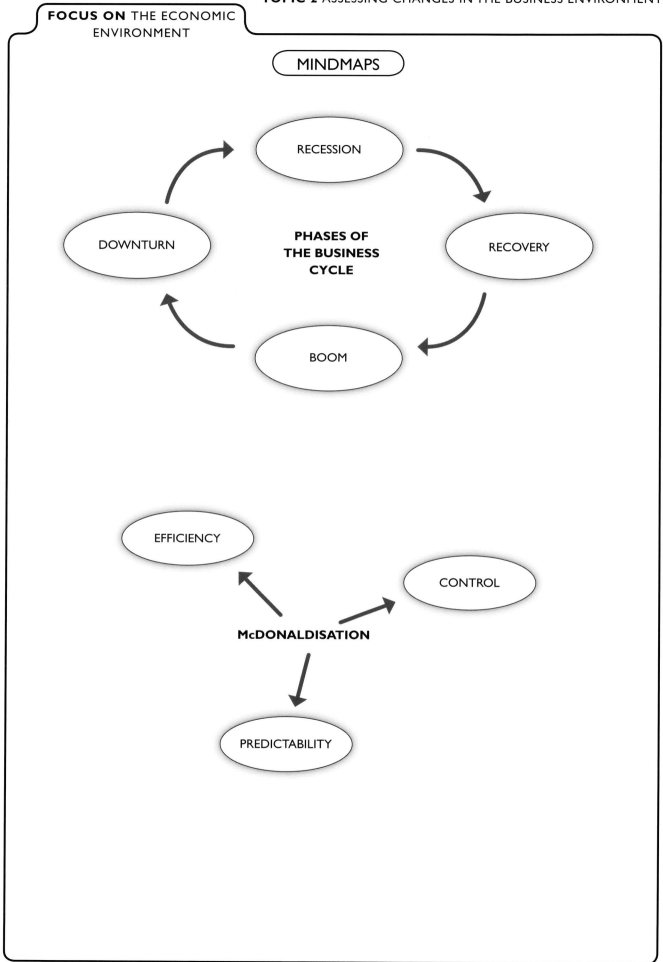

FOCUS ON THE ECONOMIC
ENVIRONMENT

MINDMAPS

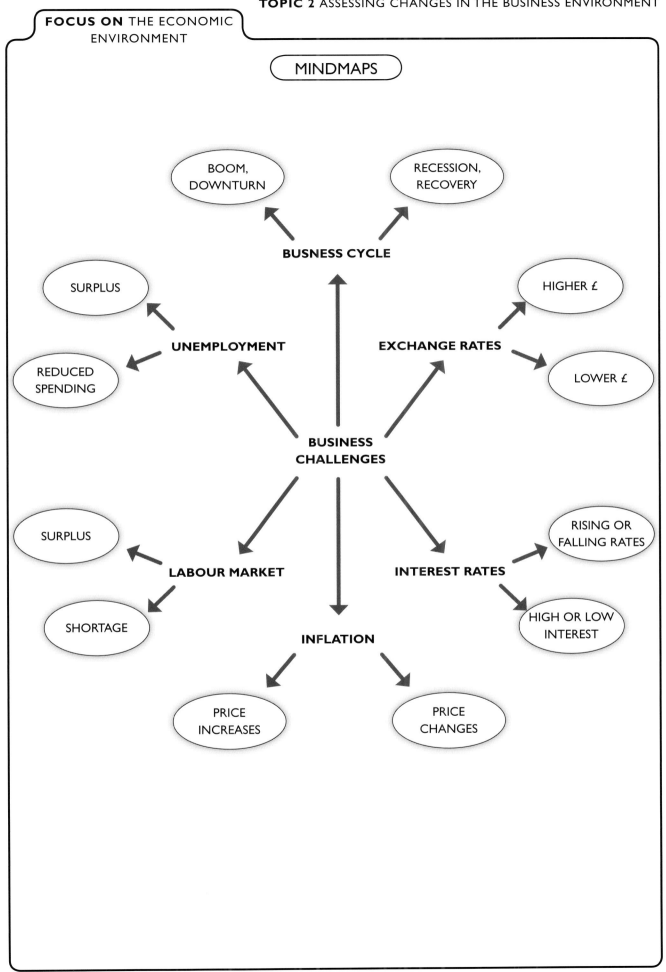

FOCUS ON THE ECONOMIC
ENVIRONMENT

(WORKSHEET)

1   What is a homogeneous product?

2   Distinguish between an oligopoly and a monopoly.

3   Briefly explain the FOUR phases of the business cycle.

Answers ▶ page 227

A2 ESSENTIAL BUSINESS STUDIES FOR AQA

FOCUS ON THE ECONOMIC
ENVIRONMENT

WORKSHEET

1 Why are changes in the exchange rate significant to a British business that exports overseas?

2 Distinguish between the economic approaches of Friedman and Keynes.

3 What do you understand by the term 'McDonaldisation' and what are its key characteristics?

Answers ▶ page 227

FOCUS ON THE POLITICAL
AND LEGAL ENVIRONMENT

Government intervention in the economy ▶ textbook pages 204–5

CASE STUDY – PRODUCTIVITY GROWTH DECREASES

What does the graph tell us about manufacturing productivity and unit wage costs? *(12 marks)*

In the fourth quarter of 2007, manufacturing productivity, on an output per job basis, was 2.2 per cent higher than the same quarter of 2006, down from a growth of 2.7 per cent the previous quarter. This decrease in the growth rate of quarterly productivity was due to a decrease in the contraction rate of manufacturing jobs.

On a quarterly basis, manufacturing productivity increased by 0.2 per cent in the fourth quarter of 2007, compared with the previous quarter, up from zero growth in the third quarter. This increase in the growth rate of quarterly productivity was due to an increase in manufacturing output growth.

Whole economy unit wage costs in the fourth quarter of 2007 were 2.7 per cent higher than the same quarter a year earlier, up from an increase of 1.8 per cent in the previous quarter. This is due to an increase in the growth rate of average wages and salaries and a decrease in the growth rate of output per worker.

Overall, manufacturing unit wage costs in the fourth quarter of 2007 grew by 1.2 per cent, compared to a growth of 0.4 per cent in the previous quarter.

Tax and subsidy ▶ textbook pages 206–7

CASE STUDY – BRITISH AIRLINES – TAXED OR SUBSIDISED?

Using the information in the case study and your own research, comment on the British airline industry in terms of its size, support for other businesses, and competitiveness. *(12 marks)*

Aviation is a major UK industry in its own right:

- contributing £10.2 billion a year to UK GDP
- generating 180,000 direct UK jobs
- exporting £6.6 billion a year of services
- investing £2.5 billion a year in the UK
- contributing £2.5 billion a year to the Exchequer.

Aviation Supports UK businesses:

- generating and supporting 380,000 indirect and induced UK jobs
- transporting £35 billion of UK exports
- maintaining unrivalled access to global markets.

Aviation underpins UK competitiveness:

- growing four times faster than the UK economy
- producing 2.5 times more output per worker than the national average
- acting as a catalyst for growth in tourism and knowledge-based industries
- attracting direct foreign investment.

FOCUS ON THE POLITICAL
AND LEGAL ENVIRONMENT

Monetary and fiscal policy ▶ textbook pages 208–9

QUESTION

There is very little difference between
monetary policy and fiscal policy. Discuss.
(12 marks)

Students should focus on the key differences,
with fiscal policy centred on taxation and
spending and monetary policies dealing with
interest rates, the control of money supply and

the manipulation of the exchange rates. Both
policy options usually have a goal of either
increasing or decreasing the level of economic
activity, and while it is preferable to have a
productive, growing economy, an economy
can also be too productive, in which case the
policies are used to slow down the economy.

Supply side policies ▶ textbook pages 210–11

QUESTION

Do supply side policies work? Discuss.
(12 marks)

Students could argue this either way, but they
should focus on whether the supply side policies
have actually improved the efficiency of markets
and the economy in general. Examples of
problems with supply side policies could include
the following:

Job insecurity – employees now no longer
feel safe in their jobs, and stress levels at work
are rising as reduced trade union power has
led to the introduction of 'lean' production
techniques which aim to minimise waste.

Access to state benefits has been reduced to
create incentives to work – hence unemployed
workers face a rougher ride in their attempts
to survive the period inbetween jobs; income

inequality has generally risen over the last
20 years, and supply side policies have played
a part in this.

An increase in the capacity of the
economy is of no help in itself unless there
is a corresponding increase in AD – in a
recession, a focus on supply side reforms may
be at best unhelpful and at worst counter-
productive (the early years of privatisation in
the UK saw large scale job losses from former
state-run industries when the economy was
only just recovering from recession. Hence
these unemployed workers found it extremely
difficult to find employment. This worsened the
government's finances (due to unemployment
benefits) and also led to deskilling, which
increased the level of 'core' unemployment in
the economy).

Political decisions affecting trade and access to markets ▶ textbook pages 212–13

QUESTION

Outline the key advantages and disadvantages
to Europe and industry of the enlargement of
the European Union. *(18 marks)*

Advantages

• *Economic growth*. Enlargement will generate
economic growth in both 'old' and 'new'

member states. In the new states, the reform
of economic systems to a market economy will
generate increased productivity and efficiency
and allow them to be able to take advantage
of the Single Market through increased trade.
In the old states, as trade and investment
opportunities increase with the new states

FOCUS ON THE POLITICAL
AND LEGAL ENVIRONMENT

Political decisions affecting trade and access to markets (continued)

there will be economic growth. Estimates suggest that job totals could increase in old member states by 300,000.

- *Stability.* Membership of the EU will bring political stability to the new democracies of Eastern Europe as they reform their legal and government institutions as part of the accession process. Such stability is important in generating investment not only from within the EU but from outside it, thus contributing to further economic development.

- *Global Presence.* The EU has a stronger global voice, as its enlargement has brought the population to over 500 million (more than the USA and Russia combined), so giving more weight in international negotiations such as trade policy.

- *Business Confidence.* Companies in existing Member States will have more confidence with those in the new Member States, as they will be operating on a level playing field in terms of EU legislation. Again, business confidence is an important factor in generating investment and encouraging enterprise and initiative.

- *Foreign Direct Investment (FDI).* Membership of the EU and the Euro will increase the amount of Foreign Direct Investment in the New Member States.

- *Structural Funds.* The regional aid which attempts to redistribute funds from the wealthier regions of the EU to the poorer ones will be made available to the New Member States. This will help develop these countries and improve infrastructure. Improvements in infrastructure will again be a benefit to trade and, in theory, all countries involved will benefit – the new member states from improved internal infrastructure and the old member states from the extra revenues earned from new trade.

Disadvantages

- *Migration.* Enlargement could produce high levels of migration as workers move from the new member states such as Poland where unemployment is high at 16.7% to those old member states where it is low such as the

Netherlands at 3.6%. It was anticipated that workers would be able to move freely as the EU operates on the principle of the Single Market – one of the 'four freedoms' inherent in the Single Market is the free movement of labour. However, the old member states have created restrictions on the entry of labour into their countries for at least the first two years of enlargement.

- *Common Agricultural Policy.* The controversial Common Agricultural Policy will be extended to the new member states, many of which have predominantly rural economies. The CAP includes measures such as subsidies and income guarantee schemes for farmers, which could prove to be hugely expensive if extended and a drain on the economies of old member states.

- *Regional Aid.* The difference in GDP per capita between the old member states and the new member states is stark. This is also reflected in the ranking of each set of countries in the UN Development Programme's Human Development Index (HDI), which combines indicators of life expectancy, education, literacy and GDP. This difference in wealth and standard of living could be another drain on old member states in two ways – firstly, old member states may need to contribute more as the demand for regional aid increases, and secondly, old member states currently receiving regional aid, such as Spain and Greece, find their aid reduced as money is channelled elsewhere.

- *EU Standards and Systems.* There are concerns that some New Member States will not have the necessary standards and systems in place, e.g. in meeting standards in food hygiene, and regulations on agricultural production. Meeting environmental standards may be too high a cost for some, while bringing public services up to standard will mean increased taxation for many citizens of the New Member States.

- *The Legacy of the Soviet Economy.* In some of the states of the former Soviet bloc, certain areas of industry may not have had time to catch up with those of the EU and find they are forced out of business when these countries join the Single Market.

FOCUS ON THE POLITICAL AND LEGAL ENVIRONMENT

Impact of legislation: employment law ▶ textbook pages 214–15

QUESTION

What are an employee's rights under sex and discrimination law? *(8 marks)*

An employer is not allowed to discriminate on the following grounds:

1 Sex of employee or prospective employee.
2 Marital status of employee or prospective employee.
3 If an employee intends to undergo, is undergoing or has undergone gender reassignment.
4 Race, (this means colour, race, nationality or ethnic origins) of employee or prospective employee.

5 Also an employer cannot victimise an employee for bringing a complaint for discrimination or giving evidence in a complaint brought by another employee.

However, following the introduction of the Human Rights Act 1998, an Employment Tribunal has decided that the Sexual Discrimination Act 1975 does include sexual orientation, *Ministry of Defence v. Macdonald*. However, the Human Rights Act 1998 does not deal with compensation for discrimination.

Impact of legislation: consumer protection ▶ textbook pages 216–17

QUESTION

British businesses have only themselves to blame for the introduction of consumer protection legislation. No wonder we are known as 'rip-off Britain'. Discuss. *(12 marks)*

The Government is backing a new anti-'rip-off Britain' offensive against shops and websites that exploit shoppers. The Government wants to give more protection for UK consumers. Ministers want to overhaul consumer protection laws and allow people to claim compensation if they fall victim to offences such as price-fixing. Britain has a reputation for some of the highest prices in the world, with global companies sometimes referring to the UK as 'Treasure Island' because profit margins are higher than in many other countries. The most radical suggestion being considered by ministers is a 'money back' law that would give consumers the right to reclaim sums as small as a few pounds without having to resort to lawyers. Former trade secretary Stephen Byers launched the original 'rip-off Britain' bandwagon in the early days of the New Labour government almost a decade ago. It led to tougher powers for the Office of Fair Trading and Competition Commission but was criticised as 'Labour spin' for not delivering lower prices. Now ministers at the Department for Business, Enterprise and

Regulatory Reform – led by Business Secretary John Hutton – believe the huge growth in Internet shopping indicates the need for a root-and-branch review of consumer law. A similar pan-European review is being carried out in Brussels. The UK proposals include:

- A new law based on Danish legislation that would allow consumers to 'piggyback' on legal actions brought against price-fixing cartels. This 'private action' system is seen as a less cumbersome method of redress than hugely expensive US-style 'class actions'. People who could show they had been ripped off using proof of purchase would be able to sue collectively to get their money back.

- A new 'super-Ombudsman' to represent the interests of consumers.

- A consumer rights card for wallets and purses enshrining five or six basic principles of consumer protection. Shoppers could refer to it when they were about to pay for goods in shops or online.

- A big tidying-up of the 'plethora' of sometimes contradictory consumer laws. For example, some laws say consumers have 14 days to return a product, others say the limit is seven days.

FOCUS ON THE POLITICAL AND LEGAL ENVIRONMENT

Impact of legislation: health and safety ▶ textbook pages 218–19

CASE STUDY – HEALTH AND SAFETY RISK ASSESSMENT

Suggest how a general health and safety risk assessment could be carried out by the manager. (8 marks)

The manager looked at HSE's web pages on health and safety in offices, and at guidance on preventing slips and trips in call centres (published by the North West Contact Centre Project). He also considered the HSE guidance 'Advice regarding call centre working practices', and at HSE's disability and risk assessment guidance web pages;

He walked around the office noting what might pose a risk, taking into consideration HSE's guidance.

The manager talked to the safety representative, supervisors and staff, including those who are wheelchair users, to learn from their experiences and to listen to their concerns and opinions about health and safety issues, as well as looking at the accident book to learn about previous problems.

The manager then wrote down who could be harmed by the hazards and how.

For each hazard, the manager wrote down what controls, if any, were in place to manage them. These controls were then compared to the good practice guidance on HSE's website. Where existing controls were not considered good enough, the manager wrote down what else needed to be done to control the risk.

The manager then implemented the findings of the risk assessment. This involved setting out when the actions that were needed would be carried out, and who would do them. These actions were then ticked off as they were completed. The risk assessment was discussed with staff, to check they understood it. It was also displayed in the staffroom and made part of the induction process for new staff.

The manager decided to review and update the risk assessment every year or straight away if any major changes in the workplace happened.

Business responses to a change in political and legal environment

▶ textbook pages 220–1

QUESTION

Explain why the government intervenes in the market. (18 marks)

Government intervention in the market sets out to attain two goals: social efficiency and equity. Social efficiency is achieved at the point where the marginal benefits to society for either production or consumption are equal to the marginal costs of either production or consumption. Issues of equity are difficult to judge due to the subjective assessment of what is, and what is not, a fair distribution of resources.

Externalities are spillover costs or benefits. Whenever there are external costs, the market will (other things being equal) lead to a level of production and consumption above the socially efficient level. Whenever there are external benefits, the market will (other things

being equal) lead to a level of production and consumption below the socially efficient level.

Public goods will be underprovided by the market. The problem is that they have large external benefits relative to private benefits, and without government intervention it would not be possible to prevent people having a 'free ride' and thereby escaping contributing to their cost of production.

Monopoly power will (other things being equal) lead to a level of output below the socially efficient level. It will lead to a deadweight welfare loss: a loss of consumer plus producer surplus.

Ignorance and uncertainty may prevent people from consuming or producing at the levels they would otherwise choose. Information

FOCUS ON THE POLITICAL
AND LEGAL ENVIRONMENT

Business responses to a change in political and legal environment (continued)

may sometimes be provided (at a price) by the market, but it may be imperfect. In some cases it may not be available at all.

Markets may respond sluggishly to changes in demand and supply. The time lags in adjustment can lead to a permanent state of disequilibrium and to problems of instability.

In a free market there may be inadequate provision for dependants and an inadequate output of merit goods.

Taxes and subsidies are one means of correcting market distortions. Externalities can be corrected by imposing tax rates equal to the size of the marginal external cost, and granting rates of subsidy equal to marginal external benefits.

Taxes and subsidies can also be used to affect monopoly price, output and profit. Subsidies can be used to persuade a monopolist to increase output to the competitive level. Lump-sum taxes can be used to reduce monopoly profits without affecting price or output.

Taxes and subsidies have the advantages of 'internalising' externalities and of providing incentives to reduce external costs. On the other hand, they may be impractical to use when different rates are required for each case, or when it is impossible to know the full effects of the activities that the taxes or subsidies are being used to correct.

An extension of property rights may allow individuals to prevent others from imposing costs on them. This is not practical, however, when many people are affected to a small degree, or where several people are affected

but differ in their attitudes towards what they want doing about the 'problem'.

Laws can be used to regulate activities that impose external costs, to regulate monopolies and oligopolies, and to provide consumer protection. Legal controls are often simpler and easier to operate than taxes, and are safer when the danger is potentially great. However, they tend to be rather a blunt weapon.

Regulatory bodies can be set up to monitor and control activities that are against the public interest (e.g. anti-competitive behaviour of oligopolists). They can conduct investigations of specific cases, but these may be expensive and time-consuming, and may not be acted on by the authorities.

The government may provide information in cases where the private sector fails to provide an adequate level. It may also provide goods and services directly. These could be either public goods or other goods where the government feels that provision by the market is inadequate. The government could also influence production in publicly owned industries.

Government intervention in the market may lead to shortages or surpluses; it may be based on poor information; it may be costly in terms of administration; it may stifle incentives; it may be disruptive if government policies change too frequently; it may not represent the majority of voters' interests if the government is elected by a minority, or if voters did not fully understand the issues at election time, or if the policies were not in the government's manifesto, it may remove certain liberties.

FOCUS ON THE POLITICAL
AND LEGAL ENVIRONMENT

Case studies, questions and exam practice ▶ textbook pages 222–3

CASE STUDY – FLEXIBLE WORKING AND THE EMPLOYMENT ACT

1 **What do you think is meant by the term 'traditional infrastructure'?** *(4 marks)*

Standardised human resource support and the assumption that the majority of the workforce consists of full-time, permanent employees. It suggests that HR will have to be far more flexible and capable of responding to new challenges.

2 **Why is it likely that more women will enter the workforce over the next ten years?** *(4 marks)*

Changes in the rules regarding flexible working will allow more women to either return to work earlier than before after having children, or be able to find a workable balance between employment and home responsibilities.

3 **Why might employers be unprepared for the increased demand for flexible working patterns?** *(4 marks)*

It will need a significant change in attitude from employers including taking into account changes in lifestyle, demographics and the changing nature of the workforce. They will have to adapt to employees working for them for shorter periods and accommodate a new home/work balance.

CASE STUDY – BRITISH ARMS INDUSTRY SUBSIDIES

The hundreds of millions of pounds saved by reducing or ending the UK arms trade could be invested in other industries, such as renewable energy and transport. This would create new, highly skilled jobs. It would also be a far more ethical use of public funds. Discuss. (18 marks)

Students should focus on government policy priorities. This question can be argued either way, providing the students back up their

suggestions with probable advantages and disadvantages to the British economy, balance of trade, innovation and technology, employment levels and workforce skills. Currently the British arms industry is a significant employer and provides major export opportunities. However, according to CAAT, the subsidies amount to close to £1 billion. The argument could focus on purely ethical issues, but the students should attempt to answer the question with clearly argued responses beyond this.

FOCUS ON THE POLITICAL
AND LEGAL ENVIRONMENT

MINDMAPS

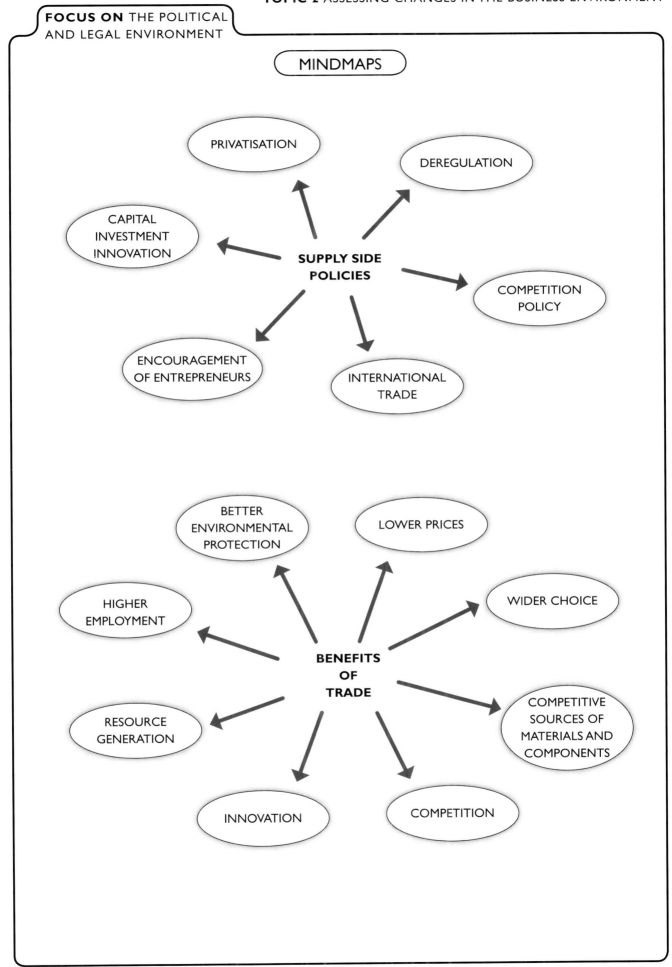

FOCUS ON THE POLITICAL
AND LEGAL ENVIRONMENT

MINDMAPS

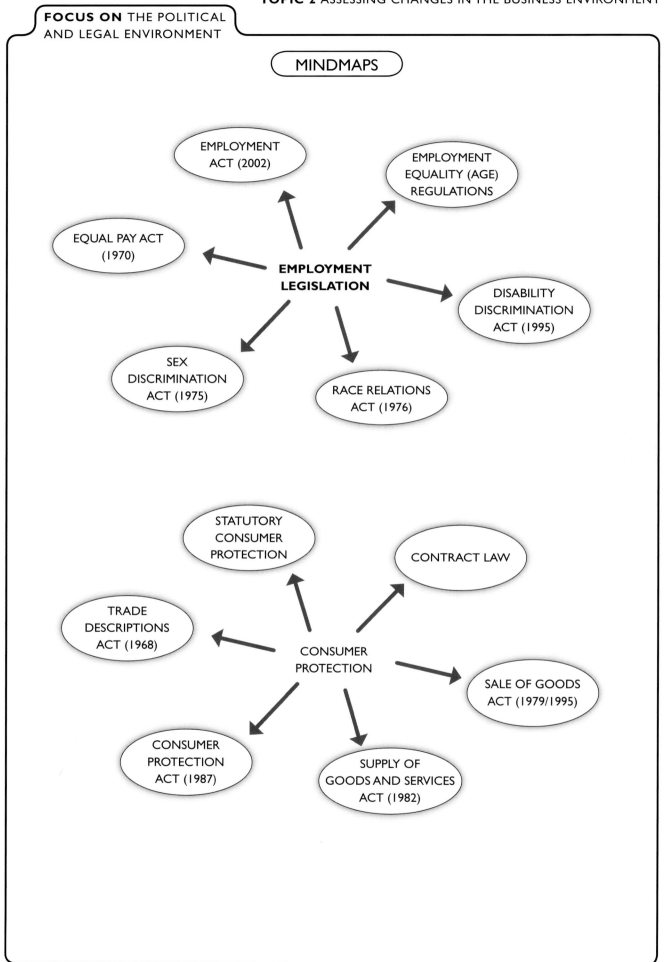

A2 ESSENTIAL BUSINESS STUDIES FOR AQA

FOCUS ON THE POLITICAL AND LEGAL ENVIRONMENT

WORKSHEET

1 What is the balance of trade, and what is the ideal balance?

2 Why might government subsidies distort competition?

3 What is the role of the Bank of England's Monetary Policy Committee?

Answers ▶ page 227

FOCUS ON THE POLITICAL
AND LEGAL ENVIRONMENT

WORKSHEET

1 Distinguish between monetary and fiscal policy.

2 What is the Public Sector Borrowing Requirement?

3 What is the purpose of supply side policies?

Answers ▶ page 227

FOCUS ON THE POLITICAL
AND LEGAL ENVIRONMENT

WORKSHEET

1   What is the purpose of the World Trade Organisation?

2   In relation to the EU, what is enlargement, and what are its advantages to existing member states?

3   What are the negative impacts of trade barriers?

Answers ▶ page 227

FOCUS ON THE POLITICAL
AND LEGAL ENVIRONMENT

(WORKSHEET)

I   What are the significance and consequences of age discrimination legislation to British businesses?

2   If a business deliberately misleads customers regarding the performance and features of a product, which piece of consumer legislation has been broken and what might be the consequences?

3   What is the purpose of occupational health-screening?

Answers ▶ page 228

FOCUS ON THE SOCIAL ENVIRONMENT

Changes in the social environment: demographic factors ▶ textbook pages 225–6

QUESTION

Peter Drucker wrote:

'One of the challenges will be using these retired people, who are in perfect physical and mental condition, making them useful to the society. It is important to learn how to work with older people; it could be an enormous competitive advantage. I even believe that, in the next 20 or 30 years, the age of retirement in the developed countries will have to be higher. Or at least, retirement will not mean coming out of the working world. Working relationships will probably become very heterogeneous and increasingly flexible.'

How might British businesses respond to this? (12 marks)

The focus should be on flexible working practices, the fact that older members of the workforce may have different motivational factors such as socialising and maintaining status, and may have greater resistance to change. The students should also focus on the stereotypes about ageing, some of which are deeply embedded prejudices. The value of older members of the workforce is enormous, as their experience is irreplaceable. Over time they can transfer their skills and experience to younger members of staff. Older people should also have access to training, qualifications and skills acquisition.

Changes in the social environment: environmental issues ▶ textbook pages 227–8

QUESTION

What is an environmental review and what is likely to be involved? (12 marks)

An environmental review establishes which issues affect a business.

The review should cover five areas:

1 What environmental impact does your business have and how do you manage it? Can it be managed more effectively?

Key areas to consider include:
- The raw materials the business uses and the products it makes
- The waste produced
- The energy used
- Any discharges or emissions from the business
- The storage and movement of materials
- How any previous incidents were handled
- The environmentally responsible credentials of the business investments

2 • What environmental risks does the business pose?
 • What environmental damage could be caused if there was an accident?
 • How likely is an accident?
 • Is the business located in an environmentally sensitive area?
 • Does the business offer advice, or manage contracts, that could result in a third party causing environmental damage?

3 What environmental standards and regulations apply to the business, now and in the future? Also what policies and legislation are being developed by the government that might affect the products, supplies or operation?

4 What do customers, employees, suppliers and others expect of the business? Sending out questionnaires can raise expectations, so informal consultations may be more appropriate.

5 Does the businesses insurance policy cover environmental risks?

FOCUS ON THE SOCIAL ENVIRONMENT

The changing nature of the ethical environment ▶ textbook pages 228–9

CASE STUDY – TRANSCO BUSINESS ETHICS

Ethical statements such as these are meaningless. Discuss. *(12 marks)*

Large businesses take business ethics very seriously, but they also often do exclusively what is in their best interests. Some of them will do things that will effectively impact on their profit margins in the interests of adhering to strong business ethics. A prime example is the cigarette manufacturers: should they dissuade people from smoking when their business is to sell cigarettes? Businesses spend large amounts of money on education and putting across their business ethics. It does have a practical place in business as it infers a moral code and a set of values a business will not step beyond, even if it affects profits.

Social environment and corporate responsibility ▶ textbook pages 230–1

QUESTION

How might a thorough stakeholder analysis help a business respond to the changing social environment? *(14 marks)*

It seems fairly clear that a stakeholder analysis is a valuable instrument in identifying key stakeholders, assessing their interests and the ways in which these interests could affect the business and its viability. Businesses carry out stakeholder analysis to draw out the interests of stakeholders in relation to issues facing the business. It helps identify potential conflicts of interest and other conflicts. It also identifies the viability of business ideas in terms other than purely financial. It assists the business in identifying the overall picture, identifying relationships between different stakeholders and encouraging mutually beneficial conditions.

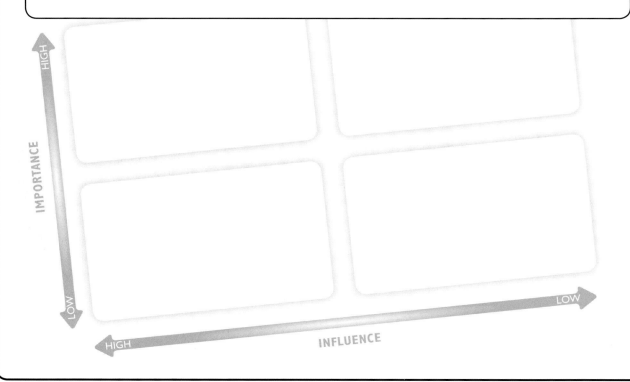

FOCUS ON THE SOCIAL ENVIRONMENT

Case studies, questions and exam practice ▶ textbook pages 232–3

CASE STUDY – BOTTLED WATER – IS IT IMMORAL?

Are products such as bottled water immoral both ethically and environmentally? (12 marks)

Research commissioned by a Swiss-based conservation group indicates that bottled water is often no healthier or safer to drink than tap water. The World Wide Fund for Nature argues strongly that bottled water is not only environmentally unfriendly but also a waste of money. The bottled water market is booming. The research by the University of Geneva shows that bottled water sells for up to 1,000 times the price of tap water, but that the quality is often no better. In 50% of cases the only difference is that bottled water has added minerals and salts, which do not actually mean the water is healthier. Furthermore, some bottled waters are exactly the same standard as tap water, without being as energy efficient. Tap water comes from underground pipes, while the manufacture, distribution and disposal of bottled water require much more energy and fuel. While the WWF does acknowledge that bottled water is generally safer in areas where tap water is contaminated, it says boiling or filtering local water is a cheaper and more sustainable alternative. The long-term solution, it argues, is to clean up municipal water supplies.

It costs 10,000 times more to create the bottled version than it does to produce tap water, say scientists. Huge resources are needed to draw it from the ground, add largely irrelevant minerals, and package and distribute it – sometimes half-way around the world. The plastic bottles it comes in take 1,000 years to biodegrade, and in industrialised countries, bottled water is no more pure and healthy than what comes out of the tap. The new study comes from the Earth Policy Institute (EPI), a Washington-based environmental group which has previously alerted the world to melting ice caps, expanding deserts and the environmental threats of a rapidly industrialising China. It points out that the world consumed a staggering 154 billion litres of bottled water in 2004 – an increase of 57 per cent in just half a decade. Emily Arnold, the report's author, said: 'Even in areas where tap water is safe to drink, demand for bottled water is increasing – producing unnecessary garbage and consuming vast quantities of energy.'

FOCUS ON THE SOCIAL ENVIRONMENT

MINDMAPS

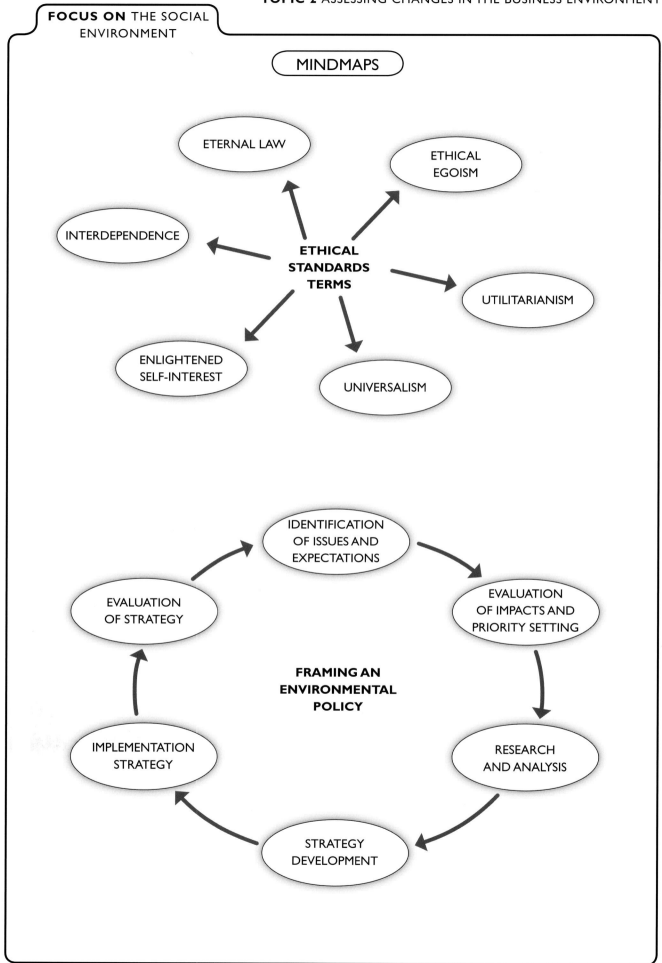

FOCUS ON THE SOCIAL ENVIRONMENT

MINDMAPS

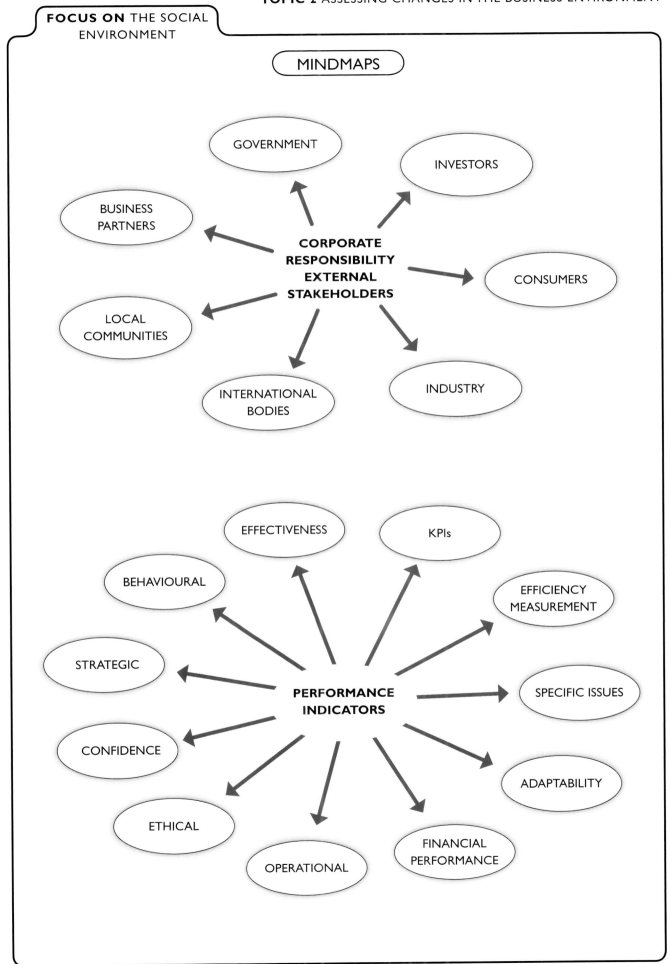

FOCUS ON THE SOCIAL
ENVIRONMENT

WORKSHEET

1 What is the effect of Britain's ageing population?

_____

_____

_____

_____

_____

_____

_____

2 What do you understand by the term 'sabbatical'?

_____

_____

_____

_____

_____

_____

_____

3 What is SCP, and what are its implications?

_____

_____

_____

_____

_____

_____

_____

_____

Answers ▶ page 228

FOCUS ON THE SOCIAL ENVIRONMENT

(WORKSHEET)

1 Distinguish between utilitarianism and universalism as ethical standards.

2 Identify FIVE key external stakeholders of a typical business.

3 What is meant by the term 'corporate responsibility' and what are its implications for a business?

Answers ▶ page 228

FOCUS ON THE TECHNOLOGICAL
ENVIRONMENT

Effects of technological change ▶ textbook pages 234–5

QUESTION

What are the benefits to a business of CRM?
(12 marks)

Implementing a customer relationship management (CRM) solution might involve considerable time and expense. However, there are many potential benefits.

A major benefit can be the development of better relations with existing customers. This can lead to:

- increased sales through better timing due to anticipating needs based on historic trends.
- identifying needs more effectively by understanding specific customer requirements.
- cross-selling of other products by highlighting and suggesting alternatives or enhancements.

This can lead to better marketing of products or services by focusing on:

- effective targeted marketing communications aimed specifically at customer needs.

- a more personal approach, and the development of new or improved products and services in order to win more business in the future.

Ultimately this could lead to:

- enhanced customer satisfaction and retention, ensuring that a good reputation in the marketplace continues to grow.
- increased value from existing customers and reduced cost associated with supporting and servicing them, increasing overall efficiency and reducing total cost of sales.

Once the business starts to look after its existing customers effectively, efforts can be concentrated on finding new customers and expanding the market. The more the business knows about its customers, the easier it is to identify new prospects and increase their customer base.

Response of businesses to technological change ▶ textbook pages 236–7

QUESTION

How has technology changed British banking?
(12 marks)

Student answers could cover interaction with banks, including telephone banking, online banking, and the use of ATMs and the closure of branches. Also the increasing reliance of banks on telephone and email communication with their customers. Also significant are the services offered by banks as a result of more sophisticated customer relationship management systems. Banks use this technology to cross-sell products and services such as insurance, mortgages and other financial

services. Other considerations are the fact that the banking system has become more competitive, with major brand names, such as Tesco and Sainsbury's selling their own banking services (which are often fulfilled by third parties).

FOCUS ON THE TECHNOLOGICAL
ENVIRONMENT

Case studies, questions and exam practice ▶ textbook pages 238–9

CASE STUDY – LEARNER SHOPPERS

What is RFID technology and what are its implications? *(12 marks)*

RFID is short for radio frequency identification. RFID chips are tiny microchips (smaller than a grain of sand) with antennae on them. The chips can transmit a unique code or other data to an RFID reader without touching it, via radio transmission. Most commonly, they turn up in retailers' supply chains, working like electronic barcodes. They're stuck to pallets, crates, cases and even individual items of stock. Then, instead of having to employ someone to count stock, you wave an RFID reader near the tag (the chips can typically be read up to a range of about 10 feet away) and it does all the counting and stock identification. Some major chains like Wal-Mart, House of Fraser, Marks and Spencer and Tesco have trialled RFID. Some, like Wal-Mart, are mad for the new technology and intend to drag their suppliers along with them whether they like it or not – Gillette even

went as far as putting the tags on their razors, much to the annoyance of some shoppers – while others are less than enthusiastic and have steered clear of the technology beyond the trial stage. The biggest and most often cited obstacle is cost – the chips are just too expensive, according to most retailers, to put on every pallet, let alone every item. The tags cost upwards of 15p and retailers are reluctant until the cost drops to a couple of pence.

FOCUS ON THE TECHNOLOGICAL
ENVIRONMENT

MINDMAPS

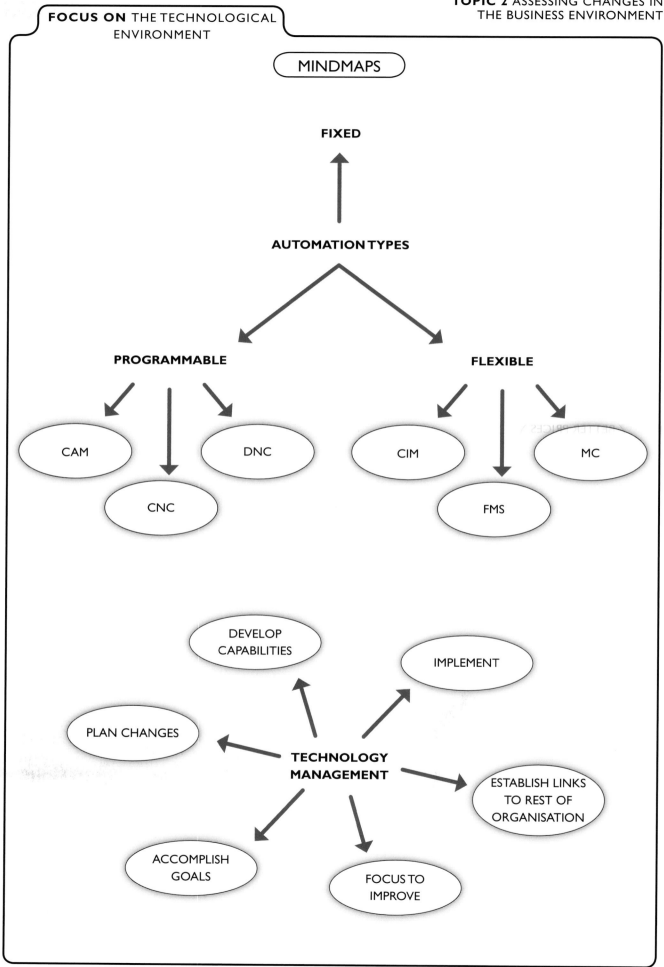

FOCUS ON THE TECHNOLOGICAL
ENVIRONMENT

MINDMAPS

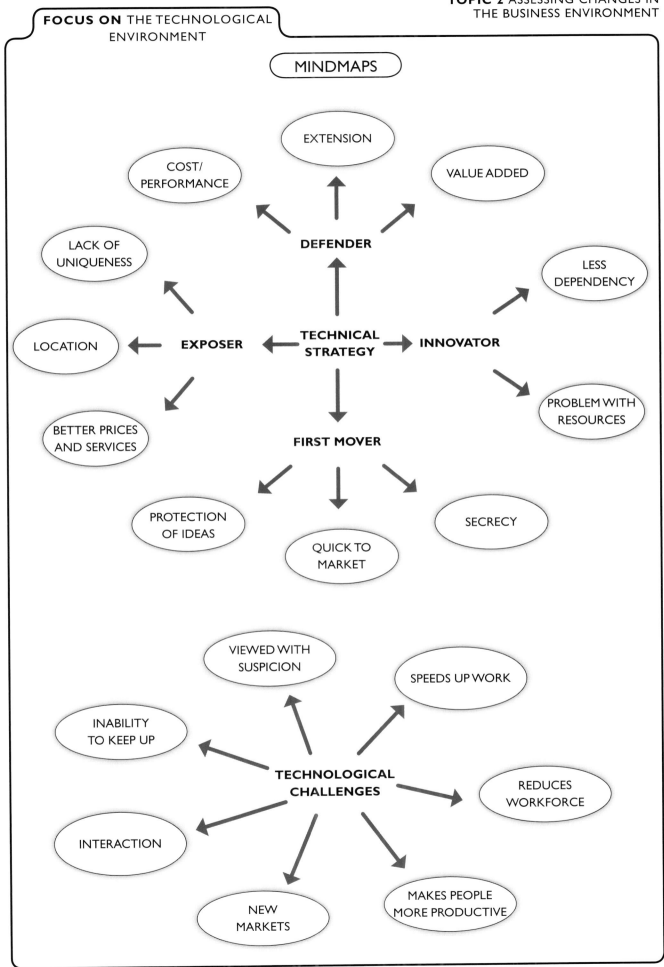

FOCUS ON THE TECHNOLOGICAL
ENVIRONMENT

WORKSHEET

I   What is CRM and what are its business applications?

2   What are the key features of fixed automation?

3   Changes in technology can offer a series of challenges to business, but outline the opportunities
that it also offers.

Answers ▶ page 228

Changes in the competitive structure: new competitors and dominant businesses ▶ textbook pages 240–1

QUESTION

How significant is rivalry as part of the competition between businesses? *(12 marks)*

Rivalry is a major driving force in competing organisations. Businesses will try to gain a distinct advantage in almost any set of circumstances. This becomes particularly prevalent when market conditions are not particularly good. Rivalry is especially high when there is a large number of competitors in the marketplace and where circumstances cause customers to routinely switch from one supplier to another. New competitors are prone to extreme forms of rivalry, where existing businesses will compete vigorously to hinder their entry into the market. There is also a high level of rivalry where products and services are standardised. Short-term pricing and promotional strategies are used to undermine competitors' actions.

Changes in the competitive structure: customers and suppliers

▶ textbook pages 242–3

CASE STUDY – VIDEO GAME GIANTS

Explain why a merger such as this represents synergy. *(12 marks)*

Synergies are the benefits that can result from combining different aspects of an organisation, rather than allowing them to act separately. In other words, organisations will seek to group complementary activities in situations where there is a strong possibility of collaboration. This means that a mutual benefit can be enjoyed, particularly when common work or activity form the basis of the alliance.

Synergies can also be enjoyed between organisations where complementary skills or production processes, or indeed knowledge of a specific market, can be brought together in order to achieve far more than the two organisations could possibly have hoped for individually. Synergies can either bring about short-term, project-based alliances between businesses, or may well prove to be the foundation of a longer-term relationship.

Business synergy is often a term applied to franchise operations – when individuals purchase a franchise they become part of a larger 'family'. All the members of the family work together and the most effective ideas are shared.

FOCUS ON THE COMPETITIVE ENVIRONMENT

Evaluating responses to a change in the competitive environment

▶ textbook pages 244–5

CASE STUDY – ARGENTINIAN BEEF

How might Porter's Five Forces explain the competitive responses by this industry?
(12 marks)

Porter considered the reason why some nations were more competitive than others, and he identified that the foundation of success lay in the 'diamond' of 'home' advantage. Four 'home' prerequisites are required to successfully launch an international challenge – the maximum use of endowed resources (natural and human); the forming of domestic networks to fully exploit these resources; domestic demand (which may involve the invitation to world-class players to help develop these resources in a country); and an industry and environmental structure (the latter provided by Government) in order that these forces can thrive.

A food system, to be competitive, must have two qualities. It must be competitive with other agricultural systems or any other system (say wildlife management) in attracting resources, and it must be absolutely competitive against

similar commodity systems or industries in other countries. The commodity system may have to compete against those industries in international markets or be threatened by them in its domestic markets. Porter refers to this as 'competitive advantage' or 'international competitiveness'. Porter concentrates on two factors in the control of manufacturing industries:

- lower-cost production and delivery – leading to under-pricing over competition
- differentiation of product – quality, image, services

Plus, in export-oriented agriculture there is a third potential source of competitive advantage:

- complementary supply – 'off season', meeting production shortfalls because of weather, disease and so on.

However, complementary supply may not be a competitive strategy in the long term, because a supplier must still look at itself as a low-cost or product-differentiated supplier.

Case studies, questions and exam practice ▶ textbook pages 246–7

CASE STUDY – NINTENDO Wii IS MARKET LEADER

How might these figures influence suppliers, customers and publishers of games for the consoles? *(12 marks)*

Sales of consoles and video game software leapt by 57 per cent to $1.7 billion in March 2008, compared with the previous year. Nintendo's Wii console was the strongest performing console, shifting 721,000 units – an increase of 67 per cent on February, according to figures from NPD Group. Sales of video game software, meanwhile, rose by 63 per cent on the same period a year ago to $945.6 million, far surpassing analyst expectations.

Nintendo was also the strongest performer in consoles, its Wii and portable DS devices together accounting for 58 per cent of the video games hardware market. Microsoft's Xbox nudged ahead of Sony's PlayStation 3, after several months of

slower sales which Microsoft had blamed on supply constraints. Americans bought 262,000 Xbox 360s in March, compared with 257,000 PlayStation 3s.

The President of videogame developer Epic Games has compared Nintendo's Wii console to a 'virus', despite having bought one himself. Epic's President also implied that the console's games are not up to much, and said that the few titles he did like would still be better off on other consoles. Microsoft appears to agree. They claimed the Wii's software attachment rate in Europe is just 3.5 titles – a lot lower than the seven or so titles it claimed Xbox 360 owners have bought. As for attachment rates, Nintendo claimed that, in January 2008 in Europe, Wii owners had bought 5.6 titles on average – rather more than the 3.5 MS claimed.

FOCUS ON THE COMPETITIVE ENVIRONMENT

MINDMAPS

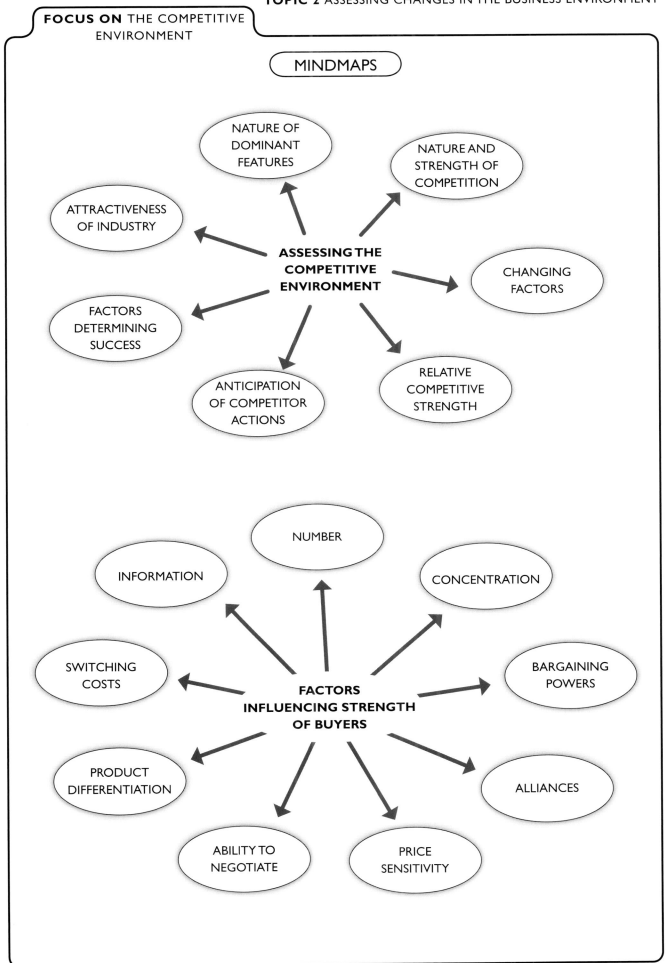

FOCUS ON THE COMPETITIVE
ENVIRONMENT

MINDMAPS

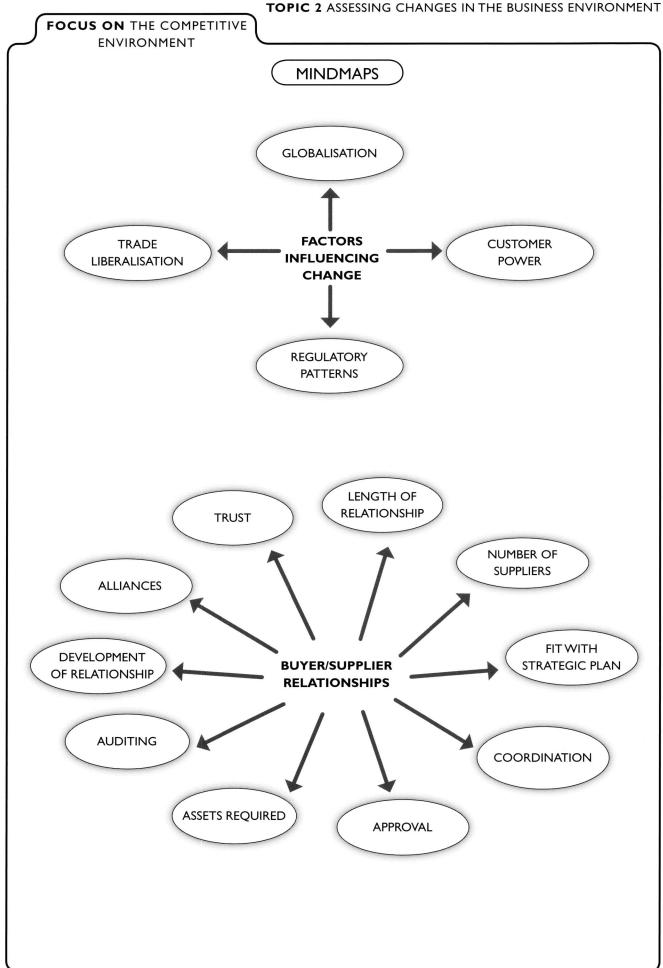

FOCUS ON THE COMPETITIVE ENVIRONMENT

WORKSHEET

1   What is a substitute product and what are its implications to a business that faces the arrival or identification of a substitute product?

2   How might a business view a merger as a means to increase its market share?

3   What are the FOUR key factors that Porter identified as driving the changing environment and the degree of competition faced by a business?

Answers ▶ page 228

FOCUS ON INTERNAL CAUSES OF CHANGE

Changes in organisational size ▶ textbook pages 250–1

QUESTION

Explain why organic growth may be the most desirable form of business growth. (12 marks)

Organic growth is internal growth, achieved by the expansion of existing business or investment in new projects. A key advantage is that any investment can be planned exactly to the requirements of the organisation. Another advantage is that organic growth is, by definition, in a related area. This overcomes problems that often arise by businesses diversifying into non-core areas of operation. This non-core diversification holds greater risks. Organic growth also avoids the payment of premiums to purchase another business by acquisition. Typically, in order to acquire a competitor, the business will have to pay over the existing market price to secure the purchase. The premium is not always justified in terms of expected savings or synergies.

New ownership, leadership and poor business performance

▶ textbook pages 252–3

CASE STUDY – POOR PERFORMANCE

1 Define the term 'restructuring'. (2 marks)

Restructuring means the reorganisation of a business. It may involve reorganising the actual structure, the operations, the responsibilities and other aspects of the business. It may also involve downsizing areas of operation.

2 What is meant by the term 'key metrics'? (4 marks)

Two of the key metrics are mentioned: productivity and cost per unit. These are important measurements of a business's performance and underlie its profitability and success.

3 What might be the consequences of restructuring for the workforce? (6 marks)

The restructuring may involve the organisation laying off staff (redundancy etc.). It may also mean re-deploying, retraining, or requiring staff to adjust their work patterns. It has serious implications for staff as they will be systematically appraised and their contribution measured. It would certainly be unsettling for the workforce.

FOCUS ON INTERNAL
CAUSES OF CHANGE

Case studies, questions and exam practice ▶ textbook pages 254–5

CASE STUDY – A LITTLE BIT OF HISTORY

1 What is a hostile takeover? *(4 marks)*

A hostile takeover is one that happens despite opposition expressed by the directors of the target (the company that would be taken over). This unique type of acquisition does not occur nearly as frequently as friendly takeovers in which two companies work together because the takeover is perceived as beneficial. Hostile takeovers can be traumatic for a target company, and they can also be risky for the other side, as the acquiring company may not be able to obtain certain relevant information about the target company.

2 How might a hostile takeover be dealt with by the target business and why are such takeovers invariably successful? *(10 marks)*

There are a number of ways in which the directors of the target company might attempt to block the takeover (beyond simply advising shareholders against it) including:

- a poison pill to make the takeover more expensive
- finding a white knight (a bidder the directors prefer)
- increasing the target's market cap by making acquisitions of its own, paid for by issuing new shares.

Hostile bids often reveal a serious conflict of interest between shareholders and directors. Shareholders are offered a chance to sell their shares, usually at substantially above the market price prior to the bid. Directors stand to lose their jobs. In theory, directors should recommend a bid unless they have a good chance of getting a better offer, or have very good reason to believe that the market is undervaluing their company. How impartial the decisions of directors will be is questionable. Some financial economists have suggested that one of the key reasons for the occurrence of hostile bids is that they offer a way in which to replace incompetent but well-entrenched management. This is because institutional shareholders rarely vote against incumbent management, making it hard to replace directors even if they underperform.

FOCUS ON INTERNAL
CAUSES OF CHANGE

MINDMAPS

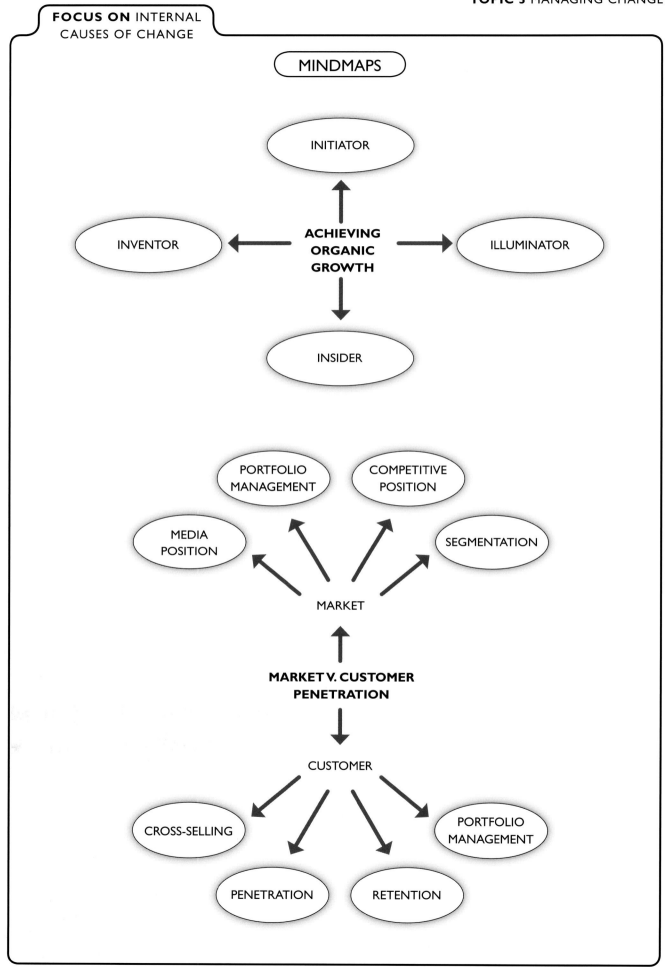

FOCUS ON INTERNAL
CAUSES OF CHANGE

MINDMAPS

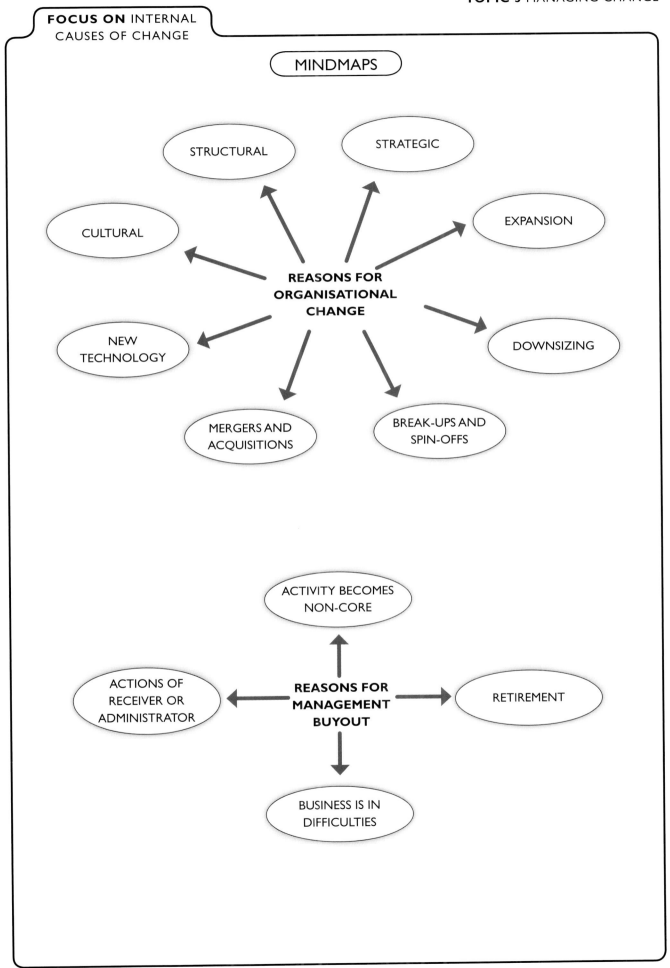

FOCUS ON INTERNAL
CAUSES OF CHANGE

(WORKSHEET)

1   What do you understand by the term 'organic growth'?

2   What is a retrenchment strategy and why might a business consider it?

3   What is the purpose of organisation development (OD) and how does it benefit a business?

Answers ▶ page 229

FOCUS ON INTERNAL
CAUSES OF CHANGE

WORKSHEET

1   Identify FIVE reasons why there might be organisational change.

2   Distinguish between a management buy-out and a management buy-in.

3   What are the options open to a company performing badly?

Answers ▶ page 229

FOCUS ON PLANNING
FOR CHANGE

Corporate planning ▶ textbook pages 256–7

CASE STUDY – TASMANIA'S CORPORATE PLAN

1 **What is meant by the phrase 'not a static document? (4 marks)**

It means that the corporate plan is open to amendment and change as circumstances arise that makes the original plan unfeasible or unworkable.

2 **Explain how the corporate plan is monitored and amended. (8 marks)**

Students should focus on and explain the seven stages of the monitoring and review process at various stages of the year. They should

note that the original corporate plan derives from experiences and conditions from the previous year and some of the aspects of the plan may be ongoing over a period of years. The operating plans are created at branch level so that a wider part of the organisation has ownership and understanding of what will be required of it. The reviews and budgets, for example, occur on several occasions during the year and involve the creation of individual work plans. All these processes are designed to make the plan fully workable and flexible.

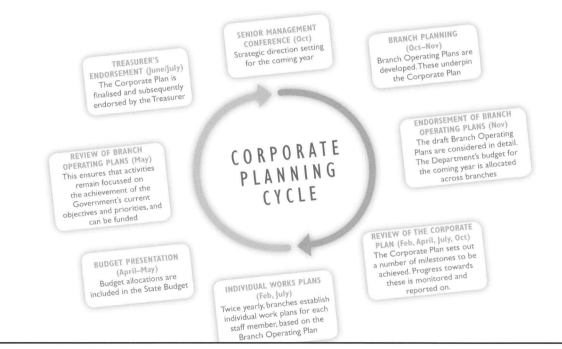

Influences on corporate plans ▶ textbook pages 258–9

CASE STUDY – BARNET'S CORPORATE PLAN

Identify Barnet Council's likely stakeholders and their influences (12 marks)

Students should include the local community, political parties, pressure groups, community groups, central government, Greater London

Authority, the mayor of London, various agencies and government departments. Influence can vary from direct to indirect and from slight to significant. Their answers are likely to reflect the nature of their own local area.

FOCUS ON PLANNING
FOR CHANGE

Approaches to planning ▶ textbook pages 260–1

CASE STUDY – THE BALANCED SCORECARD - WHO'S DOING IT?

Using the case study, and Internet research, describe the nine stages or steps of the balanced scorecard process. *(18 marks)*

Step One of the scorecard building process starts with an assessment of the organisation's Mission and Vision, challenges (pains), enablers, and values. Step One also includes preparing a change management plan for the organisation, and conducting a focused communications workshop to identify key messages, media outlets, timing, and messengers.

In Step Two, elements of the organisation's strategy, including Strategic Results, Strategic Themes, and Perspectives, are developed by workshop participants to focus attention on customer needs and the organisation's value proposition.

In Step Three, the strategic elements developed in Steps One and Two are decomposed into Strategic Objectives, which are the basic building blocks of strategy and define the organisation's strategic intent. Objectives are first initiated and categorised on the Strategic Theme level, categorised by Perspective, linked in cause-effect linkages (Strategy Maps) for each Strategic Theme, and then later merged together to produce one set of Strategic Objectives for the entire organisation.

In Step Four, the cause and effect linkages between the enterprise-wide Strategic Objectives are formalised in an enterprise-wide Strategy Map. The previously constructed theme Strategy Maps are merged into an overall enterprise-wide Strategy Map that shows how the organisation creates value for its customers and stakeholders.

In Step Five, Performance Measures are developed for each of the enterprise-wide Strategic Objectives. Leading and lagging measures are identified, expected targets and thresholds are established, and baseline and benchmarking data is developed.

In Step Six, Strategic Initiatives are developed that support the Strategic Objectives. To build

accountability throughout the organisation, ownership of Performance Measures and Strategic Initiatives is assigned to appropriate staff and documented in data definition tables.

In Step Seven, the implementation process begins by applying performance measurement software to get the right performance information to the right people at the right time. Automation adds structure and discipline to implementing the Balanced Scorecard system, helps transform disparate corporate data into information and knowledge, and helps communicate performance information. In short, automation helps people make better decisions because it offers quick access to actual performance data.

In Step Eight, the enterprise-level scorecard is 'cascaded' down into business and support unit scorecards, meaning that the organisational level scorecard (the first Tier) is translated into business unit or support unit scorecards (the second Tier) and then later to team and individual scorecards (the third Tier). Cascading translates high-level strategy into lower-level objectives, measures, and operational details. Cascading is the key to organisation alignment around strategy. Team and individual scorecards link day-to-day work with department goals and corporate vision. Performance measures are developed for all objectives at all organisation levels. As the scorecard management system is cascaded down through the organisation, objectives become more operational and tactical, as do the performance measures. Accountability follows the objectives and measures, as ownership is defined at each level. An emphasis on results and the strategies needed to produce results is communicated throughout the organisation.

In Step Nine, an Evaluation of the completed scorecard is carried out. During this evaluation, the organisation tries to answer questions such as, 'Are our strategies working?', 'Are we measuring the right things?', 'Has our environment changed?' and 'Are we budgeting our money strategically?'

FOCUS ON PLANNING
FOR CHANGE

Assessing the value of corporate plans ▶ textbook pages 262–3

CASE STUDY – ST ALBANS

Suggest some of the criteria that could be used under each of the ten themes. *(20 marks)*

The actual criteria are laid out below; students should attempt to identify two for each of the themes. These are typical performance criteria for a local authority:

Ambition

- Council has made a commitment to strive for excellence.
- Long-term ambitions linked/influenced by customers and partners and ensuring access for all (i.e Saturday opening, access for disabled people).
- Five-year ambitions set out in service plans and linked to aims and objectives of the council – reviewed annually with budget and service planning (e.g. recycling, electronic service delivery).
- To maintain long-term ambition with the balance of political control, the council has established forums in order to help focus its priorities.
- Council works closely with the Youth council and town/parish councils.
- Lead role in the development of the Local Strategic Partnership and other partnerships.
- Internal re-organisation focused leadership on fewer directors – Corporate Management Team leads corporate initiatives.

Prioritisation

- Aims and objectives historically covered all services , acknowledged to be too broad.
- Cabinet revising aims and objectives which is leading to more customer focused priorities for 2004/5, influenced by the MORI survey 2002 and the Community Strategy.
- Comprehensive service planning process now in place – developing policy-led budgeting.
- Medium-term budget strategy introduced – guides budget for five years.
- Importance of e-voting and leading the way in this area.
- Priorities communicated through members, Best Value Performance Plan, Local Press, Council Tax Leaflet – communications being addressed through the Communications Strategy incorporating Staff through Other office and awareness sessions.

Focus

- Focused through performance management systems, Best Value Performance plan and service planning.
- Service plans monitored by managers/portfolio-holders to track progress – O&S Committee to assess progress and challenge delays.
- Establishing a corporate performance management framework to ensure consistent approach to monitoring service plans and performance.
- Community Panel and MORI provide feedback.
- Consultation to be developed through Communications Strategy.

Capacity

- Difficulties in recruiting staff impacting on services, e.g. planning, tangible backlogs of work.
- Competent, experienced officers with professional skills across the council – staff appraisals identify training needs.
- Recruitment issues being addressed through HR policies; flexible working – key workers unable to access housing, being evaluated through council's housing strategy and countywide through key worker partnership.
- Morale survey 2001 compiled action plan; now being led by the head of Human Resources and Customer Services.
- Consultants employed to temporarily provide expertise – costs prohibitive.
- Officers clear about their responsibilities through job descriptions for all posts; service plans include scope of service responsibility; clear accountability laid out in constitution.
- Partnership working to deliver complex priorities (e.g. Community Safety Partnership).

Performance management

- Recognised weaknesses with current systems; reviewed and launched in October 2003 with further improvements in March 2004.
- Service planning process implemented to provide a consistent and robust approach to performance management; improve services and inform decision-making.
- Effective financial control, measured by budget-setting process was a high priority and now debt-free.

Assessing the value of corporate plans (continued)

- Information cascaded from Corporate Management Team to Departmental Management Teams to regular team meetings within departments.
- Risk Management Group regularly meets; Risk Management Strategy provides contingency plans and has been cascaded throughout the council.
- Council adheres to Procurement Strategy and Constitution to provide value for money (tendering policies) allowing council to go debt-free.
- Many services contracted out (e.g. refuse collection) with value for money a driving force behind this.

Achievement in quality of service

- Service is good and evidenced through national/local performance indicators (e.g. benefit claims, museum visits, recycling).
- Museums service received 'Quality Assured Visitor Attraction for Tourist Board'; awarded grant of £80,000 to interactive services.
- Best Value reviews highlighted high quality services (e.g Housing Repairs '2 stars') but identified areas for improvement (Planning and Transport services) with plans in place to address these.
- Successful partnership working ensured high service quality such as Community Safety.
- E-government initiatives improved service quality (e.g. Online planning applications, online payment for services).
- Chartermark awarded for Environmental Health 1999-2002; not renewed at the time due to lack of resources; building control achieved ISO 9001:2000; other awards to be identified in 2004/05 service plans.
- Residents' expectations high; service quality realistic in relation to available resources; resident satisfaction with services very high (71% in 2002).
- Comprehensive complaints procedure provides indication of customer satisfaction; further development underway and incorporated into performance management framework.

Achievement of improvement

- Quality of life indicators being considered in service plans 2004/5.

- Many services consistently improving e.g. housing, green spaces, recycling have a direct and long-term impact on the quality of life.
- Improvements sometimes reactionary but managed well across the council; also achieved through accessing external funding.
- No failing services but weak areas identified (e.g. Development control, decline in service standards due to delay in planning applications).
- Project management weak, being addressed with managers undertaking the PRINCE 2 project management training.
- Improvements in line with priorities; identified through service plans.
- Significant progress made across the council (recycling, building control, benefits).
- New political arrangements and internal structure now embedded leading to continuous improvements in service planning and delivery.

Investment

- Management structure changed to streamline and allow Strategic Directors to concentrate on corporate overview, while Heads of Service concentrate on service delivery.
- Debt-free status increased capital spending ability, e.g. significant capital programme for Housing 2003/4 in excess of £8 million.
- Procurement Strategy adopted in September 2002 to obtain skilled management of procurement and supply chains.
- Council secured £18 million of Housing Corporation Grant (largest in region) securing around 229 affordable housing units.
- Sale of Burnside to HPC Housing Association secured investment of £1.8 million and secured 36 affordable dwelling units.
- Several other investment initiatives detailed in Self-Assessment.
- Council open to external competition through market testing and competitive tendering – several services provided by external contractors (e.g. leisure, refuse collection).
- Council required having external audit and inspection always had positive Audit letter.

Learning

- Aware of areas of poor performance through Best Value Reviews and Performance Indicators.
- Corporate complaints procedure in place with

FOCUS ON PLANNING
FOR CHANGE

Assessing the value of corporate plans (continued)

reporting to members; not enough action is taken to ascertain patterns of complaint but being addressed.

- E-voting highlighted the need for good project management.
- Housing procedures are regularly reviewed and if found deficient, are overhauled. Robust monitoring process identified as good practice by Audit Commission.
- HR conducts exit interviews with all staff leaving the council and gives feedback to Heads of Service.
- Services look to learn externally and are involved in many forums at a regional or professional level e.g. Herts Policy Network.
- Information shared at senior level through Strategic Director meetings and Corporate Management Team; Cascaded down via staff meetings/sessions.

Future Plans
- Key stakeholders/customers consulted on future plans through various forums and consultation exercises.
- Peer challenge has helped the council to develop an improvement plan.
- Community Panel of 1,000 residents is actively consulted on service delivery and forward planning.
- Council acknowledges weaknesses and areas for improvements and is initiating changes through Best Value, Performance Management and Service Planning.
- Community Strategy is a key influence on the future planning of the council.
- Difficult to plan for future with contractual arrangements for services. Increased flexibility will be a feature of future contracts.

Contingency planning ▶ textbook pages 264–5

CASE STUDY – FOOTBALL LICENSING CONTINGENCY PLANS

1 What other contingency plans, such as the crowd-surge contingency plan, could be prepared by a football club? *(8 marks)*

Any of the following would be ideal answers. Fire; bomb threat/suspect package; adverse weather conditions; damage to structures; power cut or failure; gas leak or chemical incident; turnstile counting mechanism failure; closed circuit television failure; public address system failure; electronic information board failure; stewards' radio system failure; internal telephone systems failure; incursion onto the playing area; late arrivals or delayed start; lock-outs; disorder inside the ground; large-scale ticket forgery; emergency evacuation and abandoned match.

2 **Suggest the contents of a contingency plan for crowd trouble.** *(8 marks)*

The FLA's ideal blueprint is shown in the diagram on the right.

FOCUS ON PLANNING
FOR CHANGE

Case studies, questions and exam practice ▶ textbook pages 266–7

CASE STUDY – UNIVERSITY OF SOUTH AUSTRALIA

Why might the university carry out environmental scanning? *(12 marks)*

According to the university, environmental scanning (ES) is an important activity in the development of an organisation's capacity and capability for change. Environmental scanning helps identify the external forces, events, trends, issues and relationships (referred to as 'items') that might assist or adversely affect an organisation's future. Some of the benefits of ES include:

- reducing uncertainty – assisting both short-term decision-making and the development of long-term strategies
- identification and monitoring of new and emerging risks and opportunities
- benchmark assumptions
- process improvement
- enhance contextual awareness – assisting staff to develop awareness of the organisation's environment, and promote strategic conversation
- develop experience and techniques in obtaining and reporting on organisational intelligence

Environmental scanning is particularly important to universities because of the nature of these organisations. Universities have broad and permeable boundaries due to the fact that, among other things, they are intrinsically connected with the community/society, they have additional reporting, legislative and governing responsibilities, and they have strong international links.

Planning and Assurance Services (PAS) have the responsibility for the formal task of environmental scanning at corporate level. Tasks include the scanning of the corporate environment and the production of an annual environmental scanning paper.

Environmental scanning, however, is an activity that all work areas should be more engaged in. Many staff scan individually, in an informal fashion through general reading and peer contact, but the information they view is often not shared or utilised as effectively as it could be. The UniSA Environmental scanning guidelines are designed to assist work areas to conduct their own ES (or to make them more efficient and effective at it) and to provide some techniques on how they might utilise the information for planning.

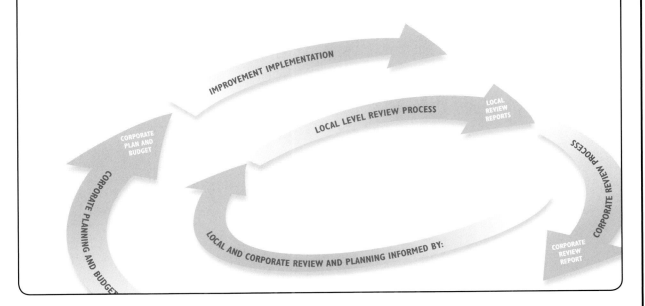

FOCUS ON PLANNING
FOR CHANGE

MINDMAPS

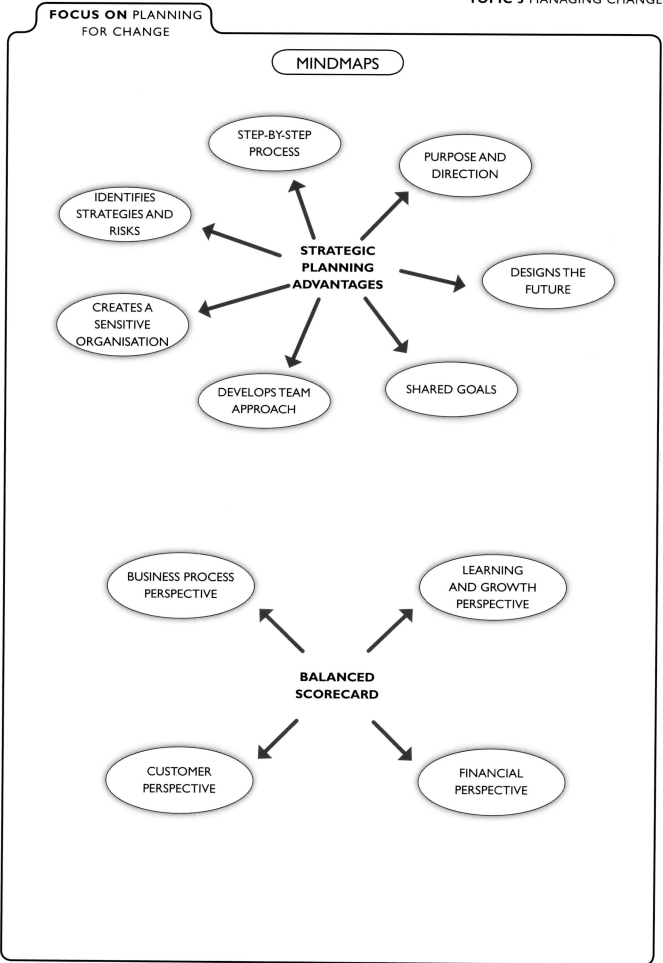

FOCUS ON PLANNING
FOR CHANGE

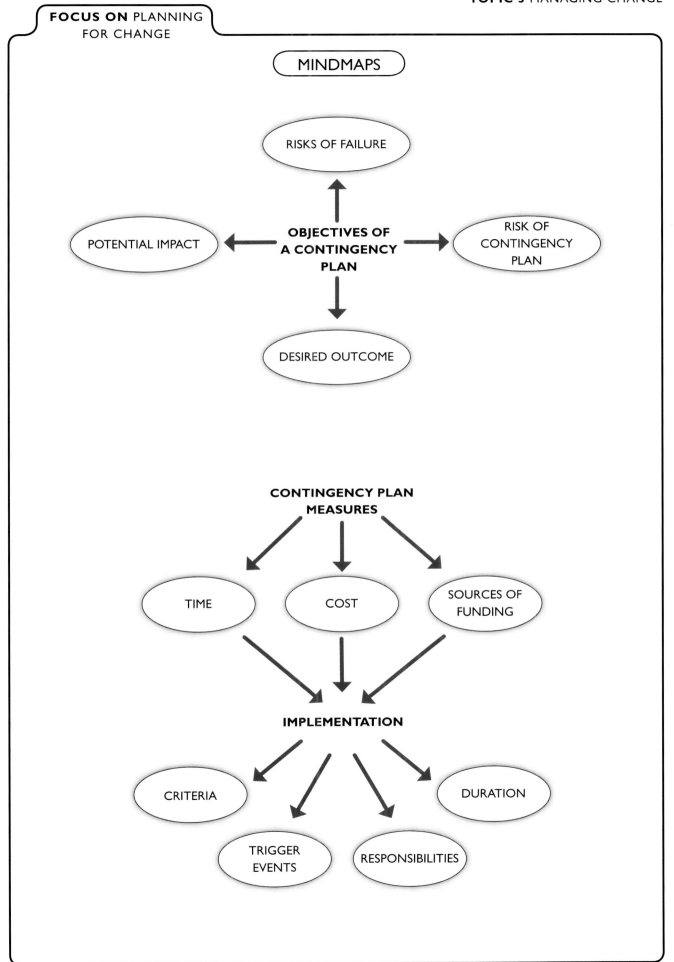

MINDMAPS

RISKS OF FAILURE

POTENTIAL IMPACT

**OBJECTIVES OF
A CONTINGENCY
PLAN**

RISK OF
CONTINGENCY
PLAN

DESIRED OUTCOME

**CONTINGENCY PLAN
MEASURES**

TIME

COST

SOURCES OF
FUNDING

IMPLEMENTATION

CRITERIA

TRIGGER
EVENTS

RESPONSIBILITIES

DURATION

FOCUS ON PLANNING
FOR CHANGE

(WORKSHEET)

1 How does SWOT fit into the corporate planning process?

2 What do you understand by the term 'balanced scorecard' and its application?

3 Identify FIVE key advantages of strategic or corporate planning.

Answers ▶ page 229

FOCUS ON PLANNING
FOR CHANGE

(WORKSHEET)

1   Identify FOUR key benefits of an integrated corporate plan.

2   What is a contingency plan and why do businesses create them?

3   What is the purpose of environmental scanning?

Answers ▶ page 229

FOCUS ON KEY INFLUENCES ON
THE CHANGE PROCESS: LEADERSHIP

The meaning of leadership and the difference between leaders and managers ▶ textbook pages 268–9

QUESTION

Distinguish between a manager and a leader. (18 marks)

Both a manager and a leader may know the business reasonably well, but the leader must know the business to a finer degree and from a different viewpoint. They must grasp the underlying market forces that determine the past and present trends in the businesses niche, so that they can generate a vision and strategy to bring about its future development and growth. A crucial sign of a good leader is an honest attitude towards the facts and objective truth. Conversely, a subjective leader obscures the facts for the sake of narrow self-interest, partisan interest or prejudice.

Effective leaders continually probe all levels of the organisation for information, challenging their own perceptions and validating the facts. They talk to their employees to find out what is working and what is not. They keep an open mind to the knowledge they gain. An important source of information for a leader is the knowledge of the mistakes and failures that have been and are being made within their organisation.

Leaders investigate reality, taking the pertinent factors and analysing them carefully. On this basis they produce visions, concepts, plans and programs of change. Managers usually adopt the truth from others and implement it without regard to the facts.

There is a profound difference between leaders and managers. A good manager does things right while a good leader does the right thing. Doing the right thing implies a goal, a direction, an objective, a vision, a dream, a strategy, a path, a reach.

Managing is as much about efficiency as leadership is about effectiveness. Managing is about how things need to be done, leadership is about what things need to be done and why these things should be carried out. Management is about systems, controls, procedures, policies and structures whereas leadership is about, trust, vision and human capital.

Leadership is about innovating concepts, inspiring others and initiating projects. Management is about carrying out these visions and managing the status quo. Leadership is creative, adaptive and agile. Leadership looks to the future while also being mindful of the financial bottom line.

Leaders base their vision, appeal and integrity on a careful estimation of the facts, trends and contradictions. They develop the means to re-define the status quo so that their vision can be realised while enrolling others into the vision of the future. Without other peoples buy-in, a vision will stall, and a period of transition will ensue. Leaders, therefore, have to empower others to accomplish the over-arching goal while also rewarding their achievements.

To manage means: 'to bring about or succeed in accomplishing, sometimes despite difficulty or hardship'. To lead means: 'to guide in direction, course, action, opinion, etc.' The distinction is important.

The most dramatic differences between leaders and managers are found at the extremes. Poor leaders are despots while poor managers are bureaucrats. Leadership is a human process and management is a resource allocation process. Both are important and in many instances managers need to also perform as leaders. Indeed first-class managers have significant leadership ability.

FOCUS ON KEY INFLUENCES ON THE CHANGE PROCESS: LEADERSHIP

The range of leadership styles ▶ textbook pages 270–1

QUESTION

How might management theory help us understand the skills needed as a manager? *(18 marks)*

Students should focus on the fact that theory of management helps us identify first the characteristics of managers and then the skills that they require in order to carry out their role in an effective manner. Management theory identifies the fact that there is a broad range of different styles of management. It does not necessarily seek to identify which is the most desirable leadership style, but helps us to recognise the fact that management approaches differ in the way they seek to provide the manager with the necessary underpinning skills and approaches in a variety of situations. Clearly many management theories recognise that some form of consultative or participative management style is a skill in itself and that this is the most effective form of management. More authoritarian approaches often suggest that the manager lacks the necessary skills to motivate and mobilise subordinates.

Transformational leadership ▶ textbook pages 272–3

QUESTION

Compare and contrast the theories of transformational leadership and action-centred leadership. *(12 marks)*

Transformational leadership aims to turn subordinates into effective leaders in their own right by empowering them and providing them with the necessary back-up in order to make decisions. There are various stages involved, but they involve stimulating an individual's desire to take control of a work situation, and the manager or leader is often seen as an innovator, encourager or coach. The action-centred model focuses on what a manager does rather than what a manager is. It recognises that managers have to balance the needs of the task, the team and the individual simultaneously. As a result of this three-part role, it is not always possible for the manager to focus on the individual or the team when often the compelling priority is to simply get the task done. An effective manager under this theory can balance the three by taking an overview.

Factors influencing leadership style ▶ textbook pages 274–5

QUESTION

To what extent can theory explain the factors that might influence leadership style? *(18 marks)*

Students should focus on how leadership styles are determined and whether this is a cognitive choice on behalf of the manager, or whether it is a feature of their personality. Other managers are clearly influenced by the way in which they themselves are motivated and their own self-concept. Equally, some managers believe that they have to adopt a specific role, as they have been allocated a degree of power and authority to carry out tasks, or at least direct those tasks. Theories also suggest that social learning or reinforcement is an integral part of a manager adopting a particular leadership style, simply, over time, they adopt the predominant type of leadership style in the organisation. It is also important to note that other managers simply react and adopt a leadership style in order to fulfil particular pressures on them in terms of performance.

FOCUS ON KEY INFLUENCES ON
THE CHANGE PROCESS: LEADERSHIP

Role of leadership in managing change and achieving success

▶ textbook pages 276–7

QUESTION

How might theories of change help us understand a leader's role in managing change and ensuring the success of an organisation?
(18 marks)

The role of leadership in change is crucial, as it often either frames the parameters of the change and/or drives that change over a period of time. The wealth of different change theories only serves to illustrate the fact that there is no set of golden rules to determine the way in which change should be managed. In fact, there is great dispute about how change should be managed and the pace at which that change should be instituted. Equally, there is a wide variety of different theories suggesting the ways in which

the resistance to change and the underlying reasons for that resistance should be handled. Cotter and Schlesinger actually identify six different ways in which this element should be handled. The theories, as with most theoretical approaches to real-life situations, are not all-encompassing and neither can they necessarily provide total solutions to what are complex and often traumatic situations.

Assessing the importance of leadership ▶ textbook pages 278–9

QUESTION

Why is leadership important to an organisation?
(12 marks)

Leadership provides a focus, direction and decision-making function for organisations. Leadership aims to visualise what may be ahead and frame the approach. Without leadership, organisations are directionless and prone to conflict. Leaders need to identify their vision and

then transmit this to the rest of the organisation and gain the commitment of the employees to that vision, which needs to be compelling. Leadership also needs to accept the fact that risks are inevitable, as is failure. Leadership also provides authority and influence within an organisation. The greater the power and authority, the wider the range of leadership skills required.

FOCUS ON KEY INFLUENCES ON
THE CHANGE PROCESS: LEADERSHIP

Case studies, questions and exam practice ▸ textbook pages 280–1

CASE STUDY – NHS LEADERSHIP QUALITIES FRAMEWORK

Explain what is meant by 'the applications of the framework'? *(14 marks)*

The seven key applications identify primarily the requirements of NHS leaders. The first recognises that personal development is important and this includes training and education on an individual basis. NHS boards also need development, specifically in terms of decision-making and teamwork. The application also recognises that clear profiles need to be developed, in order to identify key leadership qualities when recruiting and selecting management. In a large organisation, career paths are not as clear, as a degree of the hierarchy is not accessible to administrative posts, because they will be clinical posts. The succession planning refers to identifying those who will replace senior managers who have either retired or moved to another authority. The connecting leadership capability suggests that leaders with specific skills should be identified and assigned tasks relevant to their skills sets. The final application suggests that management, just like the rest of the organisation, should be subject to performance measurement.

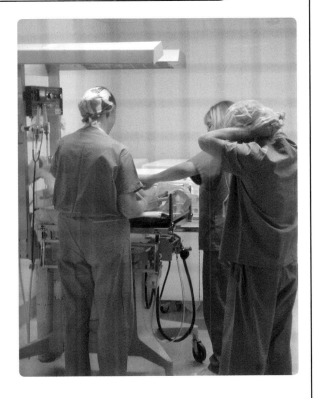

FOCUS ON KEY INFLUENCES ON
THE CHANGE PROCESS: LEADERSHIP

MINDMAPS

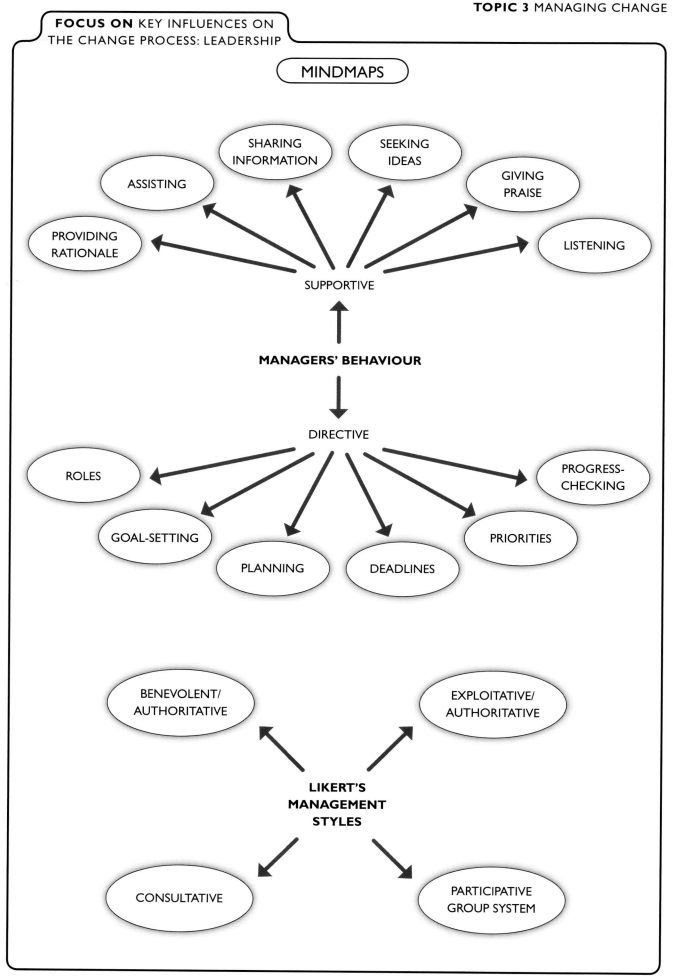

FOCUS ON KEY INFLUENCES ON
THE CHANGE PROCESS: LEADERSHIP

MINDMAPS

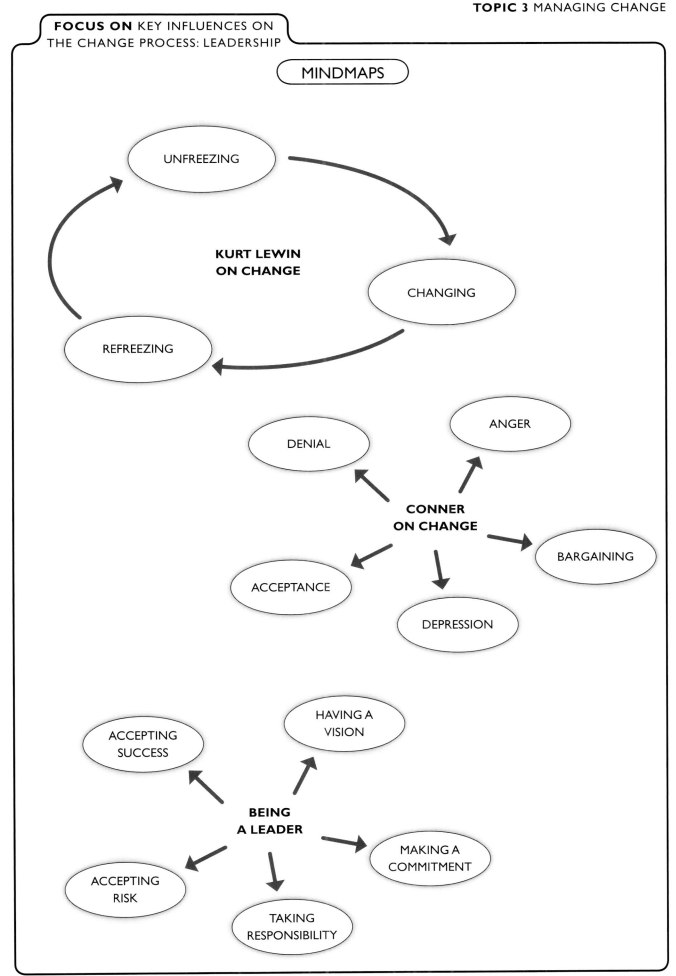

FOCUS ON KEY INFLUENCES ON
THE CHANGE PROCESS: LEADERSHIP

WORKSHEET

1   Distinguish between a leader and a manager.

2   Briefly explain McGregor's Theory X and Theory Y.

3   What do you understand by the term 'country club manager'?

Answers ▶ page 229

FOCUS ON KEY INFLUENCES ON
THE CHANGE PROCESS: LEADERSHIP

WORKSHEET

1   What are the FOUR Is of transformational leadership?

2   What did Lewin mean by 'unfreezing'?

3   What are the key characteristics of a visionary leader?

Answers ▶ page 229

FOCUS ON KEY INFLUENCES ON
THE CHANGE PROCESS: CULTURE

Types of organisational culture ▶ textbook pages 282–3

QUESTION

What is corporate culture and why is it difficult for corporate culture to adapt to changes in the wider community? *(14 marks)*

Corporate culture is the basis of any company's code of ethics and is described as being 'the way we do things around here'. The idea of an organisation's culture can be applied to any group or corporation, small, medium or large. Corporate culture encompasses such practices as fair hiring procedures, how a deal is worked out, how holiday entitlement is decided, how the company is structured, the goals of the company, and pension programmes. Essentially, corporate culture is how a company runs on a day-to-day basis, following unwritten rules that are simply understood by all employees and employers. It is important to note that corporate culture may contradict a written

code of ethics. In other words, often older, or authoritarian, or more established companies and organisations find it difficult to align their corporate culture with the changing views of society. Therefore, for an integrity-aspiring corporation, it is important to understand that while the views and ethics of the board of directors may not change, the needs, views, make-up and ethical practices of the employee base may dramatically change over time. This requires ethics testing, policy and training recalibration, social performance auditing, accountability and transparency analysis, and continuous improvement. In order to meet the needs of these new employee demographics as well as changing societal expectations, a corporation must be willing to examine its corporate culture, identify the outdated aspects, and change it for the better.

Significance of organisational culture ▶ textbook pages 284–5

QUESTION

We mentioned the Hawthorne Experiments by Elton Mayo on this spread. Find out about these experiments and explain their significance. *(18 marks)*

Elton Mayo was employed by the Hawthorne Works during the 1920s and 1930s to attempt to improve the electrical company's productivity. As a result of this work he developed a theory which has since become known as the Hawthorne Effect.

Initially, Mayo adopted the scientific management theory of F. W. Taylor in his attempt to discover which environmental features of the workplace were affecting productivity. He made amendments to the lighting, heating and availability of refreshments, and then went on to make changes to the length of the work day and week. Each time he made a change the rate of productivity increased. Puzzled by his findings, Mayo reversed his actions by removing tea-breaks and reducing the level of lighting, but productivity continued to increase. Mayo's

conclusion was that the changes had been made in consultation with the employees and that this factor had been the determining influence on productivity, together with the fact that the employees had a good working relationship with their supervisors. This research became known as Mayo's Hawthorne Effect.

Further research was then undertaken in another department of the organisation. Two different groups of employees were working on complex equipment; one group considered that their status was high because of the complexity of the job role. The second group considered themselves to be lower in status and this resulted in a degree of competition between the two groups. Both groups had established their own sets of rules and code of behaviour and each had established the pace of work and degree of output. Individuals within the group who did not comply with these standards were put under pressure from the other members of the group.

Significance of organisational culture (continued)

Each group was given a target output for the day by the management of the organisation. On some days these targets were exceeded, but the groups were simply reporting that they had reached the target figures and included the excess in the target figure for the following day. Mayo's conclusions from this were that the groups had:

- been given a benchmark. Their benchmark had been the employer's output targets and they had been able to compare this with their own output totals
- had established for themselves a concept of a fair day's output and did not feel they needed to exceed these targets.

Mayo felt that lessons could be learned from this research in that a group's needs have to be in accord with organisational rules. Consultation was the key to achieving this, together with close monitoring of day-to-day organisational activities.

Mayo made three interesting discoveries from his research that form the basis of this 'solidarity theory':

- Output and motivation improve when employees are being observed.
- Peer pressure contributes to the level of support by the individuals within the group.
- A group had strong feelings about what is possible and reasonable. This is as important to a group as its reaction to the demands of managers.

The latest edition of Mayo's book is *Social Problems of an Industrial Civilisation*, Routledge, 1998.

Reasons for and problems of changing organisational culture

▶ textbook pages 286–7

QUESTION

Why might there be resistance to changes in organisational culture? *(14 marks)*

In all organisations, you will find some measure of resistance to organisational change. Many employees have settled down into their functions which may seem both comfortable and efficient to them. Organisational change invades the personal sense of security. However, studies have shown that 70 per cent of an organisation is positive towards change. Hence, most people care about their workplace and want to contribute to its development. What the studies also show is that whereas employees have a positive attitude towards changes in general, they are reluctant to accept changes in their own work function.

When an organisation is about to undergo a major change, there are often two different kinds of resistance. One is the resistance of the management to a new management philosophy. The other is the resistance of the employees to changes in the company.

There are numerous theories about the reasons behind the resistance:

- Nature: resistance is a normal human instinct
- Lack of self-trust: we do not believe that we have the ability to learn new trades
- Indifference: we are doing fine the way we currently do things
- It is useless: the world around us does not change regardless of what we do
- The fear of the unknown: it is better to stick with what you know
- Self-interest: what do I gain from the changes?
- Group mentality: if everybody else thinks like this, why should I think otherwise?
- Ego: are you trying to say that what we do is wrong?
- Short-sightedness: we want our rewards now, and our ways are right, their ways are wrong.

When concerned with a group's resistance to change, the answers are often based on habits or comfort. Particularly, the propensity of some individuals to change is often considered suspicious as, in a group, individualism is suspect. The person who argues for changes is often considered a troublemaker and disloyal to the company. This explains the resistance to good ideas. The decisive factor is not whether an idea is good — it is whether it is shared by the majority. If it is not, it will be rejected.

Assessing the importance of organisational culture ▶ textbook pages 288–9

QUESTION

What are the major advantages of organisational culture? *(12 marks)*

Organisational culture is a system of shared values and beliefs about what is important, what behaviours are appropriate and about feelings and relationships internally and externally. Values and cultures need to be unique to the organisation, widely shared and reflected in daily practice and relevant to the company purpose and strategy. But there is no single best culture.

The research also found that it is important for organisations to create the kind of environment or culture where the positive managerial behaviours of listening, coaching, guiding, involving and problem-solving are actively encouraged and reinforced. This is where HR policy is critical as it reflects and reinforces organisational values and culture.

To build commitment and drive improved performance it needs to be:

- embedded and understood across the organisation
- integrated into relationships between stakeholders
- enduring, built around or on a legacy of past success
- habitual, with behaviours repeated, collective and routine.

The research also clearly shows a link between strong shared values and high commitment. Where strongly shared values can be demonstrated, people are more likely to be satisfied, displaying higher levels of organisational commitment, lower quit rates, greater customer satisfaction, and lower levels of dissent or dissatisfaction over levels of pay.

High performance cultures are a launching pad for new initiatives, and are characterised by the following behaviour.

- Can-do spirit – mutual support
- Bias for action
- Passion for the customer
- Collaboration – positive attitudes
- Creative/innovative
- Willingness to change

The US company, General Electric is recognised as one of the world's most successful business organisations. The secret of GE's success is its focus on a set of core values, which defines the culture. It really is the power of a healthy culture. GE leaders throughout the company demonstrate these core values. They are:

- Having a passion for excellence and hating bureaucracy and all the nonsense that comes with it
- Relishing change and being stimulated by it. Seeing change as an opportunity, not as a threat
- Understanding that speed is a competitive advantage and appreciating the organisational benefits that can be achieved from a focus on speed
- Willingness and confidence to empower others
- Commitment to work and to walk-the-talk. Not only to talk!
- Energy and the ability to energise and motivate others.

FOCUS ON KEY INFLUENCES ON
THE CHANGE PROCESS: CULTURE

Case studies, questions and exam practice ▶ textbook pages 290–1

CASE STUDY – MILLER BREWING

Mark Spear introduced a form of employee engagement. What does this mean? Give examples of this process from the case study. (18 marks)

The term engagement can actually refer to both employees and customers. Engaged employees are encouraged to use their natural talents in order to assist the business in having a competitive edge. It is believed that collectively, efforts involving employee engagement can actually assist in the engagement of customers themselves. Employee engagement requires employee understanding, not only of the business but also the management and what both hope to achieve. Managers within organisations must assist employees in realising their expectations, which have been learned by the subordinates as being the primary motivators of the business itself.

Employee engagement, therefore, involves the mobilisation of the talent, energy and resources of employees. If effective, employee engagement delivers the following:

- the development of a healthy and sustainable business
- identification of the needs and the solutions of customers
- opportunities for dialogue with the business's stakeholders
- leverage for the business in the sense that it strengthens relations with stakeholders and leads to partnerships

- more efficient use of resources
- development of skills and personnel
- benefits to leaders and team development
- bringing any form of corporate culture into sharp focus, building morale, loyalty and pride in the workforces
- the establishment and maintenance of the business's reputation

FOCUS ON KEY INFLUENCES ON
THE CHANGE PROCESS: CULTURE

MINDMAPS

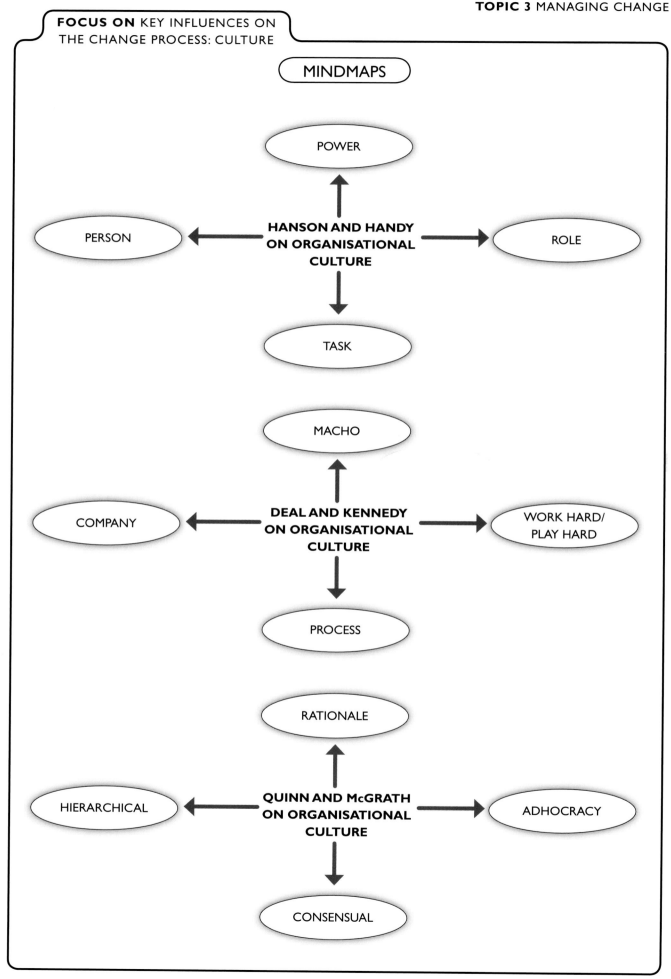

FOCUS ON KEY INFLUENCES ON
THE CHANGE PROCESS: CULTURE

MINDMAPS

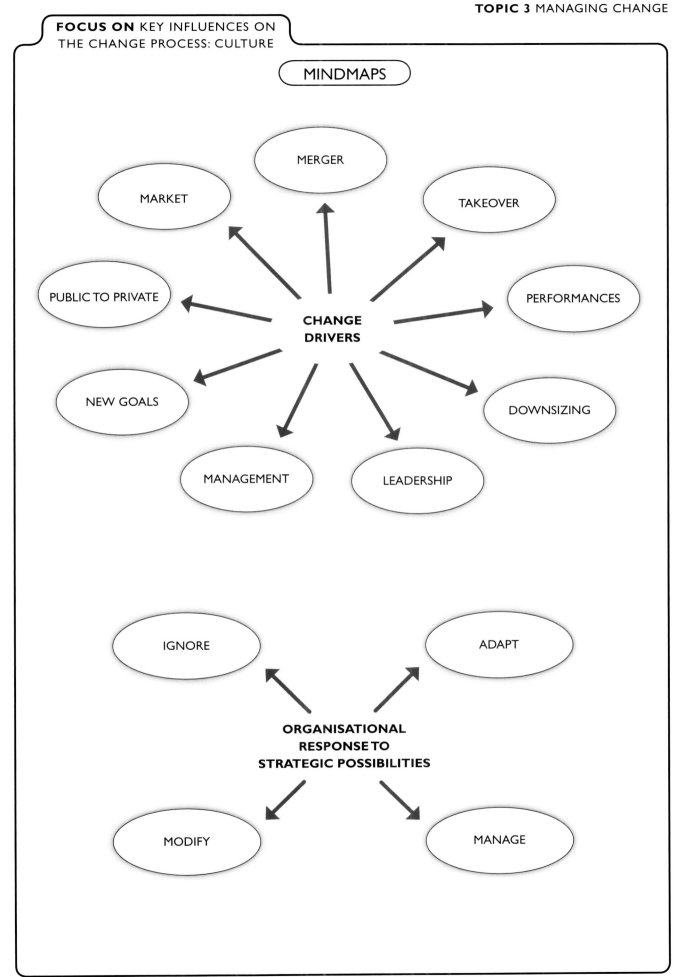

FOCUS ON KEY INFLUENCES ON
THE CHANGE PROCESS: CULTURE

WORKSHEET

1   What are the features of an organisation that has a macho culture?

2   What is meant if a business is said to have a consensual culture?

3   Why might it be valuable to examine the culture of an organisation?

Answers ▶ page 230

FOCUS ON KEY INFLUENCES ON
THE CHANGE PROCESS: CULTURE

WORKSHEET

1   What are the THREE primary objectives of organisational design?

2   What are organisational norms?

3   Suggest FIVE reasons why there may be a change in an organisation's culture.

Answers ▶ page 230

FOCUS ON KEY INFLUENCES ON THE CHANGE PROCESS: CULTURE

WORKSHEET

1   What is force field analysis and what is its purpose?

2   How can organisational culture reduce conflict in an organisation?

3   Identify FOUR reasons why organisational culture would have an influence on the strategies of a business.

Answers ▶ page 230

Significance of information management ▶ textbook pages 292–3

QUESTION

An organisation will need to consider the information requirements across all its business units and functions. It is often recommended that a life-cycle approach is used to look at the use of information in business processes. What should the organisation review regarding its use of information? *(12 marks)*

The organisation should review:

- What information is currently held, and how it can be classified
- What information needs to be collected or created by the business processes

- How the information will be stored and maintained
- How the information will be accessed, by whom and in what ways
- How the information will be disposed of, and under whose authority
- How the quality of the information will be maintained (accuracy, consistency, currency, etc.)
- How the information can be made more accessible inside and outside the organisation
- Who will be responsible for the various processes of information management
- How all staff can be made aware of their responsibilities for information management.

Value of different approaches to decision-making ▶ textbook pages 294–5

QUESTION

'Investment appraisal is the only foolproof way of underpinning decision-making'. Discuss. *(18 marks)*

Investment appraisal is a very valuable tool to be used alongside decision-making. It is relatively easy to use and provides clear answers, which can be simply applied. It is accurate as long as all available information has been used. It can measure the extent to which future cash flows will be affected, and can factor in impacts such as changes in the interest rate and the effects of inflation. It does, however, only provide a purely financial basis for the decision-making and does not take into account any qualitative or long-term factors.

FOCUS ON MAKING STRAGETIC DECISIONS

Influences on corporate decision-making ▶ textbook pages 296–7

CASE STUDY – ROYAL BANK OF SCOTLAND STAKEHOLDER ISSUES

How might the RBS have discovered this information and set of priorities for its stakeholders? *(8 marks)*

From the RBS website, they explain:

'Our stakeholder research process is designed to identify, explore and prioritise the issues that our stakeholders care about. We explore the financial services sector in general and the RBS Group in particular. The study uses both qualitative and quantitative research. We completed a stakeholder study in the UK in the last quarter of 2006. We conducted a series of focus groups with customers and employees. We interviewed key opinion formers from the media and from relevant NGOs. We met with

key SRI analysts, and followed this up with a short email questionnaire. We also conducted extensive desk research. This research enabled us to identify the issues and their overall importance on a stakeholder by stakeholder basis. We then produced a combined list of the top issues across all stakeholders. Our direct stakeholders were given more weight than our indirect stakeholders. This work enables us to focus on the real issues associated with the overall impact of our operation on society and the environment, in the eyes of our stakeholders. We plan to use it to ensure we continue to focus our time and energy most effectively for the benefit of our business and our stakeholders.'

Case studies, questions and exam practice ▶ textbook pages 298–9

CASE STUDY – DECISION TREE

Using the data from the decision tree, should the business open a new outlet in London or refurbish its existing one? Show your calculations. *(18 marks)*

The calculations are:

Full refit:			
	0.6 × £150,000	=	£90,000
	0.2 × £100,000	=	£20,000
	0.2 × £50,000	=	£10,000
			£120,000

Partial refit:			
	0.5 × £50,000	=	£25,000
	0.3 × £30,000	=	£9,000
	0.2 × £20,000	=	£4,000
			£38,000

Large new outlet:			
	0.6 × £800,000	=	£480,000
	0.2 × £500,000	=	£100,000
	0.2 × £300,000	=	£60,000
			£640,000

Small new outlet:			
	0.4 × £200,000	=	£80,000
	0.3 × £150,000	=	£45,000
	0.3 × £100,000	=	£30,000
			£155,000

Using the following maximum cost figures, it is now possible to calculate the cost savings of each option:

Full refit:
£150,000 – £120,000 = £30,000

Partial refit:
£50,000 – £38,000 = £12,000

New large outlet:
£800,000 – £640,000 = £160,000

New small outlet:
£200,000 – £155,000 = £45,000

Clearly, the new large outlet offers the greatest cost savings, but the full investment is four times higher than any of the other alternatives. The business may ultimately decide that the investment costs are actually more significant than the apparent cost savings.

FOCUS ON MAKING
STRAGETIC DECISIONS

MINDMAPS

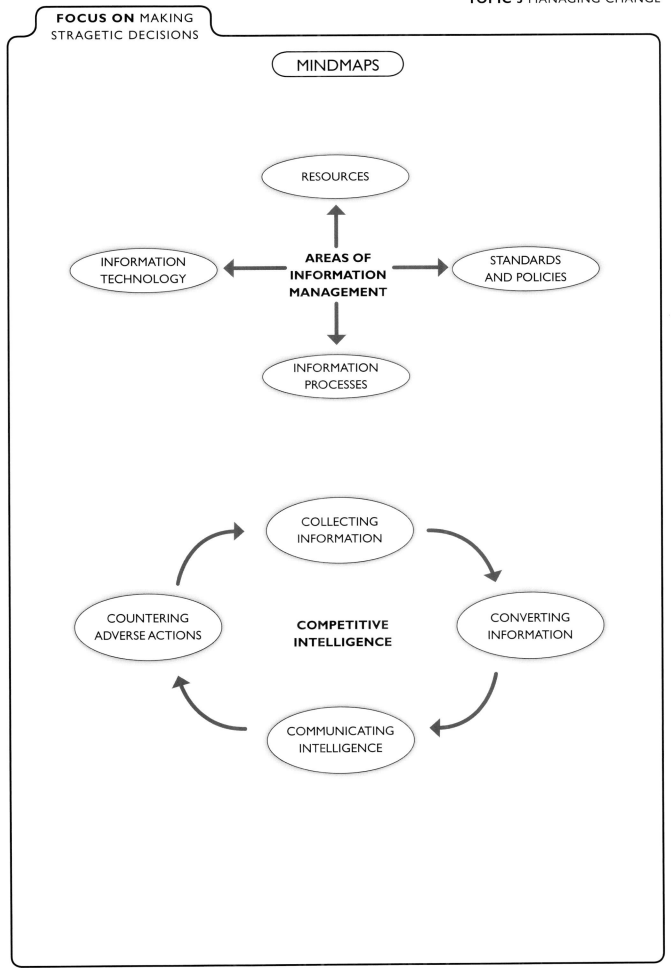

FOCUS ON MAKING
STRAGETIC DECISIONS

MINDMAPS

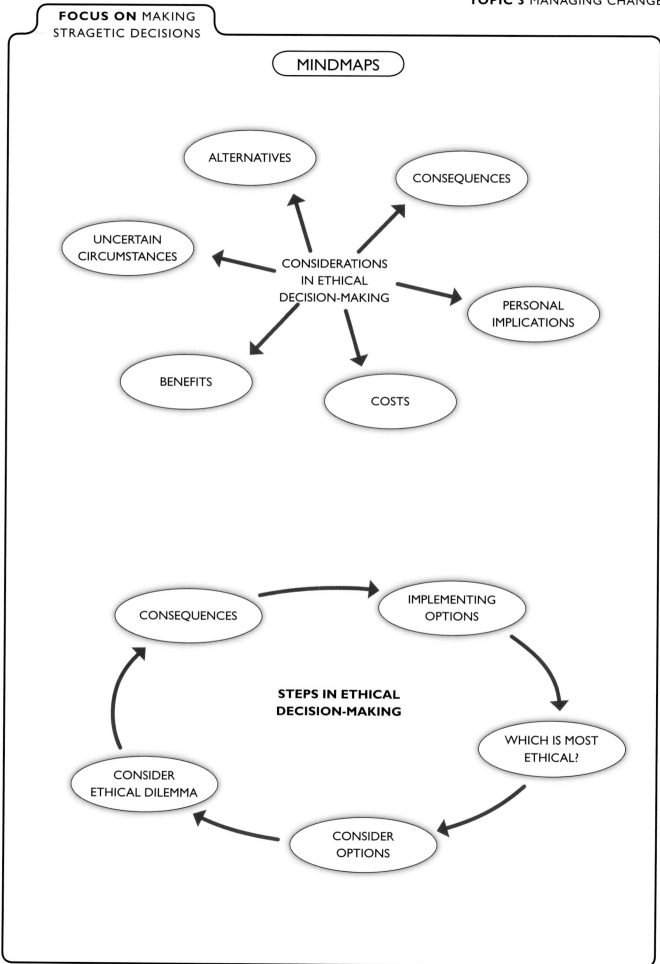

ALTERNATIVES

CONSEQUENCES

UNCERTAIN
CIRCUMSTANCES

CONSIDERATIONS
IN ETHICAL
DECISION-MAKING

PERSONAL
IMPLICATIONS

BENEFITS

COSTS

CONSEQUENCES

IMPLEMENTING
OPTIONS

**STEPS IN ETHICAL
DECISION-MAKING**

WHICH IS MOST
ETHICAL?

CONSIDER
ETHICAL DILEMMA

CONSIDER
OPTIONS

FOCUS ON MAKING
STRAGETIC DECISIONS

WORKSHEET

1 Distinguish between an MIS and a CIS.

2 What does a fishbone diagram illustrate?

3 Why has it become increasingly important for a business to embrace an ethical approach to its operations?

Answers ▶ page 230

FOCUS ON IMPLEMENTING AND MANAGING CHANGE

Techniques to implement change ▶ textbook pages 300–1

CASE STUDY – CHANGE AND GROWTH

Read the case study. Find out about the theories of Rosabeth Moss Kanter and her views of empowerment and change. What are the main points of her theory? *(12 marks)*

In her book, *The Change Masters*, Kanter puts forward approaches to achieving these. She compares four traditional corporations with six competitive and successful organisations, described as Change Masters. All findings were weighed against the experiences of many other companies, and much other material. From the six innovative organisations, Kanter derives a model for encouraging innovation.

Innovative companies were found to have a distinct, 'integrative' approach to management, while firms unlikely to innovate were described as 'segmentalist' in being compartmentalised by units or departments. The difference begins with a company's approach to problem solving, and extends through its structure and culture. Entrepreneurial organisations:

- operate at the edge of their competence, focusing on exploring the unknown rather than on controlling the known
- measure themselves by future-focused visions (how far they have to go) rather than by past standards (how far they have come).

Three clusters of structures and processes are identified as factors that encourage power circulation and access to power: open communication systems, network-forming arrangements and decentralisation of resources. Their practical implementation is discussed.

Individuals can also be change masters. 'New entrepreneurs' are people who improve existing businesses rather than start new ones. They can be found in any functional area and are described as, literally, the right people, in the right place, at the right time:

- right people – vision and ideas extending beyond the organisation's normal practice
- right place – an integrative environment fostering proactive vision, coalitions and teams
- right time – moments in the historic flow when change becomes most possible.

The ultimate change masters are corporate leaders, who translate their vision into a new organisational reality. *The Change Masters* advocates 'participation management' as the means to greater empowerment. Some major 'building blocks' for productive change are identified, and practical measures to remove 'road blocks' to innovation are discussed.

Assessing the factors that promote or resist change ▶ textbook pages 302–3

QUESTION

Suggest reasons why conflict may be desirable and why undesirable, and suggest types of conflict that could occur in the workplace due to managerial actions. *(12 marks)*

Conflict is often needed as it:

- helps to raise and address problems
- energises work to be on the most appropriate issues
- helps people to 'be real', for example by motivating them to participate

- helps people learn how to recognise and benefit from their differences.

Conflict is not the same as discomfort. The conflict isn't the problem – it is when conflict is poorly managed that it becomes a problem.

Conflict is a problem when it:

- hampers productivity
- lowers morale
- causes more and continued conflicts
- causes inappropriate behaviours.

FOCUS ON IMPLEMENTING AND MANAGING CHANGE

Assessing the factors that promote or resist change (continued)

Managerial actions that cause workplace conflicts:

1 Poor communications
   a Employees experience continuing surprises – not being informed of new decisions, programmes, etc.
   b Employees not understanding reasons for decisions and not being involved in decision-making
   c As a result, employees trusting the 'rumour mill' more than management

2 The alignment or amount of resources is insufficient. There is:
   a disagreement about 'who does what'
   b stress from working with inadequate resources

3 Poor 'personal chemistry', including conflicting values or actions among managers and employees, for example:
   a strong personal natures don't match
   b we often don't like in others what we don't like in ourselves.

4 Leadership problems, including inconsistency, absence, domineering or uninformed leadership (at any level in the organisation), evidenced by:
   a avoiding conflict – 'passing the buck' with little follow-through on decisions
   b employees see the same continued issues in the workplace
   c supervisors don't understand the jobs of their subordinates

Case studies, questions and exam practice ▶ textbook pages 304–5

CASE STUDY – THE CASE FOR MANAGING CHANGE

It is not just the business that can be affected by organisational change. What technique can be used to identify those staff who will be affected, and how should they be handled? *(14 marks)*

Change participants are all those affected by change. They come under the umbrella term of 'stakeholders' but there may also be stakeholders who are not directly affected. For instance funding bodies or governors may have a stake in seeing that a change is implemented, but the change may not have any immediate impact on their working practices.

Identifying the key stakeholders and their influence on the change as well as potential resistance will help in devising a programme that will address their concerns and fears, as well as identifying and dealing with potential conflicts.

The purpose of this analysis is:
- To identify those affected directly or indirectly by the change.
- To assess their interest, resistance and support for the change initiative.
- To identify – and to find a means of resolving – any conflicts of interest.
- To encourage stakeholder ownership and participation in the change initiative.

- To facilitate partnership and co-operation between institution and stakeholders.

The key stakeholders are those who can influence (facilitate or hinder) the success of the change project. In many cases these people will also be change participants.

Having identified your stakeholders the next stage is to concentrate on the change participants and consider for each sub-group of participants:

- the barriers to change - what reasons will this group give for not wanting to change. This is usually the easy bit.
- the levers to change - what are the factors which this group might see as beneficial about the change?
- how you can communicate with this group so you can respond to concerns and reinforce the positive messages.
- what action needs to be taken to lower barriers, reinforce the positive aspects (or these will become forgotten) and to communicate this effectively with the stakeholder group.

For large-scale changes it may be worth undertaking focus group work to see whether your intuition is matched by reality in these areas.

FOCUS ON IMPLEMENTING
AND MANAGING CHANGE

MINDMAPS

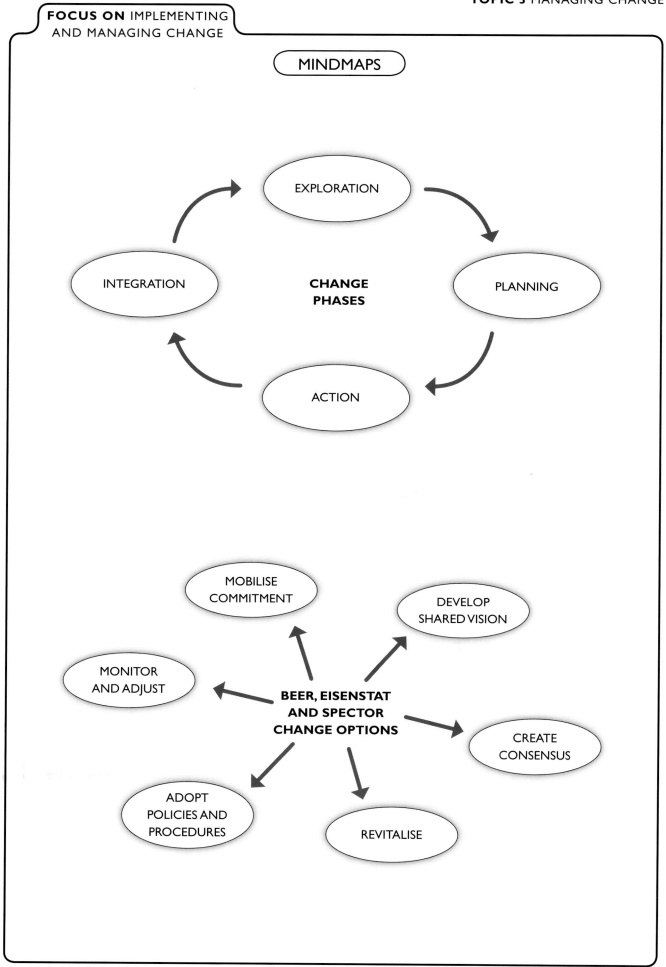

FOCUS ON IMPLEMENTING
AND MANAGING CHANGE

MINDMAPS

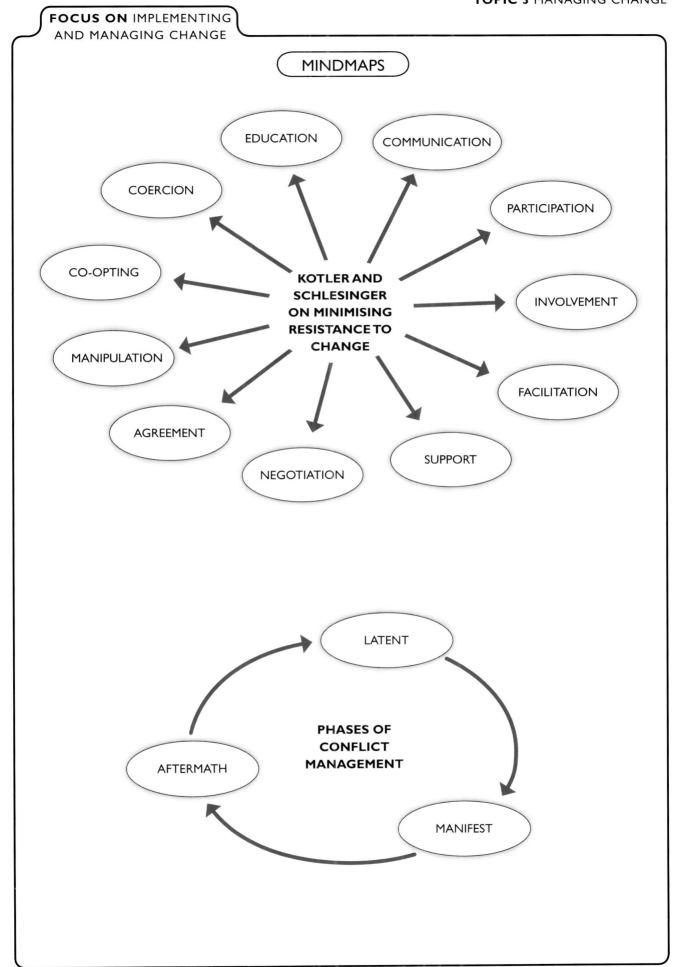

FOCUS ON IMPLEMENTING
AND MANAGING CHANGE

WORKSHEET

I   What is action research in its application to the management of change?

2   What is meant by the term 'business changeability'?

3   What is the purpose of the study of conflict management?

Answers ▶ page 230

Mock exam ▶ textbook pages 306–8

TESCO CORPORATE GOVERNANCE

1 With reference to the article above and your own research, discuss the view that corporate governance is a marketing function in that it is public relations driven. (*40 marks*)

Ethical values – as well as setting operational or business values, organisations often set themselves ethical values, which they aspire to observe in carrying out their business. These include respect, honesty, openness and responsibility, whereas business values often focus on efficiency, service, quality, growth and profit.

Ethical values guide ideas of acceptable and desirable behaviour above and beyond compliance with laws and regulations.

An ethics policy:
- sets out an organisation's ethical values, standards, and commitments to stakeholders
- confirms an organisation's leadership commitment to the above
- describes how these aims will be achieved and monitored through an ethics programme
- identifies the main ethical issues faced by the organisation or sector
- identifies other policies and documents that support and detail aspects of the ethics policy, for example: a code of ethics, a speak-up policy, a bullying and harassment policy, a gifts and hospitality policy, or an environment policy
- usually takes the form of a public declaration on values and ethics and can often be found on an organisation's corporate website.

A code of ethics is the central element of the ethics programme, and its main purpose is to provide guidance to staff. Unlike a code of conduct – which is generally 'do this or else' in tone – a code of ethics will usually be aspirational and supportive, and aim to guide staff to make decisions based on principles. The code illustrates how a company's values translate into concrete policies and procedures.

The main aims of an ethics policy code and programme:
- *values* – to embed a set of ethical values into the organisation's goals, strategies and operation
- *ethical behaviour* – to provide guidance and support to staff for making decisions and

carrying out their work in a way that is compatible with the organisation's ethical values and standards
- *corporate culture* – to consolidate and strengthen a culture of integrity and openness in order to facilitate a sustainable business
- *risk* – to minimise operational and integrity risks
- *reputation* – to enhance trust among stakeholders to facilitate business success
- *sustainability* – to minimise the organisation's negative impact on the social, economic and environmental wellbeing of wider society, and to maximise its positive contribution.

The simple test of an ethical policy involves three criteria:
- *transparency* – do I mind others knowing what I have decided?
- *effect* – who does my decision affect or hurt?
- *fairness* – would my decision be considered fair by those affected?

Many people perceive public relations as merely clever strategies to convince the public that what's wrong is right, and public relations professionals as manipulators of the public mind, rather than conveyors of truth. This may explain why almost every code of conduct, especially those targeted at the PR profession, stresses honesty above all else.

2 With reference to Articles B and C and your own research, to what extent do you believe that most businesses apply business ethics only as far as they are compelled to do so, and that ethics only really extend to their immediate stakeholders? (*40 marks*)

Business ethics should consider the right or wrong behind a decision and be based on careful stakeholder analysis. In practical terms, however, businesses face a number of different stakeholders who are directly or indirectly affected by decisions that are made by the business. The term 'focal stakeholders' can be used to describe individuals or groups that experience the direct impact of a decision – for example employees if a manufacturing plant is closed down. Primary stakeholders are all the others that are directly impacted upon by a business's decision, including

END-OF-UNIT SUMMARY AND REVISION

Mock exam (continued)

shareholders, suppliers, managers and customers. The position of the secondary stakeholders is of particular interest – some may be impacted directly and others indirectly. This group can be seen to include the government, the environment, interest groups, the community at large, and the media. Students should also make a distinction between internal and external stakeholders. Business ethics should incorporate some form of corporate transparency, which attempts to give access to their actions, operations and finances to the widest collective body of focal, primary and secondary stakeholders. Students should recognise that any business, regardless of its ethical stance, cannot cater for every stakeholder with every decision. By expanding rapidly, for example, a business might please some stakeholders, but not others, such as the community or the environment. By seeking to drive costs down, it can please customers and shareholders by being more profitable, but this is at the expense of suppliers (as the case study suggests). Business ethics is therefore a balancing act, which attempts to incorporate the desires of as many stakeholders as possible while not undermining the basic imperatives of the organisation.

3 **Leadership is essential to businesses in a rapidly moving market. Discuss. (40 marks)**

Typically, you should focus on the role of leadership and how it is instrumental in setting the initial mission of the organisation. Mention of transformational leadership would be valuable. Other impacts of good leadership include: motivation, team-building, culture-setting and culture-changing, and the ability to be able to bring about change and transformation. However, leadership is not always successful. There may be resource shortages, the leadership may struggle to cope with the organisational culture, and it is not always clear whether good leadership is enough to ensure a successful business. Examples of other key determinants include: the economic situation, the relative power of stakeholders, the state of the market, and the activities of the competitors. Some examples of strong and effective leadership can also be valuable, such as the CEOs at Tesco and Marks and Spencer. Credit should also be given if the student identifies the board as leaders

rather than a single individual, as in many cases cooperative leadership determines success.

4 **The use of ICT is essential to all business success. Discuss. (40 marks)**

ICT is essential as it facilitates efficient communication and information-sharing. Having information available allows a business to be far more effective in problem-solving and decision-making. ICT also allows a business to effectively delegate responsibility and empower staff to make decisions, as they have access to information. It also allows the business to understand its customers, the activities of the competition, and changes in the market. The business can also rapidly analyse facts and figures as they become available. ICT helps an organisation understand both its internal and external environment and allows the two to be matched. However, if ICT is not used effectively then decision-making can be muddled, and opportunities, customers and market share can all be lost.

5 **The environment in which a business operates is in constant flux, and if a business cannot adapt to the changing circumstances then it is doomed to failure. Discuss. (40 marks)**

A business needs to be able to adapt in a flexible manner. It needs to evaluate its current and future situation through techniques such as SWOT analysis. It needs to be able to adjust by offering new products and services or risk complete failure or, at best, considerable loss of market share. It is important to note that some markets are less apt to change than others, but businesses still need to be aware of impending changes and plan to react to them. Change can, of course, be social, economic, political, legal, environmental and technological. Examples of these and businesses that have adapted to them should be credited. In many cases it is in fact a business within an industry or market that creates the change to which all other organisations in that industry or market will ultimately have to adapt. An identification of businesses that are capable of, or have effected, root changes to their industry or market should also be given credit.

UNIT REVISION

Mock exam

Surname		Other names	

UNIT 4   **THE BUSINESS ENVIRONMENT AND MANAGING CHANGE**
MOCK EXAMINATION PAPER

ASSESSMENT

WRITTEN PAPER: **1 HOUR AND 45 MINUTES**

INFORMATION

THE MAXIMUM MARK FOR THIS MOCK PAPER IS 80.

WEIGHTING IS 25% OF TOTAL A-LEVEL MARK

THE MARKS FOR QUESTIONS ARE SHOWN IN BRACKETS.

THIS IS A TWO-PART PAPER. SECTION A CONTAINS QUESTIONS THAT ARE BASED ON PRIOR RESEARCH. SECTION B PROVIDES A CHOICE OF ESSAY TITLES FROM WHICH THE CANDIDATE WILL SELECT ONE. THIS IS A SYNOPTIC PAPER AND WILL DRAW ON THE WHOLE SPECIFICATION.

FOR EXAMINER'S USE			
Question	Mark	Question	Mark
1		3	
2		4	
Total column 1			
Total column 2			
TOTAL			
Signature			

TOPIC LIST

- *Corporate aims and objectives* – purpose and nature of corporate strategies, stakeholder perspectives
- *Assessing change in the business environment* – the effects of changes in the economic, political, social, ethical and technological environment and responses of organisations
- *Managing change* – planning for change, leadership and corporate culture, making strategic decisions, decision-making

Answers ▶ page 232

Mock exam (continued)

SECTION A

Answer ONE question from this section in the space provided.

Read Article A and answer the question that follows.

ARTICLE A – HARRY POTTER AND THE PRICE WAR

Half-a-million readers of the Harry Potter novels were facing disappointment in July 2007. They had hoped to pick up a cut-price copy of the final book in the series, written by J.K. Rowling, from the Walmart-owned Asda retailer. Bloomsbury, the publishers of the book, had cancelled Asda's order for half-a-million copies of the book. This was despite the fact that tens of thousands of buyers had already ordered copies from Asda.

Asda had accused the publisher of profiteering, by setting the recommended retail price at £17.99. The first book in the series, *Harry Potter and the Philosopher's Stone*, had a recommended retail price of £11.99. The sixth book in the series, *Harry Potter and the Half-Blood Prince*, had a recommended retail price of £16.99.

However, the dispute was not actually anything to do with the dispute over the recommended retail price. Bloomsbury had cancelled Asda's order because Asda had an outstanding invoice of nearly £40,000. In any case, Asda had already announced that they would be selling the book as a loss leader at considerably less than the recommended retail price. After angry exchanges of words, Bloomsbury and Asda came to an accommodation: the bill was paid and the order was reinstated.

By July, the price war for the new Harry Potter title was in full swing. Asda was offering it for £5; Morrisons for a penny less. Morrisons would allow each customer to buy only one copy; Asda allowed two. Tesco offered the book for £5 providing customers had spent £50 on other products at the same time. Amazon, the online bookseller, had received advance orders for some 2.2 million copies. In the first week of the book's release, Amazon alone was selling a copy every four seconds.

The last book in the series quickly became the fastest-selling book of all time. In the first two days, three million copies were sold – a million more than the sixth book in the series, which had previously been the record holder. Asda sold 250,000 copies between midnight on the release date and lunchtime the following day. By the end of the day, they had sold nearly all their half-a-million copies. Tesco, meanwhile, had sold in excess of 350,000.

The price war was reignited a year later, with the release of the paperback version. The recommended retail price was £8.99; Asda sold it for £1. Asda had also taken 79% of the market share of sales for the children's edition. They had sold it at 89% off its recommended retail price, and the initiative had cost them £150,000.

Mock exam (continued)

Question One

With reference to the article above and your own research, discuss the view that the competitive environment can be completely distorted and unfair to some retailers because of the sheer purchasing power of giants such as Asda. *(40 marks)*

Mock exam (continued)

ARTICLE B – HARRY POTTER AND THE GLOBAL PRICE WAR

Price cutting of the Harry Potter books was not restricted to Britain. On the other side of the world, in Kuala Lumpur, several independent book chains decided to withdraw *Harry Potter and the Deathly Hallows* from their shelves. This was in protest against the fact that Tesco and Carrefour would be selling the novel at RM69.90* instead of the recommended retail price of RM109.90. The chief operating officer of one of the independent book chains confirmed to the media that the book would not be on sale, and that a number of events that had been organised by the chain had been cancelled. In her view it was unfair that hypermarkets such as Tesco were allowed to sell a product of such importance to the book trade. In response to these additional difficulties, the publisher, Bloomsbury, refused to take any responsibility for the situation.

Once again the big-hitters had won the day and had grabbed the lion's share of the sales.

*RM = Malaysian Ringgit, the Malaysian currency

ARTICLE C – THE NET BOOK AGREEMENT

Until 1997 British publishers and booksellers had a secure agreement about the recommended retail price of books, known as the Net Book Agreement. Booksellers that sold titles at less than the agreed price would no longer be supplied by the publisher.

In the early 1990s, bookshop chains, such as Dillons and Waterstones, began offering books at a discount. A court ruled in 1997 that the agreement between publishers and booksellers over recommended retail prices – known as the Net Book Agreement – was illegal. This led to large bookstore chains and discounters, such as supermarkets, taking an enormous market share because they could buy in bulk and offer significantly discounted titles.

By the beginning of 2009, over 500 independent bookshops had been forced out of business. In Britain, more than 200 million books were sold in 2008 alone. Price wars are common. Books have become cheap, but profits in the book trade are increasingly being shared among fewer, bigger publishers, as are the profits of booksellers, including the supermarkets.

Mock exam (continued)

Question Two

With reference to Articles B and C and your own research, to what extent do you think that changes in the technological, competitive and legal environment have radically altered the market for selling books? *(40 marks)*

UNIT REVISION

Mock exam (continued)

SECTION B

Answer <u>ONE</u> question from this section in the spaces provided.

Question Three

A leader has to be a visionary in order to create a radically new mission for an innovative organisation. Discuss. *(40 marks)*

Mock exam (continued)

Question Four

Change is both inevitable and desirable for all organisations. Discuss this view. *(40 marks)*

Mock exam (continued)

Question Five

The management and use of information is one of the most important aspects of a business's success. Discuss this view. (40 marks)

UNIT 3 STRATEGIES FOR SUCCESS

TOPIC 1 FUNCTIONAL OBJECTIVES AND STRATEGIES

FOCUS ON UNDERSTANDING FINANCIAL OBJECTIVES
▶ page 6

1 A corporate objective is a broad statement made by a business. It should be broad enough for the business to be able to use a range of functional objectives to achieve it.

2 Functional objectives are still fairly broad. They include issues such as growth, profit maximisation, increase in market share and specific social, ethical or environmental objectives. They are specific steps that the business intends to take.

3 This is often the most difficult step because the broad objectives need to be quantifiable and achievable, and need to be achieved within specified time periods. A business will analyse its current situation, perhaps using SWOT. It will then develop a series of strategies or plans, and it then needs to implement those strategies and plans, supported by organisational and management systems. The business also needs to monitor and evaluate progress so that it can make necessary ongoing adjustments.

TOPIC 2 FINANCIAL STRATEGIES AND ACCOUNTS

FOCUS ON UNDERSTANDING FINANCIAL OBJECTIVES
▶ page 11

1 Maximisation of its cash inflows and a minimisation or justification of its cash outflows.

2 Students could suggest:
- checking supplier invoices for overcharging or double-billing
- eliminating unnecessary costs
- reducing over-capacity, waste, or non-value-added processes
- eliminating excessive costs such as expensive despatch methods, expensive suppliers or luxuries
- dealing with inefficiencies – for example, consolidating orders or switching to monthly invoicing to cut down on processing costs

3 The main external influence is the shareholders, although other suggestions could include the local community, the country (in terms of the economy), the government and other groups and institutions.

FOCUS ON USING FINANCIAL DATA TO MEASURE AND ASSESS PERFORMANCE (1)
▶ page 20

1 Assets are equal to liabilities; total assets are equal to the fixed and current assets; and liabilities are equal to the share capital, borrowers, other creditors and reserves.

2 Balance sheets provide a view of a business's position on a specific day. They do not cover the entire current situation, which may have changed since the balance sheet was created.

3 A profit-and-loss account shows income from sales minus direct costs (which are equal to gross profit). It shows the costs deducted from the gross profit to illustrate the business's operating or trading profit (or performance of the business). It shows the net profit before tax and the net profit after tax. And it shows what the business does with the remaining profit and how this is distributed or retained.

FOCUS ON USING FINANCIAL DATA TO MEASURE AND ASSESS PERFORMANCE (2)
▶ page 21

1 Working capital is sometimes referred to as net current assets. It is what is left of a business's funds (liquid assets) once it has paid all its immediate debts. It is the money available to pay day-to-day expenses.

2 Depreciation is used to show the real value of a business's assets throughout their life. It is meant to be an accurate figure, reflecting the true value of that asset rather than the original purchase price.

3 Good quality financial data is vital, as it provides accurate, valid, reliable, timely and relevant information to assist a business in assessing risks.

FOCUS ON INTERPRETING PUBLISHED ACCOUNTS
▶ page 26

1 A liquidity ratio is also known as a solvency ratio. It measures the actual liquid assets that are held by a business (cash or other assets that can quickly become cash). It allows the assets to be compared with short-term debts or liabilities.

2 A highly geared business has more than half of its capital employed in the form of loans. This means that the business is reliant on borrowed money, and if there are increases in the interest rate it may find it difficult to repay those loans.

3 Students could suggest that ratios are only averages, taken across the whole of the business. In isolation they say very little and can hide losses or gains. A business can distort the figures. Inflation is not often taken into account. The ratios are also based on historical figures, so working out ratios on existing accounts says little about what the business may do in the future. Ratios often pose more questions than they answer, and the figures upon which the ratios have been worked out may be unrealistic.

ANSWERS TO WORKSHEET QUESTIONS

FOCUS ON SELECTING FINANCIAL STRATEGIES
▶ page 31

1 Internal sources could include owner's capital or retained profit. External sources could include overdrafts, hire purchase, loans or mortgages.

2 Setting up profit or cost centres allows the business to look at the individual performance of particular areas, to allocate costs and to attribute profit. It shows how different parts of the business are performing and their contributions or costs.

3 Capital expenditure is spending on a fixed asset. Each budget-holder bids for capital expenditure from a limited pool of resources. The business assesses each demand and sees if it is central to the smooth running of its operations. It uses this approach to prevent the purchase of unnecessary or ill-considered fixed assets.

FOCUS ON MAKING INVESTMENT DECISIONS
▶ page 36

1 Investment appraisal involves looking at the financial viability of an investment project. It considers whether or not it is desirable and can include both quantitative and qualitative considerations.

2 A business is likely to look at capital costs, residual values of an asset, opportunity cost, revenue costs and income, or financially quantifiable benefits.

3 Quantitative influences could include payback and average rate of return, or net present values. Qualitative influences could focus on social, ethical or environmental issues, as well as issues such as responsibility for spending the business's money when there is a risk attached to it.

TOPIC 3 MARKETING STRATEGIES

FOCUS ON UNDERSTANDING MARKETING STRATEGIES
▶ page 41

1 Selling existing products into existing markets; selling new products to existing markets; selling existing products to new markets; and selling new products to new markets.

2 Different markets may have radically different characteristics, such as lifestyle, income, age, gender or geographical location. There may be different tastes and fashions, and the business needs to understand these in order to target them.

3 Available finance is the first key consideration, as it may have a direct impact on the marketing objectives. It is expensive to develop, launch and maintain new products or services. Innovative ideas may be out of the business's league. The business may also not have the necessary human resources or organisational ability. Equally, the business may not be geared up to cope with the increased demand that could be generated. It is also important to consider whether or not a specific marketing objective is consistent with the business's overall objectives.

FOCUS ON ANALYSING MARKETS AND MARKETING (1) ▶ page 47

1 A business's market position refers to whether its products or services are market leaders, followers or challengers, or indeed whether they are targeted at a market niche.

2 A business will attempt to categorise segments of the market by identifying potential customers that have similar characteristics. Each of the definable segments can then be targeted with more precision.

3 A business will try to identify patterns in sales so that they can more readily predict potential sales, fluctuations or trends. They will look to iron out seasonal fluctuations and identify underlying patterns, giving them the opportunity to prepare for future demand in line with those sales patterns.

FOCUS ON ANALYSING MARKETS AND MARKETING (2) ▶ page 48

1 Extrapolation is an attempt to predict future levels of sales by looking at current trends or the correlation between different variables and levels of sales.

2 Businesses will use market analysis software for a variety of purposes – to look at underlying trends to assist in decision-making, and to look at competitors, segmentation, demography, markets, sites and distribution locations.

3 A test market is one that is thought to have many of the characteristics of a broader, regional, national or even international market. The business will field-test its products, services and marketing campaigns in that area to gain experience, before rolling them out to a broader market.

FOCUS ON ANALYSING MARKETS AND MARKETING (3) ▶ page 49

1 Marketing Information System. This is part of a broader management information system and helps businesses to collate and analyse information.

2 Collecting secondary data fills in the gaps between what the business already knows and what they need to know. It backs up existing data and assists the business in more accurate market analysis.

3 An asset-led business looks at what the market wants and then prepares itself to deliver what the market needs. It is alert to market opportunities, in order to maximise its success and profit.

A2 ESSENTIAL BUSINESS STUDIES FOR AQA

FOCUS ON SELECTING MARKETING STRATEGIES (1)
▶ page 55

1 Cost leadership strategy means attempting to increase profits by cost reduction while maintaining average industry prices. Increased market share can be achieved by lowering prices, while the business retains a reasonable profit because of its cost reduction.

2 Using technology to bring down overall costs; efficient logistics; low labour, materials and facilities costs; and the ability to ensure that costs always remain lower than those of competitors

3 Differentiation strategy refers to a business's ability to convince customers that its products are unique in some respects, or at least identifiably different. Prime examples include Coca-Cola and Dyson, both of which have been heavily imitated by competitors.

FOCUS ON SELECTING MARKETING STRATEGIES (2)
▶ page 56

1 Market penetration; market development; product development; diversification

2 Customers can be encouraged to consume more, the business can attract customers away from competitors, market share can be taken from one large competitor or a number of smaller ones. The business can encourage more frequent purchases, it can come up with new applications or uses, or it can encourage non-buyers to make a purchase.

3 A business might replace a current product; incorporate a slight improvement to an existing product; develop an extension to its product line or a supplementary or complementary product; or release a product of a different (lower or higher) level of quality.

FOCUS ON SELECTING MARKETING STRATEGIES (3)
▶ page 57

1 Diversification involves either selling new products to new markets, or new products to new customers. A good example is Apple, which has moved into the music market with the iPod and iTunes, after being more closely associated with computers for graphic designers.

2 Horizontal diversification is when a business introduces new products to its existing markets. Vertical diversification is when a business involves itself further up or further down the supply chain.

3 A business may change its marketing strategy in order to achieve higher sales from existing products or markets. Alternatively, it might have noticed that the market has altered, or that the competition has changed its tactics. Or it might have recognised that it is better or worse at doing something than it was in the past.

FOCUS ON DEVELOPING AND IMPLEMENTING MARKETING PLANS ▶ page 62

1 A situation analysis, a marketing strategy, numerical forecasts and controls.

2 Lack of support; lack of planning; confusion over terms; focusing on forecasting rather than objectives and strategies; being too detailed; looking too far ahead; separating operational planning from strategic planning; lack of integration; poor implementation.

3 Affordable method; percentage of profits; percentage of sales; objectives and tasks.

TOPIC 4 OPERATIONAL STRATEGIES

FOCUS ON UNDERSTANDING OPERATIONAL OBJECTIVES ▶ page 67

1 Conformance is achieved when a product or service matches the specifications or requirements that have been set down by the business, usually in terms of quality or what the product or service is expected to do.

2 Students could suggest flexibility, technology, quality, speed, cost, reliability, responsiveness and dependability.

3 A business needs to supply enough products or services to meet forecasted demand, but it needs to have enough excess capacity in order to step up if demand increases, or the ability to adjust if demand decreases. It needs to be aware that many external influences can affect demand, and it needs to be able to match potential demand as closely as possible with the capacity to produce at that level.

FOCUS ON SCALE AND RESOURCE MIX
▶ page 71

1 Bulk-buying, technical, managerial, financial, marketing, risk reduction (by diversification) and capacity utilisation.

2 Diseconomies of scale occur when a manufacturing process becomes so large or cumbersome that normal economies of scale cease to apply. Unit costs are increasing, not falling.

3 A labour-intensive business focuses on individual or personalised products or services, and its labour costs are higher than its capital investment costs. A capital-intensive business invests heavily in capital equipment, such as machinery or vehicles, and its capital investment costs are much higher than its labour costs.

ANSWERS TO WORKSHEET QUESTIONS

FOCUS ON INNOVATION
▶ page 75

1 Key planning steps are: initial screening period, investigating whether the product can be produced using current production methods, testing the production process, costing the production process, market research and producing a test batch and then test marketing them

2 Dyson products – vacuum cleaners and other electrical goods – are genuinely innovative. The company holds patents for its products, which have not been successfully replicated by competitors. Therefore it can charge a premium price and make a higher profit.

3 A business's level of innovation can generally be measured in two ways: either by the amount of spending the business makes on research and development, or by the number of patents that it holds.

FOCUS ON LOCATION (1)
▶ page 80

1 Quantitative factors are primarily cost- and revenue-based, whereas qualitative factors cover issues where there is no immediate monetary value, such as quality of life.

2 A Japanese business that was just importing products into the EU would pay importation taxes, whereas it would avoid these costs if the product or service were manufactured or provided within the EU.

3 Particular locations might have a degree of prestige attached to them. Businesses will want to be associated with towns or cities that have a good reputation within their industry sector, for example a fashion designer would want to be be associated with London, Paris or Milan.

FOCUS ON LOCATION (2)
▶ page 81

1 Increased competition, rising costs, poor communication and falling sales.

2 A low-cost location may be a poor location. It may have a poor infrastructure, attract few employees or customers, or have little potential for expansion.

3 Although the business will encounter a higher level of local competition it will gain considerable advantages by being in, or close to, an area that has good communications and infrastructure, a highly trained and available workforce, a location that customers associate with that type of business, and the general support of companies that can assist the business as suppliers or contractors.

FOCUS ON LOCATION (3)
▶ page 82

1 Standardised hours ensure that each of the organisation's different sites knows exactly when the opening hours are of other sites, so they can be in regular communication.

2 They might feel that the multinational's headquarters does not understand how things work in their particular area and that the company interferes rather than provides support.

3 An autonomous business has a degree of freedom to make its own decisions and solve problems. Empowerment means having the authority to make those decisions. Empowerment is conferred upon a subsidiary by its main office.

FOCUS ON LOCATION (4)
▶ page 83

1 A business might decide to become a multinational if it has identified that there is a market for its products or services in another country, or if it can benefit from lower costs by operating in another country. It is also seen as a way of getting around protectionist policies.

2 Multinationals will often bring investment to a country, both in terms of building, improvements to infrastructure, tax payments, employment and other benefits.

3 The country may not be able to provide the skilled workers needed, so employees may be overseas nationals. The business may also not remain in the country for very long; perhaps only until incentives are removed. Multinationals also manage to siphon a good deal of money out of a country before paying tax. They may not be as ethically or environmentally careful as in their own home country.

FOCUS ON LEAN PRODUCTION
▶ page 88

1 A time study involves identifying and measuring the sub-elements of a particular job in order to work out exactly how long a whole job takes to complete.

2 Critical path analysis seeks to identify the stages through which a project has to pass. It identifies crucial activities, the order in which those activities need to be undertaken, and the earliest possible start and finish times for each activity.

3 Lean production is centred on the reduction of waste and lead time, a reduction in inventory, the creation of value and maximising customers. JIT's emphasis is on high-volume production with minimal stock levels and therefore requires close cooperation and collaboration with suppliers. Kaizen is related to the orderly, gradual and continuous improvement of a business without having to make large capital investments.

TOPIC 4 HUMAN RESOURCE STRATEGIES

FOCUS ON HUMAN RESOURCE OBJECTIVES AND STRATEGIES ▶ page 93

1 To quote Peter Drucker on hard HRM: 'Doing the right thing is more important than doing things right.' Hard HRM suggests that the primary aim of businesses is to be competitive and to be profitable; everything else is secondary to this.

2 Students might suggest: matching workforce skills; dealing with size, location and business needs; ensuring that the workforce is used to its utmost potential; minimising labour costs and maintaining good relations between management and the workforce.

3 A human resource plan forecasts the number and types of employees that will be needed by the business in the short to medium term. It can be used to set up recruitment drives, training, redeployment, redundancies, etc. It is a continually monitored process that is adjusted as the business's objectives change due to internal or external factors.

FOCUS ON DEVELOPING AND IMPLEMENTING WORKFORCE PLANS (1) ▶ page 99

1 Workforce planning is the systematic process that identifies human capital requirements in order to meet a business's goals, and incorporates the development of strategies to meet those requirements.

2 Phase IV is the evaluation and adjustment phase of the workforce planning model. It is important because the business needs to review its workforce planning efforts systematically. If a business fails to do this, it will not be in a position to respond to changes that require a rethink of its workforce planning needs.

3 Students could suggest: senior management; line management; HR professionals; IT professionals; strategic planners or budget analysts. They should also identify their role or responsibilities within the workforce planning process.

FOCUS ON DEVELOPING AND IMPLEMENTING WORKFORCE PLANS (2) ▶ page 100

1 Gap analysis looks at the difference between present workforce and future needs. It helps a business establish its priorities to deal with these skills or role gaps.

2 Legislation has developed to ensure that businesses offer more flexible working conditions to employees, so they have a better work/life balance. This is particularly true for older employees wanting to make a gradual transition into retirement and not want to work full hours. Businesses are keen to retain older and more skilled employees, as their skills and experience are difficult to replace and can be passed on to younger employees.

3 Students may suggest: demographic change; whether a business is expanding or contracting; departmental initiatives; new legislation; special programmes such as quality improvement; cyclical factors; new technology; new work processes and new workflows; budgetary constraints and new organisational structure and design.

FOCUS ON DEVELOPING AND IMPLEMENTING WORKFORCE PLANS (3) ▶ page 101

1 Students might suggest: effective and efficient use of the workforce; ensuring replacements are available; providing realistic staffing projections for budgets; a link between training expenditure and benefits; maintaining a diversified workforce; assisting in restructuring.

2 Students could suggest: understanding future skills needs; managing employment expenditure; ensuring the provision of sufficient training and development; anticipating changes in the need for different skills; delivering improved services; employee retention; implementing diversity policy; managing staff performance and attendance levels.

3 A business may wish to consider new models of service delivery, such as outsourcing. Equally, they may identify the fact that they need types of employees with skills that they had not anticipated requiring in the past. The business can also consider changes to contracts, switching over to shifts or annualised hours, or offering homeworking or flexible working.

FOCUS ON COMPETITIVE ORGANISATIONAL STRUCTURES (1) ▶ page 106

1 An adhocracy is an adaptive, creative and autonomous type of culture, where authority is based on the charisma and ability of leaders. It is a risk-orientated business. The focus is for employees to adopt the values of the organisation.

2 This type of organisation relies on the expertise of employees. Many have matrix structures, with teams. They are flexible organisations where employees are given a good deal of autonomy. They have procedures in place in order to respond to change quickly and efficiently.

3 A matrix organisation is one that has cross-functional teams. These teams deal with specific problems or projects by pulling in expertise from across the organisation. Each individual from a functional area of the business will have their own perspective and series of opinions and comments that can contribute to the problem-solving process.

ANSWERS TO WORKSHEET QUESTIONS

FOCUS ON COMPETITIVE ORGANISATIONAL STRUCTURES (1) ▶ page 107

1 Senior management can concentrate on important decision-making; the inherent empowerment increases motivation and work output; individuals lower down the organisation can use their skills and expertise to help senior management make more effective decisions; the organisation is able to respond faster to changes; and individuals tend to accept more responsibility and use that responsibility successfully.

2 Empowerment involves giving individuals more control over their contribution to the organisation – giving them authority and the responsibility to carry out their work without management intervention. Autonomy focuses on independence within the job role. It gives individuals more control over what they do, the order in which they do it and the processes that they use.

3 Organisations with a flat, or de-layered, structure have fewer layers of management and are less bureaucratic than those with a more hierarchical structure. De-layering means that layers of management have been stripped out of the business or organisation, making it flatter overall.

FOCUS ON COMPETITIVE ORGANISATIONAL STRUCTURES (1) ▶ page 108

1 A chain of command is the formal line of communication that runs down through the tiers of management of an organisation. It is through this chain of command that instructions or orders are passed. A span of control refers to the number of subordinates for whom a manager has direct responsibility.

2 'Flexi place' gives employees the opportunity to work either in their own homes, at another remote location, or in the business's premises. This flexibility is achieved through the use of telecommunication systems and computer networks. The business is prepared to allow employees to work without constant direct supervision, and the workforce can be more mobile and flexible.

3 A compressed working week breaks away from the traditional five-day, Monday-to-Friday schedule. Typically, employees might work a nine-day fortnight, where they work for 80 hours in nine days. The system has often been adopted because it allows the business to deploy more employees at crucial times of the week, and to lower staffing levels when the workload is less frantic. As far as employees are concerned, it offers them a greater degree of flexibility and it has proved to be a successful factor in businesses' staff-retention strategies.

FOCUS ON EFFECTIVE EMPLOYER/EMPLOYEE RELATIONS ▶ page 113

1 Works councils are used within organisations to discuss issues such as overtime and promotion. More broadly, they are there to encourage management to accept employee ideas and suggestions. They also operate as an early-warning system to highlight areas of potential conflict between management and workforce.

2 ACAS is essentially a mediator that deals with problems and disputes between employers and employees. It works at both the group and the individual level. When a case is referred to ACAS, both sides agree to abide by ACAS's ruling.

3 Employee engagement must be taken seriously as it contributes to the development of the business. It identifies solutions, creates dialogue and strengthens relationships and partnerships. It allows for the more efficient use of resources and the development of skills and teams, allowing corporate culture to come to the fore and helping to maintain the business's reputation. It also involves encouraging employees to use their natural talents to assist the business.

UNIT 4 THE BUSINESS ENVIRONMENT AND MANAGING CHANGE

TOPIC 1 CORPORATE AIMS AND OBJECTIVES

FOCUS ON UNDERSTANDING MISSION AIMS AND OBJECTIVES ▶ page 127

1 A mission statement might cover: the specification of target customers and markets; primary products and services; the geographical area in which the business will operate; the technology used; the company philosophy; the company self-concept and public image; an expression of commitment in respect of issues such as profitability; growth and survival and a concern for employees focusing on their value as a resource.

2 The three levels are corporate, business and functional. These are interrelated. At corporate level, strategic formulation is the broadest and then at the other two successive levels it is dealt with in more detail, but in support of the corporate level strategy.

3 Stakeholder analysis aims to identify and describe the attributes, interrelationships, interests and influence of each stakeholder group. It identifies their relative power and interest, along with their influence and any networks or coalitions to which they belong.

TOPIC 2 ASSESSING CHANGES IN THE BUSINESS ENVIRONMENT

FOCUS ON THE ECONOMIC ENVIRONMENT (1)
▶ page 136

1 A homogeneous product is one that is hard to distinguish from other products offered by competitors in a marketplace.

2 An oligopoly has a number of sellers but the market is dominated by a handful of businesses. The products are differentiated, the businesses are price makers, and there are barriers to entry. A monopoly exists where there is a single seller in the market. There are no available substitute products, so buyers have to purchase from one business that is a price maker and there are considerable barriers to entry.

3 Students should identify recession, recovery, boom and downturn. They should be encouraged to recognise that the four phases of the business cycle are interlinked, and that the periods of each phase are variable. In the current recession (2008/09), recovery is being stimulated by government policy and regulation of the financial industries. By the time you read this the recession may have ended and the economy might be well into recovery, but may not yet have reached boom. The period before the previous downturn and recession saw a significant period of boom, illustrated by gradually rising prices, particularly in the property market, but controlled inflation.

FOCUS ON THE ECONOMIC ENVIRONMENT (2)
▶ page 137

1 As the exchange rate changes, the revenue that a business receives from sales is affected. If sterling increases overseas, customers will find that products are more expensive. If sterling drops, then the British products are more affordable.

2 Friedman was a monetarist and was of the opinion that inflation could be controlled by controlling the money supply. Keynes, on the other hand, was of the opinion that a strong incomes policy was essential to keep inflation and unemployment down.

3 McDonaldisation is related to technological advances concerned with the preserving and storage of foodstuffs and growing car ownership. It is characterised by efficiency, control and predictability. It refers to the fact that consumers can now buy standardised products at relatively low prices and that the quality of those products is almost indistinguishable, whether bought in New York or Beijing.

FOCUS ON THE POLITICAL AND LEGAL ENVIRONMENT (1) ▶ page 147

1 The balance of trade is the difference between the value of products and services sold overseas and the value of products and services imported from overseas. If more is being imported than exported, then a deficit exists. If more is being exported than imported, then there is a surplus. The ideal is that these two figures are broadly the same.

2 Because they artificially set output and pricing levels at inefficient levels. They keep inefficient businesses in the market and discourage entry of efficient businesses.

3 Its primary role is to set the interest rate. It does this in order to help the government meet its inflation targets and help to ensure that there is sustained economic growth.

FOCUS ON THE POLITICAL AND LEGAL ENVIRONMENT (2) ▶ page 148

1 The main objective of monetary policy is to control inflation by government control of the money supply. Fiscal policy revolves around government expenditure and taxation – effectively how it puts money into, or takes money from, the economy.

2 The Public Sector Borrowing Requirement is the amount of money that the government would need to borrow in order to cover its expenditure commitments. Effectively this is the difference between the amount of money that the government has raised via taxation and the total amount of money it has committed to spend.

3 Supply-side policies are designed to make markets and industries more efficient and allow economic growth without inflation. This can be done through privatisation, deregulation, tough competition policy, commitment to international trade, encouraging entrepreneurs and encouraging capital investment and innovation.

FOCUS ON THE POLITICAL AND LEGAL ENVIRONMENT (3) ▶ page 149

1 The World Trade Organisation handles trade disputes and negotiations, and provides technical assistance. It handles the rules that govern free trade between countries.

2 Enlargement is the process by which new member states join the European Union, having met specific economic, social and legal requirements. Key advantages of enlargement are that it is creating the world's largest economic zone, within which trade barriers are removed and there is enormous opportunity for businesses, albeit in the face of increased competition from more efficient businesses in other member states.

3 Trade barriers distort the domestic market as they push up prices and protect inefficient parts of the domestic economy. Foreign producers are penalised and there is an inefficient allocation of resources within the domestic market.

ANSWERS TO WORKSHEET QUESTIONS

FOCUS ON THE POLITICAL AND LEGAL ENVIRONMENT (4) ▶ page 150

1   The Employment Equality (Age) Regulations (2006) outlawed direct and indirect age discrimination. This means that businesses can no longer set mandatory retirement ages, nor can they be involved in, or condone, direct or indirect harassment, victimisation or unfair practices on the grounds of age.

2   This would be in breach of the Trade Descriptions Act (1968). It is the responsibility of a business to ensure that its products and services are not falsely described. It would certainly be fined, required to change the description, or in extreme circumstances to remove the product or service from sale.

3   Occupational health screening is designed to establish and maintain a healthy working environment, to ensure that employees are in the best physical and mental health, and to ensure that the business adapts work processes and practices to support this.

FOCUS ON THE SOCIAL ENVIRONMENT (1) ▶ page 156

1   Those in employment will have an increasing burden to support those who have retired. Life expectancy in the developed world is rising and this means greater challenges, as the retired population still needs sufficient income to make purchases, otherwise the physical side of markets will diminish, leading to job losses and economic difficulties. Pensions are also less reliable, as many private pension schemes have failed, or are in a process of realignment and reconstruction, and do not offer the same benefits as they promised in the past.

2   A sabbatical is an organised and agreed extended period of leave, usually taken for family matters, travel or education.

3   SCP is Sustainable Consumption and Production. It revolves around the achievement of economic growth while respecting environmental considerations, specifically minimising environmental damage. It should lead to better products and services, cleaner production and long-term shifts in consumption.

FOCUS ON THE SOCIAL ENVIRONMENT (2) ▶ page 157

1   Utilitarianism is concerned with having sets of standards that relate to the outcome of a decision and its effects on others. Universalism is concerned with the intention of an action or decision, as opposed to the outcome of that action or decision.

2   Students could suggest a number of different options, including: government, investors, consumers, industry, local communities and international bodies, or business partners.

3   Corporate responsibility is a business's obligation to take into consideration social, economic and environmental concerns in its decision-making processes. The implications are that it may not be able to take the cheapest or the most efficient course of action but may have to compromise in order to ensure that it conforms to being a socially responsible business that does not put profit before its ethical responsibilities.

FOCUS ON THE TECHNOLOGICAL ENVIRONMENT ▶ page 162

1   CRM is Customer Relationship Management. It seeks to identify the relationships between the business or the brand and its customers. It is about managing this relationship in order to encourage long-term customer relationships and retention.

2   The key features of fixed automation are its high cost and use of specialised equipment, which is used in a fixed sequence of operations, allowing the business to benefit from low cost and high volume. It is limited in the sense that products may lack variety, and costs may be comparatively high.

3   The opportunities will often provide new markets or the ability to produce new products for existing customers. This is dependent on how the business applies these technological changes, either in terms of their use as part of processes or the ways in which they focus the range of products and services that they offer.

FOCUS ON THE COMPETITIVE ENVIRONMENT ▶ page 167

1   A substitute product is a product or service that could directly or indirectly replace an existing product or service. A prime example is email, seen as a substitute for postal services. Substitute products do not necessarily wholly replace existing products but may do so over time – for example, computers replacing typewriters or DVDs replacing VHS.

2   A merger might be a quick way for a business to join with a major competitor so that collectively they can become the dominant business in a specific market. The business gains more power in terms of costs, prices, and the number of customers that it can attract or retain.

3   Porter suggested that globalisation was a growing trend, increasing customer power, changing regulatory powers or patterns, and increasing trade liberalisation.

TOPIC 3 MANAGING CHANGE

FOCUS ON INTERNAL CAUSES OF CHANGE (1)
▶ page 172

1 Organic growth is long-term, sustainable and focused on growth. It is achieved by businesses that improve their revenue results using the resources that they already own.

2 A retrenchment strategy is effectively a scaling down of operations so that a business can refocus on its continually successful areas of operation. It involves regrouping and focusing on the reduction of costs and assets in response to a fall in sales and profits. Effectively it means reorganisation and a return to the business's core competencies.

3 Organisation development is the planned process of change. It indicates improvements in performance as the business aligns itself more closely with the market and becomes more efficient and effective. It also involves creating or developing organisational culture, values, structures, resources, processes and people. It looks at the key processes and elements and allows the business to have a better view of itself and how changes might work in practice.

FOCUS ON INTERNAL CAUSES OF CHANGE (2)
▶ page 173

1 Students may suggest strategic, structural, cultural, technological, merger and acquisition, break-up and spin-off, downsizing or expansion.

2 A management buy-out is when the existing management of a sub-unit or division of a business purchases that part of the business from the existing owners. A management buy-in is a similar process, but where an external management team buys the business from the present ownership.

3 The company could have an informal arrangement with creditors, it could seek a business rescue, or it could go into liquidation.

FOCUS ON PLANNING FOR CHANGE (1) ▶ page 182

1 SWOT is used to determine the strengths, weaknesses, opportunities and threats of an organisation. In the planning process it is used to help identify and evaluate strategic aims, providing a business with a range of possible outcomes.

2 This is a system developed in order to enable organisations to clarify their vision and strategy and then translate them into actions. The idea is that feedback is provided to facilitate the ongoing improvement of strategic performance and results.

3 Students could suggest that it gives greater purpose and direction, it helps design the future actions of the business, it allows the sharing of common goals, it develops a team approach, it makes the business aware of both the macro and micro environments, it helps the business identify strategies to respond to risk and changes in the environment.

FOCUS ON PLANNING FOR CHANGE (2) ▶ page 183

1 It increases efficiency and flexibility, encourages synergy, decreases manual planning and coordination, and illustrates the planning process in a clearer way.

2 A business develops a contingency plan to avoid, prepare for, or exploit difficult situations. The business anticipates problem situations and develops plans that would work in the majority of circumstances. It outlines major goals and targets to deal with disasters, worst-case scenarios, disruption, delays, loss of personnel or unexpected actions of competitors.

3 Environmental scanning is used to detect external changes in the environment. It looks at possible impacts on the business. It is a key tool in decision-making.

FOCUS ON KEY INFLUENCES ON THE CHANGE PROCESS: LEADERSHIP (1) ▶ page 190

1 A leader is an individual with a vision and the ability to create new systems or ways of doing things, as well as the predisposition to take risks when necessary. It may mean an individual who is inspirational and dynamic. A manager is an individual with specific supervisory or directional responsibilities. A managerial role is an executive one. Despite the differences, the two terms are not mutually exclusive.

2 McGregor's theories on how the management of a business approaches its relations with the workforce. Theory X is closely associated with what is known as hard management – tight control and punishment. Theory Y is more associated with soft management – unlocking the potential of employees. McGregor often saw elements of both approaches in the same organisation, exercised by the same management structure.

3 A country club manager is an individual who tries to avoid problems, conflict or imbalance in the workplace, and who places employee contentment above productivity.

FOCUS ON KEY INFLUENCES ON THE CHANGE PROCESS: LEADERSHIP (2) ▶ page 191

1 Idealised influence, inspirational motivation, intellectual stimulation and individual consideration. These reflect the fact that the leader should be a role model, motivator, encourager of innovation and a coach and advisor.

2 This is Lewin's three-step process of organisational change. A business will have set procedures or ways of doing things that need to be unfrozen or allowed to be changed. This moves to the change process, when the change implementation takes place. Then the situation is refrozen so that everyone knows what the procedures are.

3 A visionary leader creates a vision, mission or strategy that they communicate to others and gain support for. They provide a strategy or a path and lead the organisation or group along that path. The vision is not rigid; it has to adapt and continue to excite and motivate.

ANSWERS TO WORKSHEET QUESTIONS

FOCUS ON KEY INFLUENCES ON THE CHANGE
PROCESS: CULTURE (1) ▶ page 198

1 A business with a macho culture makes decisions very
quickly and has a tough attitude to its employees. There
is high internal competition and the business is in a high-
risk industry. It is short-term in its approach, and there is
a low level of cooperation within the organisation. These
businesses tend to have high labour turnover and a weak
organisational culture.

2 A business with a consensual culture is one that is
primarily concerned with an informal acceptance of
power and authority. It is focused on equality, integrity
and fairness. The business considers employee morale
to be very important as a primary driver in achieving
organisational objectives. Consequently, the loyalty of
employees is paramount.

3 To examine the culture of an organisation is to look at the
ways in which it coordinates itself, the extent to which it is
centralised or decentralised, and its own view of the way in
which it operates. It examines communication, management
approach, the use of power and authority, decision-making,
problem-solving, employee commitment and motivation,
and the level of risk the business is prepared to take on.

FOCUS ON KEY INFLUENCES ON THE CHANGE
PROCESS: CULTURE (2) ▶ page 199

1 The three primary objectives are: the business's objectives,
the business's resources, and the environment in which the
business operates.

2 Organisational norms are the generally accepted ways
of doing things within a business, encompassing attitudes,
opinions, communication, responsibility and decision-
making. In effect, the norms mould the attitude, behaviour,
collaboration and performance of individuals within the
organisation.

3 Students could suggest: mergers or takeovers; performance;
downsizing; changes in leadership or management; the
adoption of new corporate goals; a transformation from the
public sector to the private sector; or changes in the market.

FOCUS ON KEY INFLUENCES ON THE CHANGE
PROCESS: CULTURE (3) ▶ page 200

1 Force field analysis is a process that aims to visualise
the fact that change involves two mutually opposing
forces operating against one another. One set of forces
supports the change and the other resists it. The purpose
is for management to be able to identify these forces in
advance of a proposed change. They can then remove or
minimise the resisting forces and support or encourage the
supporting forces.

2 It encourages the sharing of assumptions, beliefs and
values. It also encourages individuals to behave in certain
ways in certain circumstances. This reduces tension,
misunderstanding and conflict.

3 Students could suggest that the business might be aware
of situations that it is uncertain about but which it can
control through a scanning process. The business can
help shape attitudes towards information and activities
emanating from the external environment. It can adapt
the way in which it behaves by collecting and interpreting
information and amending culture. It can also encourage
a dominant set of values and norms that will allow it to
respond more effectively.

FOCUS ON MAKING STRATEGIC DECISIONS
▶ page 205

1 An MIS is a Management Information System, used to
record, store and process information to assist decision-
making. A CIS is a Competitive Information System, used to
capture information about competitors and, again, to assist
in decision-making, but it is less broad in its application.

2 A fishbone diagram is a graphic representation of cause and
effect. It can be used to show the progress and content of
brainstorming, focusing on materials, machines, manpower
and methods.

3 Increasingly, there is conflict between the objectives of
businesses or industries and the ethical values of society
and consumers. They are sometimes seen as having
conflicting or mutually exclusive goals and objectives.
Businesses are increasingly concerned with ethical decision-
making and seek not just to be seen to be ethical, but to
be ethical in reality. They have come to the realisation that
an ethical stance gives them new alternatives and that
there are inherent benefits in being ethical as they take
into consideration the goals and interests of their broader
stakeholders and ensure that their objectives are not in
conflict with them.

FOCUS ON IMPLEMENTING AND MANAGING
CHANGE ▶ page 210

1 Action research is a means of problem-solving. It involves
making a systematic and rational analysis of criteria and
circumstances. Information is collected from stakeholders
and then a solution is suggested. Research is carried out
and common terms of reference are agreed. Each group's
viewpoint is taken into account and each alternative is
weighed up. It is a way in which effective change can be
imposed on an organisation.

2 This is a measure of an organisation's agility or flexibility – in
other words, its ability to adapt. Organisations are described
as being either rubber, water, concrete or wax, depending
on their degree of changeability or agility.

3 Conflict management examines situations where there is
opposition, incompatible behaviour or disruptive interaction.
It looks at the ways in which disagreements, disputes and
debates take place and are handled within organisations.
Not all conflict is negative; some is constructive and can
result in a business becoming stronger and more effective.

UNIT 3 STRATEGIES FOR SUCCESS: MOCK EXAM ▶ page 115

1 2002 gross profit percentage: 12.59%

2003 gross profit percentage: 9.59%

2004 gross profit percentage: 12.96%

2005 gross profit percentage: 13.35%

2006 gross profit percentage: 10.86%

2007 gross profit percentage: 11.07%

2008 gross profit percentage: 11.06%

During the initial growth period, 2002–05, the gross profit percentages were significant, and generally in excess of 12%. Since 2006, there has been a period of stabilisation, which has seen the gross profit percentage hovering around the 11% mark. What this indicates overall is that although the business's turnover has increased significantly, its actual gross profit percentage has not increased significantly. The business is evidently continuing to reinvest in expansion, or it could suggest that the business has not got its costs fully under control.

2 The growth figures are 11%, 21.7% and 25% respectively. However, it is important to note that the actual size of the figures in terms of the sales is significantly different. The Asia and South Africa results are better in terms of growth, but this is from a relatively low base. It is the rest-of-Europe figures that stand out as the best growth figures, as they reflect a significant amount of additional income for the business.

Students will also note that the business has focused on China as a key market. Certainly, the Chinese healthcare market is a rapidly expanding one, believed to be worth nearly £2 billion. There are significant business opportunities in China, as the Chief Executive noted that there are 14,000 hospitals. China is attempting to move its healthcare closer to European standards, so there are significant opportunities for businesses in this area, assuming that China's commitment to improving healthcare continues. There is an additional advantage for the business as its production facilities are located in China. This means it already has a route to the market, and this gives it a significant advantage over potential competitors, who may have to import similar products and thus incur higher costs.

3 Understandably, both of the statements are upbeat and positive. They both mention the term 'expansion' and are primarily focused on expansion in the Far East. Students should comment on the fact that the business is growing organically within the European market. They should also note that the growth in their industry appears to be a sustainable one and relatively protected from new entrants, as the statement 'substantial barriers to entry' reveals. The business has a significant amount of business in its order books, and it is increasing its capacity in order to cope with this. It has seen significant compound growth rates in terms of revenue, profit, etc. The business has also seen a significant increase in its value over the seven or so years. It has diversified into new markets, which spreads the risk, but also makes it more difficult for the business to coordinate. A potential investor would look at the profit before taxation, the dividend per share, and the earnings per share as primary indicators of whether the business is continuing to perform well. By all these measures, there is room for significant optimism and the business does represent a good risk and an opportunity for investors.

4 The bulk of the detail is included in the Chairman's statement, although there are references in the introductory section of the case study. It is worth noting that less than 20% of the workforce is in Britain and that the majority (over 3,000) operates in the rest of Europe, Asia and South Africa. The business states that it is committed to training and personal development, as it relies on the quality of its employees. The correct noises are being made by the business in terms of stating that their employees are professional and that they make a valued contribution to the business. This has undoubtedly been a fast-growing business and it is unclear whether it has had proper workforce planning or a human resource strategy in place for any length of time. There are no clear clues about the organisational structure and neither is there any mention of any employee dispute difficulties. A business such as this will, however, have a budget to invest in human resource development and a focus on nurturing talent, both within the existing employee base and to attract suitable candidates away from competitors, or from similar types of businesses, so that it can benefit from new employees' expertise.

ANSWERS TO MOCK EXAMS

UNIT 4 THE BUSINESS ENVIRONMENT AND MANAGING CHANGE: MOCK EXAM ▶ page 213

---

1 The focus of this question is on the relative buying power of large retailers such as Asda. It is also about their ability to offer key products as loss leaders in order to to attract customers that they hope will purchase additional products and services at the same time as purchasing the loss leader. Certainly the competitive environment is distorted, and smaller businesses that do not have the same buying power as larger retailers are often unable to purchase products for the same price. In this situation, for example, many smaller book retailers were actually buying their stock from the supermarkets, rather than from the publishers, for this reason.

2 There are several issues that students can focus on, revolving around the way in which the market for books has changed in recent years. On the one hand, there have been enormous technological changes. At the centre of this has been the development of the Internet and the fact that customers are able to purchase books and allied products from a bewildering range of sources. This has meant that customers can purchase books from overseas and (notwithstanding delivery charges) can make their considered choice purely on the basis of price from heavily discounted sources. The competitive environment has also changed; there are far fewer independent bookshops and chains, and supermarkets are key competitors. However, supermarkets tend to discount most heavily only the top titles by specific authors – the discounts are not extended across all products. This does leave room for specialist booksellers who sell titles beyond the top sellers. On the competitive and legal front, the dismantling of the Net Book Agreement – which was seen as a restrictive practice and therefore illegal – may have been initially viewed as beneficial. Certainly it has indirectly stimulated book sales, but this is because books are comparatively more affordable than they would have been if the Net Book Agreement were still in place. Issues such as quality are still important, but there has been a concentration of profit for a handful of major publishers and retailers. This has gone against the interests of the industry as a whole, both in the production and the retail markets.

3 Relevant answers could include:
- It should be the role of any leader to set a vision or a mission.
- Innovative organisations need to be different, both in terms of their organisation and their approach to business.
- The visionary leader needs to motivate.
- Team-building is essential.
- A visionary leader can set the culture of the organisation.
- A visionary leader can bring about change to the industry as a whole.

- Culture can be seen as a difficult issue to change unless the organisation is a new one.
- Resources remain a problem.
- Visionary leadership may not be enough, as there may be adverse economic conditions, the competition may respond, and there may be other stakeholders that need to be taken into consideration.

4 Relevant answers could include:
- All businesses need to be flexible, so they need to have a flexible organisational structure and take an adaptive view of change, rather than resisting it.
- A business cannot determine the rate or pace of change, particularly if it is affected by its external environment.
- Each time change happens, a series of new opportunities and threats are created.
- Change, in order to be successful, needs to build on the organisation's strengths and eliminate its weaknesses.
- The business needs to be strong and have sufficient key or core competences to deal with change.
- Change does not necessarily have to be driven by the leadership or management of the organisation, but can be led by its key stakeholders.
- Businesses often have no option but to change, otherwise they would be left behind and lose their market share and reputation.
- Some businesses deliberately create change rather than adapt to changes in the external environment. This allows them to change the market itself or create a new market and customer base.

5 Relevant answers could include:
- It is vital for all organisations to be able to manage, process and respond to information.
- The information provides them with vital data in order to solve problems and make decisions.
- By ensuring that everyone who needs access to information has it, the business can not only be better informed, but also make efficient and effective decisions.
- By providing managers and employees with information they become empowered.
- The business needs to have an up-to-date understanding of its own strengths and weaknesses, market trends and changes, and the requirements of its customers.
- If a business does not put in place good management information systems, then it will not be able to make quick decisions and will miss opportunities.
- Many businesses operate in fast-changing markets where information is vital.
- Businesses also have to be aware of the actions of their competitors and react quickly, having collected and processed the data that they have received.